Criteria
2019-2020

Discernment and Discourse
Reader and Guide

EDITED BY

Vanessa Hopper • Ona Seaney
SOUTHERN METHODIST UNIVERSITY

Kendall Hunt
publishing company

Cover image © Shutterstock, Inc.

Kendall Hunt
publishing company

www.kendallhunt.com
Send all inquiries to:
4050 Westmark Drive
Dubuque, IA 52004-1840

Copyright © 2012, 2013, 2014, 2015, 2016, 2017, 2018, 2019
by Southern Methodist University

ISBN 978-1-5249-8545-5

Kendall Hunt Publishing Company has the exclusive rights to reproduce this work, to prepare derivative works from this work, to publicly distribute this work, to publicly perform this work and to publicly display this work.

All rights reserved. No part of this publication may be reproduced, stored in a retrieval system, or transmitted, in any form or by any means, electronic, mechanical, photocopying, recording, or otherwise, without the prior written permission of the copyright owner.

Published in the United States of America

This issue of *Criteria* is dedicated to Susie Duarte for her decades of tireless service to Discernment and Discourse. On behalf of the DISC faculty, heartfelt thanks, Susie, for your professional and compassionate support of the faculty and for regularly going above and beyond the call of duty. You will be sorely missed and fondly remembered.

CONTENTS

Letter from the Editors xi

STUDENT WORK 1

Analyzing and Synthesizing, Persuasion and Argument 3

    Death, Personhood, and Experimentation: What Does It Mean
       to Be Human?
         Nathan Hites 5
    The Ethics of Somatic Cell Gene Therapy
         Jordan Hardin 10
    The End of the Road—Or Is It? Research on Euthanasia
         Sophie Vos 18
    Making Circumstance a Victim of You
         Reed Abbajay 25
    A Boardinghouse Roof for a Glass Ceiling: Evaluating Joyce's
       Mrs. Mooney
         Steven Manning 28
    The Destiny of Dirt
         Sophia Salinas 31
    Where Does Beauty Lie?
         Victoria Peters 35
    The Fruit of Their Labors for the Fruit of Their Loins
         Morgan Caldwell 40
    The Ring of Engagement
         Rasin Faruk 46

The Stark Resemblance between a Four-Hundred-Year-Old
    Play and the Now
        Isabel Muino 49
How to Become Rich
        Nicole Parmelee 52
Identity as a Political Machine: Expressing Humanity in Times of Strife
        Marina Leventis 56
A Beginner's Guide to Feminism
        Samantha Hites 65
Twentieth Century Women: By Men, for Men
        Shara Jeyarajah 68
Read All about It! Chapter Three of *A Room of One's Own* as
    Required Reading for Men
        Maria Katsulos 71
The Importance of Art and Elisabeth Demand in *Autumn*
        Sydney Maddox 74
The Damaging Effects of Materialism
        Mary-Wesley Maddox 81
Now Let's Get Information: An Examination of the Socio-Political
    Parallels between *Gentleman's Agreement* and the Time's Up
    Movement
        Zoe Kerr 85
The Last Refuge of the Soldier
        John Berry 88
Another Dead Fool: The Value of Christopher's Journey in *Into the Wild*
        Christopher Wood 91
Finding the Value of Life: Sean Penn's *Into the Wild*
        Aja Tom 95

Learning and Reflecting: Education and the College Experience 99

Blazing New Trails: Undertaking Life as a Minority Student
        Briana Rollins 101
Something Permanent
        Lauren Alexander 109
A Helping Hand
        Kevin Quinn 113

The Value of Ownership
   Amanda Oh..117
A Liberal Education: Choices Are the Foundation of Freedom
   Tina Hirt..121
Claiming My Degree
   Megan Meinecke...126
A Community in Education
   Ryan Mendez..130

TIMED WRITING..135

Undeveloped Humanity
   Sophia Paolo..137
In-Class Timed Writing
   Sarah McCafferty...139
In-Class Timed Writing
   Sunjoli Aggarwal..141
In-Class Timed Writing
   Bailey Sprague..143
Structural Parallels and Character Formation in "Tiny, Smiling Daddy"
   Anna Wright..145
Spotlight on Daddy
   Mary Meehan...147
Works Cited..149

ENGLISH AS A SECOND LANGUAGE (ESL).......................151

How to Make Progress in GO
   Yinzhe (Mark) Qian.......................................153
Natural Beauty
   Steven Zhang...157
Mother Mary and Virgin Mary
   Yuxuan Zhou...160
Why People Love Watching Soccer at Stadiums
   Phuoc Dinh Le..163
The Effects of Chinese Education on International Chinese Students in the US
   Linda Chen...167

LEARNING TOOLS **173**

Writing at the University: Insight and Advice from a Professor Who Cares
   Vanessa Hopper 175

Some Chronic Essay Issues
   Joan Arbery 179

What Is a Thesis?
   Joan Arbery 184

A Good *BET*: Forming the Thesis
   LeeAnn Derdeyn 187

Ten Steps to Building the Brightest Essay
   Vanessa Hopper 190

Newton's Four Laws on Writing
   Pauline T. Newton 193

Aristotle's Proofs of Rhetoric
   Vanessa Hopper 194

Note-Taking Techniques
   Lori Ann Stephens 195

Writing with Your Own Voice
   Joan Arbery 205

The Art of Embedding Quotations
   Lori Ann Stephens 207

Introductory Paragraph Evaluation Exercise
   Vanessa Hopper 212

Says/Does Exercise
   Marta Krogh 214

Loving Lit: A Conversational Response to the Question, "Why do I have to read this book?"
   Vanessa Hopper 215

Universal Peer Draft Evaluation Guidelines
   Vanessa Hopper 218

Tips for Writing a Timed Essay
   Pauline T. Newton 221

Planning Rubric: How to Create an Excellent Oral Presentation
   Vanessa Hopper 222

Advice for New Discernment and Discourse Students 225

APPENDIX 227

Discernment and Discourse: Course Descriptions 229
Awards 231
Class Attendance 232
Office Conferences with Your Professor: What to Expect and
    How to Prepare 233
The Writing Center 236
The Altshuler Learning Enhancement Center 238
How the Library Can Help You with DISC 240
Researching Like a College Student 242
Computers on Campus 243
On Grading 244
D&D Rubric for Evaluating and Grading 245
Avoiding Bias 247
On Plagiarism 248
Statement on Academic Honesty 249
The Revising and Editing Process 250
Revision Worksheet 252
Editing Worksheet 253
Basics: Some Conventions of Correct Writing 254
Discernment and Discourse Department-Wide Grading Scale 260
MLA Format Sample Page 261

FROM THE EDITORS

To the Professors

Welcome to the latest edition of *Criteria*. As always, this text offers a selection of excellent student writing, so your students may benefit from and find inspiration in the writing of their peers. Essays are followed by questions for consideration that could be used for discussion, or as individual or group writing exercises. There is a selection of timed writings and a selection of essays from ESL. The "Learning and Reflecting" section this year is composed of highlights from the previous three editions; each of these essays demonstrates at least one of the skills showcased in the "Analyzing and Synthesizing, Persuasion and Argument" section, but they also offer the priceless gift of insights into the journey to becoming a well-rounded human right here on the SMU campus.

The Appendix includes information that can answer many of your students' questions about the course, including the department-wide grading scale, the Discernment and Discourse grading rubric, information on libraries and the A-LEC, reinforcement of the policy against plagiarism, and a segment on what to expect from and how to prepare for a conference with a DISC professor.

Keep in mind that many of the items in the "Learning Tools" section are ready-made assignments, which is one good reason to have the students bring the book to class. Evaluation exercises for creating strong introductory paragraphs, guidelines for building an effective oral presentation, and much more can ease the burden of your class preparation and enhance your students' learning experience.

Our sincerest thanks to those who have supported this book, recognized its worth, truly utilized it, and contributed to its content. This book would not exist without the diligence of the students who commit themselves to writing and revising with heart—but it is you who inspire them to find the courage to think critically and facilitate this vital step in their climb into the realm of good citizenship.

—V.H.
—O.S.

STUDENT WORK

The work in this section represents a variety of responses to a range of assignments that students encounter in their writing classes: assignments that allow them to analyze texts of all sorts; to research issues that hold meaning for them; and to evaluate and synthesize sources as they discover and articulate the point they want to make to their readers. We hope that these examples of first-year writers' work will stimulate thought and class discussion while also providing models of effective writing.

The editors of *Criteria* offer these essays as examples of original expression by the students for the Discernment and Discourse classes of Southern Methodist University. The ideas contained in them are those of the individual writers and do not necessarily reflect the opinions of the editors, the faculty, or the university.

Analyzing and Synthesizing, Persuasion and Argument

Nathan Hites illuminates the gray areas that complicate attempts to define "human" and "person" in this argument.

Death, Personhood, and Experimentation: What Does It Mean to Be Human?
Nathan Hites

1   In much of the philosophical discourse on personhood, the terms "human" and "person" are used almost interchangeably, as if it has been accepted that to be a person one must be human, or vice versa. The question becomes, then, what does it mean to be a "human" or a "person?" The purpose of this paper is to argue against using a typical definition for either of these two terms as the basis for judgments. We cannot use physical, empirical evidence to determine who is and who isn't a human or a person, as the distinction between those that are and those that aren't is a subjective field of study that we—as corporeal, temporal entities—cannot engage in. It is impossible to please everyone, as invariably certain "humans" may be considered nonhuman by some and certain "nonhumans" may be considered human by some. This problem also exists for the overarching concept of personhood and how it relates to human-ness. Invariably, any ability-based or merited classifications will exclude certain individuals in the eyes of some people for any number of reasons. Thus, there must be another definition for these two terms that can be used: one that does not rely on simply what we can see, touch, feel, or do. Personhood is not an intrinsic value but rather a moral relation defined by a duty to other entities; it is this definition of personhood that we need to foster and guard by examining the boundaries of humanity, personhood, and death.

2   The distinctions between *human* and *nonhuman*, and *person* and *nonperson*, are paramount to the concept of personhood, and to understand this difference, we must first examine our "working" definitions of both a human and a person. According to *The Oxford English Dictionary*, a human is "a human being," while a person is "a human being . . . regarded as having . . . rights, dignity, or worth." Notice the inherent use of "human" in both definitions, especially in that of "human" itself. The dictionary suggests that both these terms *must* indicate humanity, but if that is the case, what is the difference between a human and a person? We will now examine the West African conception of the person as seen by the Akan people, through the debate between Akan philosophers Kwasi Wiredu and Kwame Gyekye. Kwasi Wiredu defends the Akan word *onipa* (a word

that refers to a member of a biological species) as the main difference between a human *onipa* and a "person." Next, he cites former Zambian President Kaunga's explanation that "personhood is not an automatic quality of the human individual; it is something to be achieved, the higher the achievement, the higher the credit" (Wingo, Section 1). Wiredu argues that personhood is achieved through works and duties, as opposed to each individual human intrinsically possessing it, which is reflected in the Akan *oye onipa paa* (real person) and *onipa hun* (useless person) for those who have and have not served their community. However, this is in contrast to Kwame Gyekye's idea of personhood: that "we are human persons *before we are anything else* and it is the human *person* that matters from the moral point of view" (Wingo, Section 1). In other words, humanity and personhood are inextricably linked, and using "person" as a label like some sort of social status is reprehensible. To him, it is "only our essentially human capacity for reason . . . that serves as the basis for moral worth [and personhood]" (Wingo, Section 1). Both philosophers agree, though, that the "human" is simply a physical body that possesses reason—closer to the species-related tags "cat" and "dog"—while a "person" is a morally obligated being who is irrevocably linked to a community's values and morals.

3   Now that we can differentiate between humans and people, we will explore common assumptions about personhood, discovering who "is" and "isn't" a person based on the original dictionary definition. The most common distinction is between animals and humans. Who is worthy of the moral consideration we give to "people" and who is not? Of course, we cannot merely use sentience or cognitive capabilities to answer this question, as every animal, human, and even plant possesses one or both of these traits (Gruen, Section 1.4). Each of these nouns is simply a label for a species and thus cannot possibly be used as an objective criterion for personhood. Bioethicist Carl Elliot treats the personhood of animals similarly to that of critically-impaired humans, such as those with Alzheimer's and other such diseases, or even babies; neither group possesses the human standard of reason. Elliot asserts, "To treat a severely neurologically damaged child as a person . . . involves taking up a certain attitude towards him . . . such as the recognition that a person deserves a special kind of respect, that he or she is to be given a proper name . . ." (qtd. in Johnson 378). With this mindset, it is possible to address common human feelings (most owners of a cat or dog believe that their precious pet has feelings and is a person, too) without redefining personhood based on some arbitrary merited quality and thus exclude a human with certain disabilities.

4   While this is subjective ground, it rectifies many of the contemporary theories about who and who is not a person and still opens some rather dangerous doors.

For instance, if we use this attitude-based definition, arguments over common controversies like abortion now boil down to questions like, "Do I feel that this mass of cells is a *baby* or a *thing*?" However, now the follow-up question that can be asked is "*why am I taking the attitude that this being might not be a person?*" (Johnson 379). It is this latter question that can then be subject to the moral scrutiny given to each person, because the answer will reveal the values of a particular individual human. Therefore, no single definition for personhood truly works, as every person possesses a different set of values and thus, every living thing may or may not be a person, depending on who is asked.

5   If personhood is subjective, then, is there any validity to the argument that a being "is" a person one moment and then "isn't" the next? In other words, if gaining personhood is possible, what about losing it? This is a direct corollary to the Persistence Question—the potential criteria required of a person to remain a person from one time to another (Olson, Section 2), and the answer relies on how death is addressed. One answer is the organismic definition, in which death is defined as "the irreversible loss of functioning of the organism as a whole" (DeGrazia, Section 1). This means that death is both common and inevitable for any given entity; thus, the only way to lose personhood once it is attained would be to stop being an object capable of fostering relations due to total functional collapse. This is commonly misconstrued as the brain's cessation: "Bereft of mechanical assistance, the body from which the brain was removed would surely die [because there is now nothing directing it]. But this body was the living organism, one of us. So, although the original brain continues to function, the human being, one of us, would have died. [Therefore, total] brain failure, then, is not strictly necessary for human death" (DeGrazia, Section 1). Some beings do not even have brains—like single-celled organisms, plants, and fetuses—but they can clearly die. However, our previous definition of organism cessation does not capture patients such as those with removed mental faculties or situations related to genetics. Say that one could accurately and completely transfer the brain activity of a person into a robot or computer, which then outlived the original donor, such that the robot acted and behaved exactly as the original did. Who, then, is the person: the dead body or the new "organism"? The answer to this question *must* be subjective if we are to remain consistent in our definition of "person." Those who believe in the personhood of the body would believe that the robot is still the same person, and they would treat the robot the same way they did the brain's former occupant. Clearly, the barrier between life and death is not nearly as obvious or as simple as one would hope: "Although no organism can fully belong to both sets [life and death], organisms can be in many conditions (the very conditions that have created the debates about death) during which they do not fully belong to either . . .

Death is a fuzzy set" (DeGrazia, Section 4) and to truly "die," one must lose *all* of one's essential properties—either at once, or over a period of time. Otherwise, that individual is still alive enough to participate in the previously-discussed moral debate surrounding personhood. Thus, those with transplants, those with mental disabilities, and even the hypothetical Frankenstein monsters of science fiction are all technically eligible for personhood.

6   Factoring in all the gray areas in and around human-ness, personhood, and death, it is rather difficult to accurately portray who is and who is not a person. While almost anyone can glance at a human being and determine that he is indeed a human, it is not nearly as easy to treat the concept of "person" the same way, due to the moral consideration that is then granted with such a label. In fact, for entities bounded by rules that we have created ourselves, it is impossible; the distinction between persons and non-persons must be subjective, or there would not be such controversy over the term. Some humans would be called non-humans (or vice versa), and some persons would be called non-persons based on an objective checklist, even when this is clearly not believed to be the case. Thus, personhood must not be an intrinsic value or based on some corporeal tie to the world, be it a physical body or some specific bodily function. Instead, it must be grounded in the ethical descriptions that each community values and protects. If we wish to address the distinctions between persons and nonpersons—and humans and nonhumans—with this philosophical discourse, we must respect this definition.

Works Cited

DeGrazia, David. "The Definition of Death." *The Stanford Encyclopedia of Philosophy*, plato.stanford.edu/archives/spr2017/entries/death-definition/. Accessed 15 Oct. 2018.

Gruen, Lori. "The Moral Status of Animals." *The Stanford Encyclopedia of Philosophy*, plato.stanford.edu/archives/fall2017/entries/moral-animal/. Accessed 15 Oct. 2018.

"Human." *Oxford English Dictionary Online*. www.oed.com/. Accessed 22 Oct. 2018.

Johnson, Jennell. "Disability, Animals, and the Rhetorical Boundaries of Personhood." *JAC*, vol. 32, 2012, pp. 372–382.

Olson, Eric T., "Personal Identity." *The Stanford Encyclopedia of Philosophy*, plato.stanford.edu/archives/sum2017/entries/identity-personal/. Accessed 15 Oct. 2018.

"Person." *Oxford English Dictionary Online*. www.oed.com/. Accessed 22 Oct. 2018.

Wingo, Ajume, "Akan Philosophy of the Person." *The Stanford Encyclopedia of Philosophy*, plato.stanford.edu/entries/akan-person/. Accessed 15 Oct. 2018.

For Consideration:

1. Revisit Hites' title and consider the list that opens it up: "Death, Personhood, and Experimentation." Does this list accurately represent the essay's focal concepts and prepare you for what the essay is about? Explain your answer and then, on your own or in a small group, brainstorm alternate titles.

2. Highlight the sentences in the final paragraph where Hites draws his final conclusions about what personhood really is. On your own or with a group, come up with examples—from your own experiences and observations, or hypothetical—to reinforce this definition.

3. Which of Hites' supporting examples do you find to be the strongest? Choose two or three and explain what makes them work. Be thorough and specific, and use the language of rhetorical analysis, demonstrating your understanding of logos, ethos, and pathos.

Jordan Hardin offers a well-researched examination of the controversies surrounding cell gene therapy. He looks reasonably at the perspectives of the medical community and the public, and closes with thoughtful suggestions for opening the lines of communication and understanding between the two groups.

The Ethics of Somatic Cell Gene Therapy
Jordan Hardin

1 As a student studying English and biomedical anthropology, I have always been fascinated by the dynamic between humanities and the sciences, and any subject that brings these two seemingly distant fields together. Somatic cell gene therapy caught my interest as an ethical topic that acts as the collision between past and future medicine, as well as society and the sciences. Since the first trials of gene therapy in the 1990s (Kaufmann et al. 1647), both the public and the medical community have struggled with the concept of altering an individual's genetic information in both generationally isolated and consequential forms. On one hand, the medical community strives to see gene therapy remedy chronic and life-threatening diseases; from this perspective, they promote optimism despite complications in the research and defend gene therapy as a natural progression of medical technology. On the other hand, while the public approves of gene therapy as a means to address debilitating diseases, many worry about the implications of the medical community's unfettered desire to fix any condition that does not adhere to their concept of health. Many fear that gene therapy could potentially eliminate the variations that contribute to individuality and, worse, create a society intolerant of disabilities and any traits that do not align with an accepted view of normality. Given these worries, I would argue that the true ethical concerns about gene therapy are rooted in the heart of what society considers healthy and the role that gene therapy will play in shaping that concept in the future.

2 Since the first gene therapy treatment in 1990 (Sadler and Zeidler 429), somatic cell gene therapy has continued to grow as a field alongside improvements in medical technology and general knowledge. Somatic cell gene therapy is the process of using external genetic sequences to replace defective or missing sequences in *body* cells (Karpati and Lochmüller 273); this term encapsulates all cells except reproductive ones (eggs and sperm), which are accounted for by the term "germline cells." Thus, somatic cell gene therapy is restricted to affecting only the individual receiving the therapy and not future generations. Over the past

two decades, various experiments have shown promising signs of future medical applications of gene therapy, particularly in single-gene disorders such as hemophilia and SCID (Smith 249).

3   Though numerous treatment successes defend the therapeutic import of gene therapy, critical concerns about the treatment continue to generate ethical debate. Although the medical community grapples with issues of delivery, safety, and treatment longevity, researchers continue to pursue gene therapy with optimism for its therapeutic benefits; to many, addressing genetic diseases previously without cures is the next logical step in the evolution of medical technology (Kaufmann et al. 1642). Still, while various groups in the public acknowledge its therapeutic benefit, many remain concerned about the implications of gene therapy. The Deaf make up one such group—one which gene therapy could eventually target, and many of whom wonder what metaphysical and social consequences such treatment could produce in the future (Scully et al. 1421). To these individuals, therapeutic benefit fails to outweigh the risks of drastically altering a person's identity and creating a society hostile to disability (Scully et al. 1421). From my own past experiences working with this group of people, I have seen how integral deafness is to their identity and how hard the community has fought to combat discrimination over time. Other groups worry about the direction gene therapy will go once therapeutic treatment is readily available. Parents in particular express concerns that enhancement gene therapy will create a culture that demands this technology be applied to all children—even if it is not an economically realistic or philosophically desirable option for many families (Dickens 195). Although different groups have different anxieties, they share a fundamental concern: where to draw the line between conditions and diseases that are acceptable to treat, those that are not, and what choices should and will be available.

4   As with the majority of medical advances, the most obvious argument in favor of gene therapy emphasizes its future benefits. Although experimental complications have posed issues for researchers, the medical community refuses to surrender its support of gene therapy. In fact, according to a survey conducted by Isaac Rabino, 79% of the surveyed scientists "believe that gene therapy will one day become as routine and pervasive as immunizations or antibiotics" (39). I believe that this optimism sources from the medical community's unique orientation of their expectations. Bernard M. Dickens aptly captures this perspective in "Legal and Ethical Challenges in Gene Therapy," wherein he asserts that gene therapy should be regarded as innovative treatment rather than research. Instead of viewing gene therapy as a series of clinical experiments, the medical community looks at gene therapy as they do many experimental cancer treatments: "an

alternative therapy for terminally sick patients who failed conventional treatment" (Kaufmann et al. 1656). In this role, gene therapy acts as a well-intentioned attempt to save a patient's life, rather than an experiment for the sake of scientific progress. Karpati and Lochmüller's article corroborates this idea, asserting that gene therapy "cannot be considered a failure . . . particularly in relation to the timetable of its successful implementation" (276). In other words, considering the short history of gene therapy, it is unreasonable to demand a high degree of success, then brand it a failure without providing adequate time to prove its therapeutic benefit.

5   Additionally, although the failures of gene therapy trials tend to overshadow their successes, researchers argue that the technology is growing in safety and size. So far, research indicates that gene therapy has a promising future; successes in addressing single-gene disorders at such an early stage in the development of this technology engender optimism in the scientific community (Smith 249). According to Kaufmann et al.'s article "Gene Therapy on the Move," even the risks, which comprise one of the fundamental points of opposition, are "already being successfully addressed" (1656) as the field develops. Furthermore, Smith and Kaufmann et al. detail the expansion of gene therapy's applications. Whereas gene therapy research began primarily with treating single-gene disorders, researchers have started to apply the technology to polygenic disorders and even cancers (Smith 254). To me, it seems that the medical community argues that, through improving safety and expanding application, gene therapy's future is much brighter than the public perceives it to be; that is to say, if the treatment were truly dangerous and without evidence of therapeutic benefit, gene therapy research would not continue—much less expand into other disease areas, and increase in study frequency and size (Kaufmann et al. 1656).

6   On a less technical note, the medical community argues that the metaphysical concerns of the public are largely irrelevant to gene therapy ethics. Smith asserts that philosophical concerns regarding gene therapy lack credibility; largely based in ideas of particular cultures and religions, these concerns are not applicable to the public as a whole (Smith 247). Essentially, given that gene therapy is a society-wide concern, these specialized views are irrelevant to the larger dialogue at hand, since they are opinions rather than facts. Moreover, many of the metaphysical concerns are grounded in misconceptions. As da Fonesca et al. notes in their article "Human Transgenesis: Definitions, Technical Possibilities, and Moral Challenges," the public places an undue emphasis on the importance of genes. To the scientific community, genes are no different than any other component of the human body, and the public's reverence of them stems from the very cultural and religious myths that Smith argues should be dismissed from the debate (247).

Additionally, da Fonesca et al. argue that somatic cell gene therapy operates on perfectly natural mechanisms. Homologous to natural processes such as horizontal gene transfer, a method through which organisms such as bacteria exchange genetic information, gene therapy incorporates transgenic mechanisms already present in nature (da Fonesca 516). Therefore, even if the technology is artificial, the fact that similar processes take place in nature demonstrates that gene therapy is a useful, natural mode of treatment. To the medical community, all of this evidence serves as sufficient reason to see metaphysics as irrelevant to gene therapy's future.

7   Unlike some ethical issues in which each side is staunchly committed to being for or against an idea, many opponents of gene therapy recognize and support some of its applications. In fact, in the aforementioned study conducted by Isaac Rabino, as high as 88% of a sample reflecting the American public approved of gene therapy when applied to fatal genetic diseases (41). However, beyond this point, opponents grow wary of gene therapy.

8   One area that draws concern from both sides, but particularly opponents, is safety. Presently, while somatic cell gene therapy has largely been conducted in a safe manner, multiple complications along the way call into question the risks associated with participating in gene therapy research. The most notable cases of complications, which continue to garner attention in medical literature, are the death of research participant Jesse Gelsinger (Teichler Zallen 272) and the development of leukemia in two other participants in a separate study (Smith 249). In both cases, while the presence of a pre-existing disease appeared to have some degree of influence on the outcome, the vector through which the gene sequences were delivered appeared to be the root cause (Smith 249). The safety concerns regarding the vector issue continue to generate much public unease and mistrust regarding gene therapy. Many members of the public fear that the scientific community is brashly compromising the "generous human beings who are putting their bodies on the line on behalf of science" (Teichler Zallen 275) for a treatment that may not even be ready for human application. I found this particular argument relevant to material covered in my Discernment and Discourse class this semester—particularly Kantian ethics. To me, the public adopts an approach grounded in the concept of the categorical imperative (Kant 8). That is to say, the public seems to argue that, even if the medical community is well-intentioned in the pursuit of gene therapy research, the moral duty to protect the lives of research participants should ultimately take precedence.

9   Even though safety is a critical argument of the opponents, the highest profile and most vociferous argument attacks the technology's trajectory; that is, many individuals fear that acceptance of somatic cell gene therapy will lead to nefarious

applications of the treatment. Public anxiety heightens around any treatment that ventures into correction of traits "not associated with disease" (Sadler and Zeidler 432). To the public, this description encompasses characteristics such as personality and physical traits. Although the public does acknowledge that technology such as cosmetic surgeries demonstrate that society is comfortable with altering personal characteristics on grounds other than health concerns (Dickens 194), they refuse the idea that gene therapy is of equal nature. While many scientists concur with the dangers of enhancement applications, Rabino's statistics indicate that the public's fear of gene therapy extending beyond its therapeutic purview is not unfounded. A majority of 51% of the researchers surveyed approved of gene therapy applied to reducing "propensity for aggression" (Rabino 40). While this figure indicates that there still is a large portion of the community that disapproves of this application, the fact that such a large number approves of altering a personality characteristic (albeit a negative one) alarms the public. It seems to me that this statistic foreshadows the attitude that the public fears the medical community will adopt in guiding gene therapy's future; they worry that the medical community's desire to fix traits transgressive to 'normality' will lead gene therapy down the wrong path.

10   Consequently, the public argues that gene therapy has the potential to threaten identity. Intelligence, height, eye color, and a multitude of other characteristics are fundamental to an individual's identity; if someone who was previously five feet tall grew to a towering seven feet, that person's identity would dramatically alter. For better or worse, chronic and life-threatening diseases similarly become a critical component of a patient's identity, since a person is often born with them (Reindal 93). While some patients are eager for treatment options, others resist the idea of gene therapy targeting their diseases or disabilities. Scully et al.'s study analyzing the difference between the ethical concerns of the medical community and patients, then patients of different disease backgrounds, demonstrates this anxiety. The medical community and patients with chronic, debilitating illness were optimistic about gene therapy, focusing on issues related to resources and technology; however, patients who were deaf or had achondroplasia (dwarfism) were concerned that gene therapy would strive to eliminate the conditions so fundamental to their identities and life experiences (1421). My own experiences with the Deaf community support this concern. Without hearing loss, the Deaf would not possess the language and history that unite the community; thus, their identities would change dramatically.

11   With the identity argument in mind, the long-term concern involved with using gene therapy to correct diseases and disabilities is that it will create a

society resistant to them. Fearing the revival of eugenic attitudes that have caused many tragedies in the past, opponents of gene therapy are alarmed by the fact that potential disability application proves that there is a dominating, misconstrued idea of what is considered healthy in society (Reindal 92). In his counter-argument of another scholar, Solveig Magnus Reindal reminds the medical community that many of the conditions society strives to correct do not actually impede the lives of those who experience them (93). Therefore, Reindal argues that these ideas of health that rule the medical conscience have dangerous consequences. In terms of social dynamics, a biased definition of health could eventually become "an instrument of power in relation to minority groups and in the oppression of, and discrimination against" (Reindal 93) these patients.

12   I found this concept evocative of Zygmunt Bauman's "The Dream of Purity" and Flannery O'Connor's "The Life You Save May Be Your Own." Similar to Reindal, Bauman asserts that purity (analogous to health) is relative rather than an "intrinsic quality" (Bauman 50). Deaf people, for example, do not perceive their hearing loss as a crippling disability; my experiences with the Deaf community have shown me that many of these individuals do not feel as though they are missing out on crucial life experiences simply because they cannot hear. Their culture is grounded in hearing loss, which is normal for them. Similarly, O'Connor's story depicts how society perceives disability far differently than the disabled people themselves do; while the old woman views Mr. Shiftlet's missing arm as crippling to his success, Mr. Shiftlet himself does not find that his disability impacts his quality of life (O'Connor 152). Both of these literary examples support the idea that there is no objective definition of health.

13   Although it would be a disservice to the importance of the issue to say that a simple dialogue is sufficient for working towards a compromise, I believe that communication is fundamental to building trust between the two communities. Throughout my research, I frequently identified evidence of the scientific community's inability to comprehend the issues that plague the conscience of the public. As the scientific community is comprised of individuals with a highly technical and vast scientific knowledge, it makes sense that their comfort with the gene therapy would prevent them from truly understanding the concerns of the public. However, as with many other issues, members of the public need to properly educate themselves on a subject before developing an opinion grounded in fear. I believe that the most realistic, direct option is establishing a dialogue between the communities through education programs and panels. Political agitation to increase the lacking oversight identified in Doris Teichler Zallen's article, while definitely necessary, is something that would play out over a large period of time,

potentially requiring a reformation in the "fad"-like way in which the public has the tendency to support many issues. Personally, I find that community outreach via education is the best way of helping each side come to an understanding. To enhance the public's understanding of the technical aspects of gene therapy, medical experts could host community outreach events and engage the media in order to increase general understanding. Additionally, to grow their own understanding of the identity and health concerns of their patients, the medical community could conduct interviews similar to Scully et al.'s with patients in the community. While it is impossible to say whether these efforts would ultimately result in a compromise between the two sides, I think that they would be highly beneficial in allowing each side to understand the other's perspectives; perhaps, in the future, this type of dialogue would pave the way for reconciliation.

Works Cited

Bauman, Zygmunt. "The Dream of Purity." *Theoria: A Journal of Social and Political Theory*, No. 86, Dimensions of Democracy, 1995, pp. 49–60. *JSTOR*. www.jstor.org/stable/41802659.

da Fonesca, Flávio Guimarães, et al. "Human Transgenesis: Definitions, Technical Possibilities, and Moral Challenges." *Philosophy & Technology*, vol. 25, no. 4, 2012, pp. 513–524. *SpringerLink*. doi:10.1007/s13347-012-0074-7.

Dickens, Bernard M. "Legal and Ethical Challenges in Gene Therapy." *Transfusion Science*, vol. 17, no. 1, 1996, pp. 191–196. *ScienceDirect*. doi:0955-3886(95)00073-9.

Kant, Immanuel. *Fundamental Principles of the Metaphysic of Morals*. Translated by Thomas Kingsmill Abbott, *The University of Adelaide Library*, ebooks.adelaide.edu.au/k/kant/immanuel/k16prm/.

Karpati, George and Hanns Lochmüller. "The Scope of Gene Therapy in Humans: Scientific, Safety, and Ethical Considerations." *Neuromuscular Disorders*, vol. 7, no. 5, 1998, pp. 273–276. *ScienceDirect*. doi:S0960-8966(97)00051-5.

Kaufmann, Kerstin B., et al. "Gene Therapy on the Move." *EMBO Molecular Medicine*, vol. 5, no. 11, 2013, pp. 1642–1661. *PubMed*. doi:10.1002/emmm.201202287.

O'Connor, Flannery. "The Life You Save May Be Your Own." *The Complete Stories*. Farrar, Straus and Giroux, 1971, pp. 145–156.

Rabino, Isaac. "Gene Therapy: Ethical Issues." *Theoretical Medicine*, vol. 24, no. 1, 2003, pp. 31–58. *SpringerLink*. doi:10.1023/A:1022967623162.

Reindal, Solveig Magnus. "Disability, Gene Therapy and Eugenics—A Challenge to John Harris." *Journal of Medical Ethics*, vol. 26, no. 2, 2000, pp. 89–94. *PubMed*. doi:10.1136/jme.26.2.89.

Sadler, Troy D. and Dana L. Zeidler. "Negotiating Gene Therapy Controversies." *The American Biology Teacher,* vol. 66, no. 6, 2004, pp. 428–433. *JSTOR.* doi:10.2307/4451709.

Scully, Jackie Leach, et al. "Non-professionals' Evaluations of Gene Therapy Ethics." *Social Science & Medicine,* vol. 58, no. 7, 2004, pp. 1415–1425. *ScienceDirect.* doi:S0277-9536(03)00336-8.

Smith, Kevin R. "Gene Therapy: Theoretical and Bioethical Concepts." *Archives of Medical Research,* vol. 34, no. 4, 2003, pp. 247–268. *ScienceDirect.* doi:S0188-4409(03)00070-5.

Teichler Zallen, Doris. "US Gene Therapy in Crisis." *Trends in Genetics,* vol. 16, no. 6, 2000, pp. 272–275. *ScienceDirect.* doi:S0168-9525(00)02025-4.

For Consideration:

1. Re-read the solutions that the author presents in the conclusion. What other possibilities could be added to the list? Explain each thoroughly, including why it is reasonable and specifically how it would be effective.

2. Did you have any opinions on gene therapy before reading this essay? If so, what were they and how did you come by them? Did reading this essay enhance or alter your original perspective in any way? If so, how and why?

3. Do a close review of the Works Cited entries. Choose one of the sources and, as practice for honing your own documentation skills, write an annotated bibliography summary for that source based on how Hardin used the text in his essay.

In her essay, Sophie Vos explores sides of the euthanasia debate while emphasizing the importance of keeping the focus on the situation and needs of each individual human.

The End of the Road—Or Is It? Research on Euthanasia

Sophie Vos

1   All humans die. No matter what pains we take to maintain health and happiness, all human life must come to an end eventually. Many of us feel great dread and fear when contemplating death and all its uncertainty—but what do we make of people who not only welcome death, but actively seek it? The question of whether to end a life or not brings in a whole host of other questions: *Why would one wish to end his or her life? Ought we to choose when and how to die? What should doctors do when approached by patients who wish to end their lives?* A hotly-debated topic in contemporary Western thought, euthanasia divides physicians, public policy experts, academics, and laypeople into strong supporters and sound opponents. Each side holds that their view champions the most ethical society. Regardless of the implications of any side, we cannot forget the patients behind the practice. Considering the utter finality in the ending of a human life, we must necessarily examine the influences and motivations behind patients' suicidal intentions; we cannot take their individual concerns lightly if we intend to build a more caring and understanding society. I believe that the better doctors understand their patients' needs, the better doctors can care for their patients. Thus, I suggest that when dealing with conscious patients capable of making autonomous decisions, doctors should focus on getting to know patients and offering them a breadth of resources and choices in order to best meet the patients' end-of-life needs.

2   Given the ubiquitous nature of death itself, it comes as no surprise that the debate over euthanasia spans thousands of years. As outlined in McDougall and Gorman's *Euthanasia: A Reference Handbook*, a nonpartisan, informational overview of euthanasia, the debate traces back to the years BCE. Pythagoreans rejected euthanasia on the grounds that "only God had the right to take life" and opposed the Athenians, who "could obtain a dose of poison which would allow them to choose death" (McDougall and Gorman 3). As we might guess from the Pythagoreans' stance, religious groups have historically condemned euthanasia; Christianity and Judaism condemned euthanasia and suicide as "murder" in the first century and middle ages (McDougall and Gorman 3–4). With the scientific

and medical advances brought by the Renaissance era, some began to reflect on the validity of euthanasia, considering the "new dilemmas" of "increased suffering" caused by physicians' new abilities to "prolong life" past the patient's natural end, while religious groups held fast to their condemnation of euthanasia (McDougall and Gorman 5). With the Age of Reason came even more physicians and lawmakers willing to consider euthanasia and the concept of justified suicide in light of increased knowledge of the human body, exemplified by "six of the thirteen [American] colonies no longer mandate[ing] legal penalties for people who attempted suicide [by 1798]" (McDougall and Gorman 5).

3   Edwin DuBose, in his non-partisan handbook on physician-assisted suicide with emphasis on religion and policy, attests to the role of religion today in shaping notions of euthanasia. Since "religious groups . . . have longstanding beliefs about the sacredness of life, the nature of human beings, suffering" and other related topics, religious groups have much to say about life and death issues (23). DuBose notes that although religious groups today still condemn euthanasia overall, "religious believers sometimes support PAS [physician-assisted suicide or voluntary euthanasia]" because they think "the moral evil present in other forms of taking innocent life may not be present" in these situations (21–22). Looking at the history of euthanasia discourse, we observe an overall trend that with technological advancement has come more voices in favor of euthanasia, or at least existing voices have made themselves more vocal. McDougall and Gorman observe that today's "vaccines for polio, certain new medications, pacemakers, and surgical techniques" advance at the same time as "increased patient requests for assistance in dying" (6). While the pro-euthanasia side might see the greater patient interest in dying as an opportunity to consider euthanasia practices, the against-euthanasia side sees the greater interest as a sign to take more caution in understanding patients' requests before rushing to make policy. In any case, the simultaneous increase in life-saving technology and the call for euthanasia suggests that patients, rather than wanting to cut their lives short, express more concern over prolonging their lives past some perceived limit. Thus, in examining both sides of the euthanasia debate, we must essentially find out why patients do not want to live longer. In uncovering patients' concerns over the "extra" time added to their lifespans, doctors can assess their patients' needs and wants with better end-of-life care options.

4   To understand patients' concerns, we must first distinguish between different types of euthanasia requests. Although "good death" captures the main idea of euthanasia, "derived from the Greek *eu* and *thanatos*," not all practices have the same implications (McDougall and Gorman 264). On the broadest scale, we

differentiate passive euthanasia, or "forgo[ing] actions that could save someone's life," from active euthanasia, or "someone other than the patient actually performing the action" (McDougall and Gorman 265). Under active euthanasia, we obtain three distinctions: voluntary euthanasia (otherwise known as "assisted suicide," which the patients themselves or another person can carry out), nonvoluntary euthanasia, and involuntary euthanasia. The differences between these three types of active euthanasia lie with the patient: voluntary euthanasia means the patient requests it, nonvoluntary euthanasia means the patient has not requested it, and involuntary euthanasia means the patient cannot request it "due to incompetence" (McDougall and Gorman 265). The bulk of euthanasia debates concern passive and voluntary euthanasia, as many people on both sides see nonvoluntary and involuntary euthanasia as unethical practices. Of course, killing another person without his or her explicit consent amounts to homicide or murder, but some contend that even this situation may fall into a gray area. For example, Thomasma and Graber, pro-euthanasia experts in bioethics and ethics, respectively, make a case for accepting non-voluntary euthanasia by giving the analogy that if a boy looks at your cookies with yearning in his eyes, you may presume he wants one (52–53). However, the level of seriousness in ending a life far exceeds the seriousness in giving a boy a cookie, and the debate continues over whether we can ethically presume a patient wishes to end his or her life if the individual never explicitly say so.

5   Before considering the increasingly vocal pro-euthanasia side, let's first understand the arguments against euthanasia. Traditionally, religion has and continues to play a "central" role in moral arguments against euthanasia (DuBose 45). *The Churches Speak On: Euthanasia*, a collection and analysis of official religious statements on euthanasia by J. Gordon Melton, explains that "the Roman Catholic Church has been the most prolific source of statements on euthanasia" stating "the primary concept undergirding Roman Catholic consideration of euthanasia [as] the sanctity of life" (Melton xvi). In addition to our responsibility to protect and treasure life because of its sacred nature, Melton also points out that Roman Catholics distinguish between active euthanasia, which "is to be opposed" no matter what, and passive euthanasia, which "is permitted when prolongation of life requires extraordinary means which impose a greater burden than benefit" (xvi). Following the Roman Catholic lead, "conservative Protestants . . . tend to oppose legalization of any form of euthanasia" from their "doctrines of dominion, stewardship, and the absolute sanctity of life" (Melton xvii). In the same vein, Dr. Arthur J. Dyck, a retired professor of ethics and population ethics at Harvard Divinity School, makes his case against legalizing euthanasia because "current

laws presuppose a shared moral outlook that characterizes life as sacred, and as an inalienable human right" (7). Dyck argues that the right to live outweighs a patient's request to die because "the wishes of patients . . . are very much dependent on the relationships they have with their physicians and other individuals at the time they are faced with the prospect of dying" (17). Because a patient's wishes may change depending on their relationships and circumstances, Dyck argues that physicians cannot support patients in forfeiting their right to live. Dyck cements his point by providing evidence that hospice physicians report that, after receiving care that alleviates pain and suffering, previously suicidal patients "change their minds," which speaks to the malleability of human desires in differing physical circumstances (47). Since a patient's feelings about the meaningfulness of life differs circumstantially, the anti-euthanasia side would argue that doctors should hold off on assisting in a patient's death in favor of giving alternative care and time to reevaluate life's value.

6   In addition to moral concerns, another compelling anti-euthanasia argument comes from Dr. Herbert Hendin, medical director of the American Suicide Foundation and professor of psychiatry at New York Medical College, who studies the Netherlands' decriminalization and wide acceptance of euthanasia in his book *Seduced by Death*. Hendin argues that widespread acceptance of euthanasia in the Netherlands, rather than helping suicidal patients, offers nothing more than a quick and irreversible "cure" to the problem of suicide that disregards important considerations about the well-being of the patient (224). Hendin relays "that euthanasia is basically out of control in the Netherlands" because rather than delving into the patient's fears, concerns, suffering, and depression to find the best possible end-of-life care, physicians increasingly administer euthanasia with alarming ease (14-15). Hendin's book provides damning evidence that the Netherlands has fallen down a "slippery slope" from accepting limited practices of euthanasia to legalizing "wrongful deaths" (13). Both Dyck and Hendin's arguments echo the famous philosopher Immanuel Kant, who reasons that we cannot justify suicide as a universal natural law because there is no natural system by which we can seek to end life without contradicting our ultimate natural motivation, which is to improve life. In other words, a person would contradict himself or herself in desiring to both better his or her life as well as to end it; one's life cannot improve when dead. Dyck and Hendin follow Kant's philosophy by championing palliative care over euthanasia to best improve patients' lives. To protect patients in some of their most vulnerable moments, perhaps doctors should focus on developing a caring and attentive relationship with the patient to address physical, emotional, and psychological needs.

7   While the anti-euthanasia side views euthanasia and suicide as incompatible with morality, formal logic, and rationality, pro-euthanasia advocates contend that this view is too narrow. To begin, Thomasma and Graber explain that to understand euthanasia, we must understand that "rather [than an enemy, death] is considered to be a friend for the patient, whose life itself has now become a burden" (3). Even though death often carries negative connotations, Thomasma and Graber ask us to put aside those negative predispositions toward the concept of death so we can consider the possible benefits of euthanasia. Proponents like Dr. Charles F. McKhann, as explained in McDougall and Gorman's book, say "suicide is sometimes a very rational choice" justified by "the desire to avoid unnecessary suffering" and "the desire to exercise one's autonomy and self-determination" (33–34). Indeed, to speak to the first justification, the avoidance of suffering provides one of the strongest bases for euthanasia. For example, in Art Spiegelman's graphic novel *Maus I*, the narrator's aunt Tosha poisons herself and the three children in her care upon learning the Nazis will take her and the children to Auschwitz (109). Whether or not we can justify Tosha's drastic decision to avoid the gas chambers remains up for debate, but we can all understand and empathize with the desire to evade the horrors and what Tosha sees as certain painful death at the hands of Nazis in a death camp.

8   The averting of suffering also plays an important role in pro-euthanasia arguments because of doctors' clear "duty to control pain and suffering" in their patients (Thomasma and Graber 192–193). By "pain and suffering," Thomasma and Graber explain that "pain is an interpreted experience" that includes not only physical pain, which patients may feel at varying levels of intensity, but also deep emotional and psychological suffering (194). Coupled with the argument that "a person has a right to do what he or she pleases with the body," or the constitutional right to privacy, Thomasma and Graber call for "a rethinking of the goals of modern medicine" to include more than just control of bodily suffering through technological means that may cause the patient emotional and psychological distress (192, 195). To prolong life no matter what, Thomasma and Graber argue, constitutes "biological idolatry" because it ignores death as the universal and inherent end to human existence (201). Since we will all die one day anyway, why should we not choose to die when and how we want? To hearken back to McKann's two justifications of "avoid[ing] unnecessary suffering" and "exercis[ing] one's autonomy and self-determination," we find that the second justification provides another pillar of pro-euthanasia argument: the patient's choice (McDougall and Gorman 34). Thomasma and Graber assert that "when a person decides that continued life is meaningless, that decision ought to be respected" (192).

9   Thomasma and Graber's argument that patients should have the right to choose their own life's meaning and fate mirrors the wishes of Thomas Youk, the man famously euthanized by Dr. Jack Kevorkian in 1998. As explained in Nichol and Wylie's book on the relevant, adult life of euthanasia advocate Dr. Jack Kevorkian, "death—on his terms—really was what [Youk] wanted" (6). Nichol and Wylie state that since Youk could assess the level of pain and suffering he felt resulting from his ALS, a neurodegenerative disease that eventually shuts down all muscle movement, Youk deserved to choose his fate "and it would be an act of cruelty to force him to keep living" (6). Surely the wishes of patients like Thomas Youk, whose irreversible medical conditions make each day more painful and challenging as the disease progresses, "ought to be respected" (Thomasma and Graber 192). In order to respect the values and goals of the patient, Thomasma and Graber insist on respecting the patients' decisions, even decisions as weighty as ending their own life. From their language, it seems that Thomasma and Graber would agree that doctors should get to know their patients to better understand and respect the patients' true wishes. Doctors would do patients a disservice if they simply took any patient's requests at face value without understanding the patient's individual circumstances, needs, and personal goals behind the request.

10   In weighing the fine arguments on both sides of the euthanasia debate, discussions about intangible things like morality, rationality, the ethics of avoiding suffering, and choice can distract us from the very real patients at the heart of the issue. We should not let our discomfort with tackling notions of death distance us from those who face the real prospect of death every day. If we encourage doctors to get to know their patients, they can direct the depressed suicidal patient to possible medication and counselors to lift them out of a depressed state. If we train doctors to learn how "to comfort and help those [terminal] patients they cannot cure," they can ease terminal patients through their end-of-life stages more peacefully (Hendin 217). I firmly believe that doctors who know their patients' personalities, pain, suffering, anxieties, family support (or lack thereof), goals, and values can much more effectively treat patients than doctors who do not. Caring for others involves so much more than caring for physical needs only; all humans have needs beyond the physical. Since the end of a life contains just as much importance in the human experience as the beginning of one, doctors, as well as the rest of us, would do well to consider the meanings we place on death and force ourselves to face it with tough questions. We must contemplate how we choose to view death and the dying process, what cultural and religious meanings we bring to death, and how we treat others during their dying processes. I believe such reflection would serve to orient ourselves within our values, purpose, and place in society with more maturity and confidence.

Works Cited

DuBose, Edwin. *Physician-Assisted Suicide: Religious and Public Policy Perspectives.* The Park Ridge Center, 1999.

Dyck, Arthur J. and the Center for Bioethics and Human Dignity. *Life's Worth: The Case Against Assisted Suicide.* Eerdmans Publishing Co., 2002.

Hendin, Herbert. *Seduced by Death: Doctors, Patients, and the Dutch Cure.* W. W. Norton & Co., Inc., 1997.

Kant, Immanuel. *Fundamental Principles of the Metaphysics of Morals.* Translated by Thomas Kingsmill Abbott, pdfs.semanticscholar.org/b2a1/f5dcbf8bf21674acdf fa76bd50db05d9ea4a.pdf.

McDougall, Jennifer and Martha Gorman. *Euthanasia: A Reference Handbook.* ABC-CLIO, 2008.

Melton, J. Gordon. *The Churches Speak On: Euthanasia—Official Statements from Religious Bodies and Ecumenical Organizations.* Gale Research Inc., 1991.

Nicol, Neal and Harry Wylie. *Between the Dying and the Dead: Dr. Jack Kevorkian's Life and the Battle to Legalize Euthanasia.* U of Wisconsin Press, 2006.

Spiegelman, Art. *Maus I: A Survivor's Tale: My Father Bleeds History.* Pantheon, 1986.

Thomasma, David C. and Glenn C. Graber. *Euthanasia: Toward an Ethical Social Policy.* Continuum Publishing Co., 1990.

For Consideration:

1. If you have not already done so, read the previous essay by student Nathan Hites. What correlations do you see between the conclusions drawn by Hites and by Vos in this essay? How does each essay "inform" the other in terms of key concepts and the conflicts addressed?

2. Before you read this essay, what was your position on euthanasia? Did reading this essay influence your position in any way? If required to do so, which of Hites' or Vos's sources would you be most interested in locating and reviewing? Explain your answers.

The following two writers argue for a sympathetic perspective on the character of Mrs. Mooney, a character generally seen as mercenary and unlikeable, from James Joyce's Dubliners *story collection of the early 1900s. Both students utilized their understanding of Karl Marx's critique of capitalism in building their arguments, which are different but equally effective. Study questions for these essays follow the second essay.*

Making Circumstance a Victim of You
Reed Abbajay

1   A child is born to overbearing parents who chiefly value his academic success; he will one day be a doctor. In terms to be found in Karl Marx's *The Communist Manifesto*, a bourgeoisie-proletariat relationship between the parents and child results, in which the child is commodified for the achievements which serve as extensions of his parents' egos, and without an exceptionally open mind that child will grind diligently all his life, never really living for himself. To resist controlling circumstances is to take the road less traveled by, epitomizing the potential of human free will. A powerful example of this is Mrs. Mooney from James Joyce's "The Boardinghouse," who turns her very unfortunate circumstances into an independent life that successfully resists the patriarchal status quo of her time.

2   As the daughter of a successful business-owner, Mrs. Mooney would be a step ahead of many in terms of having what it takes to be well-off on her own, particularly with her knowledge of how to run her father's butcher shop. When a man entered her life, however, things seemed to just get harder; her husband inherited the rights to her father's business, which he ruined by buying bad meat and arguing in front of customers. His destructive professional behavior and privately abusive behavior made Mrs. Mooney realize she would be better off on her own, and when this man went after her with a cleaver, she knew it was time to do things her own way.

3   After the Catholic Church approves a separation from her husband, she takes charge of her life with an air of independence that would certainly be considered masculine at the time. In opening her own boardinghouse, Mrs. Mooney is symbolically flipping the patriarchy on its head: although women were typically commodified for sex, reproduction, and raising children, and although men had practically seized the means of earning money independently in society, now a woman was in charge of taking care of working men, making a living in the process. Her exploitation of the patriarchy is further exemplified by the fact that she

brings her daughter to the boardinghouse to flirt with the men, exploiting their sexuality and the way they commodify attractive women in order to keep the men inside and paying. In a society where so many men reduce women to a means to an end, Mrs. Mooney does not hesitate to commodify them right back.

4 Although her behavior might make it seem as if she detests men, the nature of her son proves that this is not so. It's not men in general that Mrs. Mooney has a problem with; it's the prevalent kind of man who participates in the patriarchal bourgeoisie, investing his sense of self in having control over the women in his life as if they are proletarians. It's very likely that Mrs. Mooney had well-developed thoughts about this inequality in society and hence raised her son to contribute to breaking the cycle. This is evident in Jack Mooney's disposition and general attitude towards men and women—he made it clear that he would do some serious damage to any man who took advantage of his sister, demonstrating his high value for female dignity and his low value for sexual conquest. Considering Mrs. Mooney's experiences with her husband, Mrs. Mooney is sure to have felt that bringing another one of those men into the world would be unacceptable, and instead she raised her son in her image of what a man has the potential to be.

5 As for her daughter, Mrs. Mooney likely sees a version of herself who has the potential to live a better life. Although it might seem that the way she handles her daughter's affair with Mr. Doran is solely motivated by material means, the reality of her own past marriage and the way she feels about patriarchal bourgeois morality hint at a more complex thought process. Her hesitation to intervene in the relationship between Polly and Mr. Doran, allowing it to progress naturally on its own, suggests that she was predicting that things might go too far, which she could use as leverage to secure a marriage between a middle-class girl and a wealthy man that would never happen otherwise. Mrs. Mooney was not inclined to accept money for Mr. Doran's moral transgression like many other women at the time would have—there was no chance that she would let a man get away with reducing her daughter to a sex object and running away from it having paid a mere monetary price. It might seem odd that Mrs. Mooney approves of Mr. Doran's older age—Polly is nineteen and he is in his thirties—but Mrs. Mooney knew that an older man in a high-class position would almost certainly not turn out to be a man like her own lowly husband. Furthermore, the way she handles the whole situation screams rebellion against the status quo of women at the time—practically reducing a man to his knees and eliciting from him a commitment to the very thing that many men considered the end of life's pleasures and freedom: marriage.

⁶   Ultimately, Miss Mooney serves as a model for anyone who has been acquainted with unjust, controlling circumstances. Given her own, she very practically made the best out of what her life could have been by being an example of what women are capable of. By living independently and reacting against a patriarchal society, she shows that commodifying the female is a grave mistake, and that a society in which men have such a controlling upper hand is unsustainable if more women start to follow suit. Like Miss Mooney took her circumstances head-on, so too should young people who find themselves victims of parents who care more about academic achievement than individuality. Find inspiration in Mrs. Mooney, because she proves that being a victim of bad circumstances can mean the opportunity to live a life that is inherently redeeming: choosing oneself, denying to conform to what others egotistically dictate, and contributing to a greater movement that has the potential to radically change society itself.

Works Cited

Joyce, James. "The Boarding House." *Dubliners*. Penguin, 1976, pp. 61–69.
Marx, Karl, et al. *The Communist Manifesto*. Signet Classics, 2011.

A Boardinghouse Roof for a Glass Ceiling: Evaluating Joyce's Mrs. Mooney

Steven Manning

1   It's common to hear traditional folks moan about how modern society is out of touch with healthy family values. Of course, for Mrs. Mooney and others living in an age we look upon with such nostalgia, life was totally different. Had she been any less tough, an abusive relationship would have destroyed her life, and she needed the blessing of the church at fault for the marriage to begin with to escape. In the same way that modern society gives a pass to children known to have grown up in abusive households, it's appropriate that we do the same for Mrs. Mooney and recognize that beneath the tough skin lies a well-intentioned mother.

2   Though coarse, every time Mrs. Mooney runs roughshod over her daughter's feelings it's important to remember the alternative: her husband running roughshod over the both of them. Having been cursed once with an abusive relationship, it's apparent that Mrs. Mooney wants to do better for her daughter, and Bob Doran—the middle-aged man who has begun a love affair with her daughter—is the best way of making that happen. Mrs. Mooney's attitude to Mr. Doran and Polly's relationship—which has been clandestine, and right under the noses of all those in the boardinghouse—may seem callous. However, the normal path—a lengthy courtship and prearranged marriage—wasn't viable since it's possible that Polly is expecting Mr. Doran's baby. Additionally, given how poorly traditional courtship worked out for Mrs. Mooney, it's unsurprising that Mrs. Mooney should choose to take an alternative track. As she became aware of her daughter's pregnancy, the narrator refers to "constant peals" from a nearby belfry and mentions the worshippers in their "little circus before church" (63). Nothing in the depictions of Catholicism anywhere in the story is complimentary, and the bells may as well be the objections of the church (and its patriarchy) to Mrs. Mooney's approach to marriage without regard to social expectations.

3   Her struggle against the prison of femininity defines Mrs. Mooney and greatly influences how she approaches her daughter's relationship. Imagine, from her perspective, the gift she is giving Polly: a marriage in which the husband doesn't have ultimate authority over his wife. That gift was made possible by Mr. Doran impregnating her daughter out of wedlock; both Bob Doran and Mrs. Mooney know that if the community finds out, this could cost Mr. Doran his job, a comfortable and prestigious position at a famous wine mercantile where

he's built a reputation for over a decade. Though it's never explicitly discussed, one can infer that in a boardinghouse full of rowdy young men, an older lady like Mrs. Mooney would be under constant pressure to conform to the expectations society had for women, mostly cooking and cleaning, and this must have been degrading. Having spent a lifetime struggling to make ends meet within the limits set forth by her society, Mr. Doran is an opportunity to free her daughter from that struggle. We don't typically think of settling down and becoming a housewife as an accomplishment, but in early 1900s Dublin, Ireland, it was probably the best option available.

4   Mrs. Mooney's at times seemingly callous behavior is a product of her past and the experiences she's had with society. In a culture and within a family that treated her as incapable of making her own decisions or succeeding as a professional, she has had to work hard and be tough to succeed. In the way she runs her business and commodifies everything from beer to her daughter, it's clear that material well-being will always be in the front of Mrs. Mooney's mind. Karl Marx believed that in a capitalist setting like Joyce's, humanity is often exchanged for material wealth, and one lesson is simply that the scars of poverty never fully heal. In his manifesto, Marx describes how—under bourgeoise rule—the emotional connections within families is destroyed, damaging the capacity of individuals to empathize, and the family relation is "reduced . . . to a mere money relation" (66). In Mrs. Mooney's case, money defined both her relationship with the family and her business, and this fact alone is compelling evidence that the attitude she brings to Polly's relationship isn't intentional. Given her materially-focused priorities, Mrs. Mooney's vision for marriage is very different than what ours is today. Foremost on her mind was ensuring Polly find a husband who would always provide for her, and to her their relationship was more of a financial partnership than a romantic one. Since love is totally absent from that equation, it's unsurprising that her intervention bore no consideration for the emotional well-being of the couple. Given the poor experience that Mrs. Mooney had in her own marriage, which was likely arranged and ended up costing her everything, it's not necessarily appropriate to evaluate the marriage she arranged for Polly on modern standards. Her vision of a perfect couple was a safe and materially comfortable one, and within these criteria it seems probable that she succeeded.

5   As Joyce describes her, Mrs. Mooney's life is dominated by struggles against her husband, father, and society, simply because of her gender, and this unceasing conflict created a uniquely tough person. I doubt she would ever be nominated for mother of the year, but in all important respects she succeeded in raising two good children as a determined single mother, positioning them to lead fulfilling

and comfortable lives. The most basic duty of a parent is to give one's child a better life than you had, and though Mrs. Mooney's life was a struggle to survive, she's given her children the opportunity to have a stable and fulfilling future.

Works Cited

Joyce, James. "The Boarding House." *Dubliners*. Penguin, 1976, pp. 61–69.
Marx, Karl, et al. *The Communist Manifesto*. Signet Classics, 2011.

For Consideration:

1. If you have not read *The Communist Manifesto*, what understanding of the terms "bourgeoise," "proletariat," and "commodity" can you discern from reading these essays? After writing your own definitions, look up formal definitions and see how they compare.

2. How would you describe the differences in tone and style between Reed Abbajay's essay and Steven Manning's essay?

3. These students were working within strict length requirement, and their assignment did not require research. With a group, brainstorm the following: If these students were required to expand this assignment into a major research paper, what sources would you suggest they use? Choose one essay as your focus. Be very specific about where in the essay, why, and how research might be applied to strengthen the argument.

Marginalization, oppression, and racism have consequences. Sophia Salinas examines the strikingly similar effects of anti-Semitism upon a fictional character from the 16th century and an actual Holocaust survivor of the 20th century.

The Destiny of Dirt

Sophia Salinas

1   Zygmunt Bauman's essay "The Dream of Purity" explores the implications of a collective that not only views purity as ideal but as a goal attainable with the removal of what it deems to be society's "dirt." Bauman emphasizes that this demeaning label is often applied to people—outsiders, strangers, and minorities—who "become dirt and are treated as such" (Bauman). The effects of said treatment may be exemplified in the examination of two individuals who seem worlds apart: Shylock, a Jewish moneylender from Shakespeare's *The Merchant of Venice,* and Vladek Spiegelman, a Holocaust survivor memorialized in Art Spiegelman's autobiographical *MAUS I* and *MAUS II*. Though at the surface these men appear very different, Vladek and Shylock both face persecution and respond to its influence similarly in their reliance on community, their relationships with family, and their general attitudes. In their respective situations, we may observe the shared destiny of the outsiders who have been isolated and marginalized by society, and who reveal the symptoms of this oppression in their everyday lives.

2   One effect of Shylock and Vladek's mutual marginalization is their tendency to cling to those like them and reject all others. There is a clear hostility between Shylock and the Christian characters of the play, and while Shylock seldom provokes Antonio and his friends, the situation often deteriorates rapidly once the first insult is thrown. We can contrast these unfriendly interactions against Shylock's scene with Tubal, a prosperous fellow Jew. It is in this relaxed conversation that Shylock has the freedom to deliver his most sympathetic lines in his "Hath not a Jew eyes?" speech (3.1.50–69) and reveal much of his character's humanity in his fond recollection of his dead wife, Leah. Tubal doesn't just provide emotional support to Shylock but also more practical assistance by helping Shylock in his search for Jessica and providing Shylock with the ducats necessary for Antonio's loan. This sense of community is necessary for Shylock as a reprieve from the everyday anti-semitism of Venice, offering him a sense of equality and justice he wouldn't otherwise experience as a second-class citizen. Likewise, Vladek relies

on the Jewish communities of America to cope with the tragedy that befell him in Poland. Despite the fact that many of the other survivors view Vladek as annoying and eccentric, we still see a clear network of support as Vladek's neighbors contact his son, Art, to look after him when he and his wife separate or his father becomes ill.

3   In both cases, we see reasons for these men to retreat into their communities for solidarity, but at the same time both men exhibit prejudice towards a group that they perceive as outsiders. For example, Shylock openly expresses hatred for the Christians, the group responsible for his oppression, and admits that this is due to him sinking to their level after years of mistreatment. Comparably, Vladek exhibits signs of racism towards Americans outside of his own circle. We see Vladek react strongly against Francois picking up a black hitchhiker as he makes the racist generalization that all black people are thieves. While this racist generalizing is certainly hypocritical of Vladek, it sourced from previous trauma, as surviving the Holocaust often meant judging others based on their race alone. While a strong sense of heritage and community helps these men to cope with the tragedies their people have experienced, their children may see these feelings as harmful to all communities involved.

4   Shylock and Vladek's experiences with persecution noticeably affect their approach to parenting and strain their relationships with their children. Their attempts at communication with their children are always shadowed and often limited by the trauma they've lived through and the constant fear of what they have being taken away. Modern readers may view Shylock as an overly controlling father to Jessica, but Shylock's need to isolate Jessica directly relates to the social climate of 16th century Venice. Shylock likely confines Jessica to the house due to a fear of violence against her, as we know that upstanding citizens like Antonio not only verbally berate Jews on the street, but spit on them. The grim possibilities only multiply when one factors in that Jessica is not only a Jew but a woman; a court of law would not convict any man who kidnapped, abused, or sexually assaulted her. Similarly, Vladek's often overbearing opinions about and requirements of his son Art are connected to protecting Art from the world Vladek's PTSD has constructed. Vladek's belief that a war may happen at any moment reflects what Bauman describes as a major effect of surviving persecution in a society that constantly conformed to purity: "[T]he stranger is now as resistant to fixation as the social space itself" (Bauman). Vladek's obsessive striving for perfection and criticism of his son are an attempt to make his son as handy and quick-witted as the Vladek who survived Nazi Germany. This projection of Vladek's past experiences onto Art is made all the more real when one learns that Vladek lost one son to

those who saw Jews as the dirt of society. As Vladek calls Art "Richieu" (the name of the son who died during the Holocaust at the age of four) at the end of *Maus II* (Spielman 136), the reader understands that Art's fears that Vladek compared him to a perfect dead son are wrong, and that Vladek sees the same child he would do anything to protect in Art. In the end, these tendencies stemming from their persecution drive their children away, creating an irony that these outsiders must be outsiders even within their families.

5   In addition to their sometimes domineering parenting, both Shylock and Vladek develop what readers see as flawed characteristics that derive from their marginalization. Both individuals may be interpreted as stingy, but within context their attitudes towards money and other resources are logical. For Shylock, his money lending business determines his livelihood within Venice. Shylock was somewhat forced into this profession as Jews were limited to few careers, but with his business comes the little influence he has over those who abuse him. If Shylock's business failed or if he held less economic importance, the abuse would be worse for both him and his family. Similarly, Vladek's extreme frugality correlates with the resourcefulness that saved his life during the Holocaust. When readers watch Vladek insisting the telephone wire on the street is valuable, they must also remember the lengths Vladek went through to simply acquire paper to write to Anja, salvaging cheese wrappers and paper from the latrine. Because Vladek exists in a constantly vigilant survival-mode, he feels the need to acquire and stockpile all such resources should anything happen.

6   In this same vein is the men's manipulative and stubborn nature towards those around them. Shylock's manipulation comes in the form of his contract with Antonio as Shylock recognizes the rare opportunity for justice in a world that is constantly unjust towards his people. Shylock must constantly be persistent and calculating in order to work within a system that thinks of him as foreigner. While Shylock is cunning enough to operate within a loophole, we are reminded of how necessary this craftiness is when another loophole is the cause for his subsequent forced conversion. For Vladek, it was his stubbornness and ability to manipulate his situation that saved his life during the war. When Art complains of his father trying to influence Francoise, Art's wife, and himself to stay in the Catskills for the summer, the readers may see the situation through Vladek's eyes. Vladek expresses fear that without Mala, there is no one to care for him and his weak heart, which could result in his death. From Vladek's perspective this manipulation is simply advocating for what he needs, and it is this obstinance that both motivated him to get through the war and inspired his wife Anja to survive, as echoed in his words to her, "[T]o die, it's easy . . . but you have to struggle for life!" (Maus I 122).

7   Despite the fact that these men share such similar consequences of their marginalization and trauma throughout many facets of their lives, it is not to imply that every survivor shares the exact same experience. The resemblance of their experiences is meant to highlight what Bauman implies within his essay, that persecution is cyclical and that these consequences of casting out individuals for a dream of purity cannot be avoided. While the demands of purity may change, the outsider remains. It is not enough to simply mitigate the damage of such marginalization after such prejudices have taken root; we must work to prevent the projection of society's issues onto a people before we can ever begin to solve the issues at hand.

Works Cited

Bauman, Zygmunt. "The Dream of Purity." *The Greylodge Occult Review*, Issue 15, www.greylodge.org/occultreview/glor_015/purity.htm.

Shakespeare, William. *The Merchant of Venice*. Edited by David Bevington and David Scott Kastan, Bantam Classics, 2005.

Spiegelman, Art. *Maus I: A Survivor's Tale: My Father Bleeds History*. Pantheon Books, 1986.

Spiegelman, Art. *Maus II: A Survivor's Tale: And Here My Troubles Began*. Pantheon Books, 1992.

For Consideration:

1. Do you find it surprising that the central figures of Salinas' study—Shylock and Vladek—lived centuries apart, and that one is a fictional creation and the other is a person who actually lived? Why or why not? Explain your answer.

2. Do you think that the long-term effects of "surviving persecution in a society that constantly conform(s) to purity" leaves people similarly scarred today? Support your answer with hypothetical examples or your own personal observations and experiences.

3. Weak conclusions are common in first-year writers' work. What do we have to learn from Salinas' conclusion, which is strong? On your own or with a group, identify what works and make a list of strategies to avoid when closing. For a review of methods for building a strong introductory paragraph, repeat this exercise with her opening paragraph.

This student addresses questions of beauty while merging literary analysis with the cultural theory of Thomas Kuhn's influential book, The Structure of Scientific Revolutions.

Where Does Beauty Lie?
Victoria Peters

1 In its most basic definition, beauty is a combination of qualities that produce a pleasing aesthetic. While humans possess some ability to create a version of beauty for itself in the "man-made" world, ideal beauty resides in the natural world, characterized by spontaneity and unpredictability. By that token, Esteban in Gabriel Garcia Marquez's work "The Handsomest Drowned Man in The World" represents a spontaneous, natural beauty that it takes the villagers time to recognize but eventually come to welcome. The short story initially appears to signify fascination with the extraordinary; however, reading the work across Kuhn's principles of paradigms and the importance of a gestalt switch, the reader sees how the reactions of the villagers towards the extraordinary can benefit society. Esteban radically alters the village's existing paradigm in that, after him, houses are built with wider doors, time elongates, and various languages come into play. In the new paradigm that emerges, true beauty combines the past, present, and future. Unable to create this ideal beauty for itself, society more realistically stumbles across it—as it does Esteban in the story—allowing for humans to come closer to what true beauty actually is.

2 Oftentimes the existing paradigm prohibits one from seeing the beauty right before one's eyes. For example, the villagers are first unaware of the magnitude of Esteban's beauty because they can only define Esteban's beauty within the parameters of their existing paradigm. The villagers clarify "accepted examples" that "provide models" (Kuhn 11) for what their way of life is and for what beauty means to them. The attempts of the children and men to define the extraordinary characteristics of Esteban by means of what is already known makes their need for a paradigm apparent. The children attempt to classify the drowned man first as an enemy ship and later as a whale. Relying solely on observational skills, the children represent the laymen of society who operate within the very limited knowledge of accepted paradigms. Their attempts to classify Esteban exemplify the human need to have a proven, factual explanation for the extraordinary. While the children feel confident in the natural beauty of a whale, they aren't so sure about Esteban so they repeatedly bury him and then dig him back up, hoping

that in doing so perhaps one time when they dig him up, his beauty will be fully revealed and defined. The men of the village, assumed to be more educated and to have all the necessary tools, fall into the same cycle as the children even though their paradigms operate on a larger scale. They suggest that he'd been in the water so long that it had begun to alter him, changing his very bones, or that his height stemmed from him "growing after death [which] was part of the nature of certain drowned men" (Marquez). The knowledge of these pre-existing paradigms, although unhelpful in identifying the anomaly, prove integral. Without them, "all of the facts that could possibly pertain" to the explanation "are likely to seem equally relevant" (Kuhn 15). The men still, however, detract from the radiating beauty of Esteban in their attempts to attribute his beauty to some proven fact of their current paradigm. The villagers must come to realize that beauty proven by the past does not prohibit new beauty from also existing in the present, even if the new beauty cannot be defined by the past.

3   In order to see the beauty of the present, a gestalt switch proves necessary so that the community does not solely know that something beautiful exists but also might know the identity of the beauty. It isn't enough for the villagers simply to know that Esteban exists; the villagers also must know how to define him. The discovery of the "what" is an essential that works in conjunction with knowing simply that it exists in the first place (Kuhn 55). The lack of knowing the "what" acts as fuel for resistance because Esteban has the potential to change "fields that had already existed" (Kuhn 59).

4   Within the resistance lies a hierarchy as seen in the debate over whether the drowned man's name is Esteban or Lautaro. The young women insist that his name might be Lautaro and the older women believe them to be naïve in their adamance. The moment that the drowned man becomes truly Esteban for all of them rather than Lautaro marks the exact time that the community of women no longer see "something as something else; instead, they simply see it" (Kuhn 85). The women don't see Esteban as once a drowned man and now Esteban, but simply just Esteban, similar to how Kuhn notes scientists might see a duck at the start of a revolutionary change and a rabbit afterwards. However, this rabbit is not defined as once being a duck and now a rabbit, but simply just a rabbit (Kuhn 112).

5   The groups that advocate for a new paradigm "may not, however, be drawn at random from society as a whole, but is rather the well-defined community" (Kuhn 167). In this village, while the men are assumed to be the educated ones, the women make up the well-defined community that ultimately decides the "what" and its given value. The well-defined community represents society's need for a "professional" to assign the beauty value. While a painting can be interpreted by

anyone who comes into contact with it, society more willingly accepts the meaning given by either the person who painted it or those that are well known in that specific field of study. Undergoing the gestalt switch first, the women are the community that defines the "what" and thus become the professionals that are capable of defining the beauty of Esteban. While the women saw that Esteban "was the tallest, strongest, most virile, and best built man" (Marquez), the men attributed the women's fascination with Esteban to "womanish frivolity" and saw Esteban as trouble that should be eradicated. However, at the moment one woman reveals the "what" by removing the handkerchief from Esteban's face, the men can no longer deny his beauty. The women of the community first undergo the gestalt switch and then in a Platonic manner are able to bring the men to this same enlightenment as to who Esteban is, allowing for the community as a whole to fully recognize the beauty that is found in the presence of Esteban.

6   This newfound beauty allows for beauty in the future to be reconfigured as well, thus paving the way for a more accurate image of beauty as a whole. The new paradigm still has a backbone molded of beauty concepts based on previous paradigms. For example, Esteban did not fit into the box of what was known, but pieces of the known world still fit into him as he was made: his pants are fashioned from a piece of sail and his shirt is made from what appears to be bridal linen. As the ambiguity concerning Esteban clears up, the transition between him simply being a drowned man to "becoming all the more Esteban for them" (Marquez) becomes apparent. This gestalt switch incites the shift in which people are now operating out of a new paradigm, one where the houses take on a different shape and are made larger and stronger to accommodate a man such as Esteban.

7   As Esteban's village begins to shift, it becomes "the anticipated" (Kuhn 64). Still, however, the villagers do not completely leave the customs of the old paradigm to be forgotten. The villagers never lose touch with their identity in that they remain fishermen and do not completely rebuild the houses, but alter them. The villagers remain pleased with the beauty of where they have come from and merge this with the beauty they have found in Esteban, one of these things being time. Fourteen lines long, the last sentence signifies how time shifts in this revitalized community. In this new paradigm, however, the villagers do not get it all right. The "sun [being] so bright that the sunflowers don't know which way to turn" (Marquez) mimic the village people under the illusion that the new paradigm they have built for themselves completely defines beauty. In essence, in their attempts of working towards an end goal of making space for Esteban's memory, they have put themselves back into the cycle of paradigms. Similar to how the villagers stumbled upon Esteban, the possibility for them to stumble upon

something new and extraordinary again in the future remains high. In the future, when faced with an anomaly, they will likely attempt to explain it through the past beauty of Esteban; upon failure, they will once again have to merge them together. Even though merging the beauties of the past, present, and future together helps the villagers come closer to understanding beauty in its true form, they still must see beauty as ever-changing. Moreover, they cannot ever paint ideal beauty in its entirety.

8 Attempts to create beauty for oneself leaves one in the continuous cycle of paradigmatic life, which is not necessarily harmful as we need paradigms from which to operate. Paradigms are a way of understanding and ordering the world, and communities should strive for awareness of paradigms' power and functions. Largely because of vain attempts to classify beauty solely on the past, or the present, or the future, an understanding must arise that society cannot create quintessential beauty for itself. Additionally, communities fail at creating an ideal beauty because the beauty of the future remains unpredictable. The villagers stumbled across Esteban, but had they stumbled across a blind man or perhaps an extraordinary animal instead of a man, the beauty seen in the object would vary greatly and so would the beauty of their present, thus affecting the beauty of their future. Beauty mixes elements of the past, present, and future—elements we ourselves lack control over, making paradigm shifts inevitable.

Works Cited

Kuhn, Thomas S. *The Structure of Scientific Revolutions*. U of Chicago P, 2012.

Marquez, Gabriel Garcia. "The Handsomest Drowned Man in The World." www.ndsu.edu/pubweb/~cinichol/CreativeWriting/423/MarquezHandsomestDrownedMan.htm.

For Consideration:

1. Peters utilizes the terms "paradigm," "anomaly," and "gestalt switch." If you are already familiar with these terms, define each as you understand it, and consider whether your understanding is reflected in Peters' use of each one. If you have never encountered these terms before, revisit each one and do your best to discern the meaning of each from the context of the essay.

2. Consider Peters' claim in the introduction that "humans possess some ability to create a version of beauty for itself in the 'man-made' world," but ideal beauty resides in the natural world, characterized by spontaneity and unpredictability." Do you agree? Why or why not? Be thorough and clear in your explanation.

3. What does Peters mean near the end when she asserts that "society cannot create quintessential beauty for itself"? Respond on your own, or work through this question with a group.

This student's meditation on the American Dream focuses on the history of our national conception of childhood and the detrimental effects—financial and emotional—of the current paradigm upon parents.

The Fruit of Their Labors for the Fruit of Their Loins
Morgan Caldwell

1   In his 1961 masterpiece *The Giving Tree,* Shel Silverstein tells the story of a little boy who becomes dear friends with the apple tree in his backyard. As the boy ages, however, time reveals the unhealthy give-and-take relationship of the boy and tree. Throughout the story, the tree provides the boy with apples, her trunk, and eventually even her stump without so much as a "thank you" for her generosity. This American classic is a powerful metaphor for the relationship between a child and his or her parents, underscoring the self-sacrificing measures a parent will take for his or her child. Meanwhile, society expects these same Americans to strive for some arcane "American Dream" which a farmer defined in 1782 as "each person work[ing] for himself" towards the greatest version of him or herself (Crevecoeur 1). However, 236 years have come and gone since Crevecoeur contrived that definition. In 1782, children were "adults in training" that required only minimal instruction to become self-sufficient laborers who could contribute to the household funds (Mintz 9). In present society, these ideas are not just invalid, they can be considered grounds for a call to Child Protective Services. This shift in society's paradigm included the metamorphosis of childhood over the last two and a half centuries as the family shifted from an adult-centered unit to a child-centered one. Unfortunately, due to this focus on the next generation, 21st century American parents are sacrificing the American Dream in an attempt to ensure their children's success.

2   The American Dream deeply embedded within our society dates back much further than James Truslow Adams, the 1930s writer who popularized the phrase; the American Dream's origins can be explored in one of the earliest American texts by J. Hector St. John Crevecoeur. Having published his work months before England signed the Treaty of Paris which officially ended the American Revolutionary War, Crevecoeur attempted to define the nationalistic identity of the new country in his paper, "What is an American?" In the process of creating post-Colonial propaganda, he uncovered the American Dream. Crevecoeur

depicts a utopian country with equal opportunity unheard of in Europe. He claims, in fact, that in America, instead of working for a European aristocrat, an American's "labour is founded on the basis of nature" and "*self-interest*" where "his industry follow equal steps the progress of his labour" (Crevecoeur 3). In simpler words, Crevecoeur encapsulates the American Dream as that in which a man (and, for the sake of the 21st century, we'll add *or woman*) reaps the full reward of his or her work.

3   Of course, as a French-nobleman-turned-farmer who had experienced the British mistreatment of Colonial America and the Revolutionary War that followed, his idealism is rooted in comparisons. In comparison to France and England, America appeared to be "the most perfect society now existing in the world" (Crevecoeur 1). For the sake of argument, we will allow his declarations to stand uncontested in the 18th century. Ignoring slavery, the subjugation of women, and the terrible crimes done against Native peoples, white Protestant males in the new United States of America could indeed enjoy the fruits of their labors without having to cede a large portion to some "despotic prince" (Crevecoeur 3). However, today the era of Crevecoeur is impossible for the eighty percent of Americans that are or will become parents (Nelson et al. 850). Even if they were given the opportunities to receive the due reward of their labors, because of the current parenting mentality, parents are no longer working for themselves. American parents are giving up their time and money in sacrificial dedication to their own often-despotic princes and princesses: their own children (Coleman 416).

4   Crevecoeur's idea that children of America "gladly help their father clear those fields" represents the heavy Puritan influence on American child-rearing (Crevecoeur 3). In Puritan culture, "they considered crawling bestial and play as frivolous and trifling," expecting children to work and act like adults from even the earliest ages (Mintz 10). Throughout the 1700s and early 1800s, it was not uncommon for state and federal laws to be written referring to "Children and Servants" as equivocal positions (Mintz 13). In Crevecoeur's era, a child would work just as their parents worked for their food and lodgings. However, the industrialization of the United States marked a huge shift for America. As any middle schooler can hopefully tell you, the Industrial Revolution caused occupations to change from farming to factory work, the American lifespan to extend significantly, and the average size of the American family to drop. In fact, comparing the averages from the 1780s to the early 1900s, the average number of children a married woman bore dropped from ten to three (Mintz 77). Due to this economic and demographic metamorphosis, upper- and middle-class parents began to regard

their children "not as sources of labor but as 'social capital' requiring substantial investments of time and resources," taking up a practice that the English aristocracy had adopted centuries prior (Mintz 77).

5   Activism against child labor ratified the parenthood metamorphosis. In the uproar calling for the political officials to remove children from horrible factory conditions (partly because they were taking jobs from adults), a fervor arose to abandon the Puritan values and intensify the inclinations already present in the middle-class. Suddenly (although it had been building for the past two centuries), a 'parent' was essentially redefined a "divinely appointed guardian" with a "duty to serve as their [children's] steward" (Mintz 183). The result? The "middle-class family grew more democratic, affectionate, and child-centered" (Mintz 215). By altering the definition of childhood from a clinical description of physical growth to a nuanced social construct involving frivolity and innocence, Americans dismembered the Puritan construct of parenthood and created a new model in its place. The new definition of parenthood affected the old American Dream both financially and emotionally.

6   The easiest way to consider the gravity of children's siphoning is to examine the financial burden that parents undergo by having and raising children. A *U.S. News* article appropriately titled "The Truth About the Cost of Kids" illuminates the severe financial burden of 21st century American parents who are spending more on their children than any generation previously. Citing 2015 statistics calculated by the United States Department of Agriculture, "the cost of raising a child born in 2015 to a middle income married couple [is] $233,610" (LaPonsie). That's nearly *a quarter of a million dollars*, and that figure does not include the cost of higher education that parents often choose to shoulder for their children. For those same middle-income married couples, a quarter of a million represents the cost of a house and two cars, or a large chunk of their retirement plan. Still, we live in a society that is driven by the consumer, and American parents today choose to spend an unprecedented amount of their earnings on their children. The proof is in the economy. In the United States, we spend about "$15 billion a year on marketing to children"—that's fifteen million on *unemployable* Americans (Coleman 148). The products industry is dominated by toys, children's books, G-Rated and PG-Rated movies, youth clothing, colorful snack foods, and everything else branded "Youth." Parents are focusing their disposable income on purchasing youth culture for their children. As children went from being servants of their parents and society to the self-serving boy who takes apples from his friend, parents have gone from enjoying the individualistic American Dream to ceding all the fruits of their labors to their children.

7   The emotional repercussions of this transformation are more difficult to quantify, but equally significant. Dr. Joshua Coleman, family psychologist and writer of *When Parents Hurt: Compassionate Strategies When You and Your Grown Child Don't Get Along,* underscores the emotional anxieties today's parents feel to provide for their children. He discusses how we, culturally, have become a society that believes that "only through constant vigilance, dedication, and education" are parents successful (Coleman 122). Coleman's work focuses on parents whose grown children have cut ties with them. They experience anguish and intense guilt, but these emotions all stem from the evolution of parenthood. As Coleman points out, while in past generations "children were expected to earn the parents' love and respect, today's parents are worried that they won't have their children's love and respect because they're not enough" (Coleman 146). This anxiety present in American parents causes them to dedicate their independently earned benefits to their children so that they may avoid the nasty guilt and shame that comes from failure. As a society, parents and non-parents alike have reconstructed our economy, our pastimes, our holidays, and our definitions to create *Childhood* for American children. Along the way, the American value system evolved. Parents no longer work for their own fiscal American Dreams; they dedicate their lives to their children and make huge sacrifices for them, expecting to earn the emotional rewards of being "successful parents" in return (Coleman 98). However, meta-analysis research by Nelson et al. expresses the imperfections in this attempt. This research shows that many types of parents (including young parents, unmarried parents, parents with high socioeconomic status, and parents with low social support) consistently demonstrate *less* well-being than individuals without children. This symptom arises within the insecurities of parenthood. Evidence suggests that "negative emotions, sleep disturbances and fatigue, strained partner relationships, and financial strain" are common among parents, especially among those aforementioned (Nelson et al. 876). The researchers conclude that most of these negative effects stem from constant worry over their children's health and safety, experiencing more anxiety about possible scenarios (such as cancer or kidnapping) "than the statistical risk of such outcomes warrant[s]" (Nelson et al. 876). However, despite what the data suggests, the study also shows that parents who do not reside in the same home as their child(ren) experience "more severe symptoms of depression and anxiety than resident parents" (including all the groups previously mentioned). Even with the daily financial burdens and the emotional stress of raising a child, "the stress of not having one's own children at home and missing out on the pleasures of parenting" ends up outweighing all the pain (Nelson et al. 883).

8 The original American Dream did not stand the test of time. The pure, unfettered individualistic pursuit of prosperity is not something that today's American parents are striving to achieve. Instead, American parents choose to dedicate their time, their money, and the resources they have earned to their children. It has become an attitude so often practiced that devoting oneself to one's children is the new American Dream. However, we must be vigilant that this new American Dream does not take the same extreme path that the last one did. Pursuit only based on self-interest did not last, and pursuit solely based on children cannot either. Otherwise, parents will continue to struggle with the intense emotional stress that results from being an American parent. The answer to our parents' problems is not to reinforce or encourage the twisted relationship between the giving tree and the self-centered little boy who took everything from that tree, but instead to find a balance and to enjoy the fruits of interdependency—and maybe, just maybe, children should say thank you every now and again.

Works Cited

Coleman, Joshua. *When Parents Hurt: Compassionate Strategies When You and Your Grown Child Don't Get Along.* Collins Living, 2008.

Crevecoeur, J. Hector St. John. "What is an American?" web.utk.edu/~mfitzge1/docs/374/Creve_brief.pdf.

LaPonsie, Maryalene. "The Truth About the Cost of Kids." *U.S. News & World Report*, U.S. News & World Report, 6 Apr. 2017, 10:51, money.usnews.com/money/personal-finance/family-finance/articles/2017-04-06/the-truth-about-the-cost-of-kids.

Mintz, Steven. *Huck's Raft: A History of American Childhood.* Belknap Press of Harvard University Press, 2004.

Nelson, S. Katherine, et al. "The Pains and Pleasures of Parenting: When, Why, and How is Parenthood Associated with More or Less Well-Being?" *Psychological Bulletin*, vol. 140, no. 3, American Psychological Association, May 2014, pp. 846–95, doi:10.1037/a0035444.

Silverstein, Shel. *The Giving Tree.* Harper and Row, 1964.

For Consideration:

1. Maddox asserts that the pressure to give everything to their children has decreased parents' well-being. On your own or with a group, work through the logos of this cause-and-effect relationship. How and why, exactly and specifically, do you think a parent is more likely to become anxious or depressed due to working with the sole goal of providing his or her child with what culture dictates is the best possible material existence?

2. After answering the first question, on your own or with a group, formulate a thoughtful and logical response to this question: How might the current paradigm, as Maddox defines it and his research supports it, not only be detrimental to parents but to children as well?

3. It's doubtful that many Americans—especially those under the age of eighteen—would find a return to the colonial childhood paradigm appealing. Based on the information in this essay and your own knowledge of history, first define in as much detail as you can your understanding of the typical treatment of and social place of children before the 1900s. Then articulate what could be perceived as the *benefits* of that paradigm—for parents and children, and for society as a whole.

The following two students use Shakespeare's play The Merchant of Venice *to argue the value of studying classic literature for the vital and applicable lessons it has to teach us about human behavior and possibilities for navigating the social and political landscape of the world today. Study questions for these essays follow the second essay.*

The Ring of Engagement
Rasin Faruk

1   *Lard-laced bullets. Discarded Qur'ans ready to be lit. White nationalists' words and guns.* One *jummah* (Friday prayer), after someone claiming to share my faith orchestrated a terrorist attack, those headlines came to life when armed protestors lined the front of my mosque. Many disengage—or stand by—while trends, like anti-Muslim sentiment, take root. I walked the line: engaging when absolutely necessary and disengaging to seem "normal." I brushed off comments about being an "Osama." I resisted, silently, when my mother was judged for her hijab. As I walked to the mosque, I wondered: "Will they shoot?" Although no one was hurt, that day left me with questions that extended far beyond safety: Why were so many people protesting places and people that actually condemn terrorism? Why were so many of my neighbors, Muslim and non-Muslim, not counter-protesting? Although it was published centuries ago, William Shakespeare's *The Merchant of Venice* warned its audience of the harms of identity-based bigotry and xenophobia. The play remains invaluable because it sheds light on issues—animosity based on faith, the tendency to be apathetic, and the links between religious intolerance and extremism—that still exist today.

2   The cliché that no one is born racist holds merit; most grow up following what they observe and seldom question it. Antonio, the title character of *The Merchant of Venice*, was not born anti-Semitic; he was socialized in an anti-Semitic society, and therefore never came to personally know any Jewish people. Similarly, most of the people protesting at my mosque had never intimately known a Muslim. Antonio blindly seized each opportunity he had to attack Shylock for his Judaism by verbally dehumanizing him and physically assaulting him. In Venice at the time, Jews had a separate community and were not allowed access to the same services that Christians were. This kind of abuse is often coupled with some form of segregation, self-imposed or otherwise.

3   One would expect identity-based discrimination to be rare, particularly among the respected elites of a leading city. However, it is common, and the actions of

the most prominent have a trickle-down effect so that others follow along. Since President Trump's election, his rhetoric in office has been linked to an increase in hate crimes. Likewise in the play, Antonio's entourage looks up to him and follows his lead, thus they readily become complicit in his mistreatment of Shylock. It is notable that Shylock treats his servant, Lancelot, quite well. Lancelot had copious free time and food, and there is no evidence that Shylock is anything but a fair employer. However, Lancelot pins his status insecurities on Shylock and Judaism, and seeks employment with a Christian who has very little in terms of character to commend him. In another example, Portia sets a brutal trap for Shylock. In Act IV, in the guise of an attorney defending Antonio, she asks him to forgive Antonio for breaking the terms of the loan—terms Antonio readily agreed to. Shylock declines, citing Antonio's unjustified and constant maltreatment of him as justification. Then, after twisting the contract to give Shylock no choice but to concede, she refuses to give him the same mercy she desired, going so far as to take his fortune and make him convert to Christianity. In essence, the law is twisted to protect the Christians and punish the Jewish Shylock, although he has technically committed no crime.

4   The limiting of rights, freedoms, and opportunities of a marginalized group often goes unnoticed until the most oppressed lash out. Shylock was envious of the freedoms that were associated with being a Christian: Christians could roam freely, engage in any occupation, and were not segregated. As opposed to joining them—and stripping himself of his identity—he sought to succeed without conforming. Although he is financially successful, he isn't even treated like a citizen or a human being by his Venetian peers. In demanding a pound of Antonio's flesh, Shylock sought to strip Antonio of *his* identity, one piece at a time. This vindictive desire was the result of years of subjugation to unfair practices and the pain of being abused and disregarded. Reading this play may help people understand why people who are disregarded, oppressed, abused, and insulted sometimes decide that extremism could be suitable retribution.

5   It does appear that Shylock has materialistic values, but money is a form of protection from oppression, and he also has many positive qualities. He, in short, is a complex character who cannot be reduced to one single facet of identity: that he is Jewish. He is a loving father to Jessica and shows sincere devotion to the memory of his late wife, Leah, by cherishing the ring she gifted to him years ago above all else. Shakespeare presents a key juxtaposition between Shylock and his Christian counterparts here: Lorenzo and Jessica squander the love ring for a valueless monkey while Gratiano and Bassanio give away the rings symbolizing love from their wives.

[6] Bigotry is a common method of reinforcing one's superiority or that of one's group, but with it comes social disintegration. Engaging—and not just standing by—when these issues surface are pivotal in their mitigation.

Works Cited

Shakespeare, William. *The Merchant of Venice*. Edited by David Bevington and David Scott Kastan, Bantam Books, 2005.

The Stark Resemblance between a Four-Hundred-Year-Old Play and the Now

Isabel Muino

1   The first thing I heard after I walked into my dorm room last week was the *thunk* of my roommate's copy of *The Merchant of Venice* hitting the floor. Following a heated conversation, my roommate and I came to the conclusion that the play isn't so much a comedy as it is a blatant mockery festering with schadenfreude, specifically targeting a character that we both deeply relate to. My roommate and I walk through the world differently as gay women of color attending this university in Texas. Seeing a character like Shylock—a complex, multi-faceted Jewish person—experience social mutilation at the hands of bigoted Christians was like looking in a warped, grotesque fun-house mirror of our own lives. Some readers see Shakespeare's play as a fun, fanciful tale, but this story left a bitter taste in my mouth. The maltreatment that Shylock's character faces too closely mirrors the struggle and subsequent dehumanization that people of color, specifically Black people, face in America, and despite Shakespeare's numerous attempts to lighten the mood, the play exemplifies the harsh reality of the power imbalance in society between the majority and the minority.

2   It should be noted that the judgments placed on Shylock are those spoken by other characters almost exclusively in conjunction with criticisms of his religion; his character and religion are inseparable, and hateful stereotypes are flung at him throughout the play, painting him as a greedy, unmerciful, money-making Jew. Shylock's first conversation with Antonio depicts him as cold and vindictive, and even when using the logic of Christianity against his oppressor, he is demonized with the remark, "The devil can cite Scripture for his purpose" (1.3.96). Our society today copies this same formula as hateful stereotypes about Black people permeate our media. News outlets have reported many Black Lives Matter protests—Ferguson, Charlotte, St. Paul—as violent riots with many of their protesters labeled as thugs. In reality, those peaceful protests turned awry due to violent White supremacists, and the media sided with the White perspective. It is the same situation as in the play: the majority has put the minority down using community pressure and has caused the minority to become the stereotype.

3   Stereotype or not, moneylending is Shylock's only choice of profession in Venice as a Jewish man, and that exact societal system has set him up for failure; he is permitted only that profession and yet is condemned for attempting

to make a reasonable living off of it. Many Black Americans today are stuck in a vicious loop of systematic poverty, a situation our society has historically set them up for. Menial jobs refused by White people are taken up by Black people, who until the 1960s could legally be denied jobs that would've helped them become upwardly mobile, and they are paid a paltry minimum wage that has been proven as inadequate for the standard of living today. Black Americans then request monetary welfare, for which they are strongly criticized and asked why they don't try harder. Both of these instances are catch-22s; Shylock needs to collect interest as a moneylender to survive, and Black Americans request welfare because they could starve without it. The circumstances are different, but the concepts are the same: both parties exist in a negative feedback loop in their societies.

4   Perhaps the grossest transgression Shylock experiences is the shameless disregard of his rights during the trial. His jury is hardly one of his peers; they are the very same men that spit at him and call him names. The Duke of Venice himself, in front of a court of law, describes Shylock as an "inhuman wretch / Uncapable of pity, void and empty" (4.1.4–5). Before Shylock has even made his case, the court is already against him. This same mistreatment is far from foreign for Black people. Countless Black men and women have undergone unfair legal trials, receiving sentences far more severe than their White counterparts committing the same crime. Some don't even get the luxury of a trial and die mysteriously in detention, like Sandra Bland and Freddie Gray. Some don't even get the luxury of detainment and die at the hands of trigger-happy policemen. Black people time and time again have been wronged by the prejudiced justice system in America. In this way, Shylock's justice system failing him reflects a reality we too often see in the news today.

5   Reading a play that is more than four hundred years old and finding such close modern-day parallels is very unsettling. It is *absurd* to me that we still have to argue about the inherent value of Black people. How can we call ourselves educated and civilized when people die every day due to our ignorance? We cannot. It is essential that we recognize parallels like these. Perhaps this play is technically fictional, but Shylock's character is based on real concepts, and if we can't learn from history, as humans ought to do, then perhaps we can try to learn from fiction.

Works Cited

Shakespeare, William. *The Merchant of Venice*. Edited by David Bevington and David Scott Kastan, Bantam Books, 2005.

For Consideration:

1. Muino closes her essay with the suggestion that "if we can't learn from history, as humans ought to do, then perhaps we can try to learn from fiction." How is the experience of reading a novel or play, or watching a film, that is historically accurate different from reading a history book? What feeling, ideas, and realizations might these mediums provoke in us that simply reading recorded facts might not?

2. Both authors utilize logos, ethos, and pathos effectively to make their arguments. Create a three-column log for each essay and, with a group, break down examples of each proof by category and discuss how each contributes to the essay as a whole.

3. Think of a play, novel, story, or movie that takes place in another century in which you recognize parallels to our current society. Write a well-developed paragraph in which you explain your observations, giving supporting evidence in the form of details you remember from the text.

This student analyzes a contemporary film about business ethics, Tony Gilroy's Michael Clayton, *across philosophical idealism and Plato's "The Allegory of the Cave."*

How to Become Rich
Nicole Parmelee

1   In our society, we often employ the word "rich" as an adjective to describe someone with copious amounts of money. However, this isn't the only definition; "rich" also means plentiful and abundant. Our materialistic culture has overemphasized the first definition, unfortunately making it seem like the most important, but Plato would argue otherwise. His philosophy requires individuals to put less emphasis on tangible possessions, including money, in exchange for true enlightenment of one's spirit. *Michael Clayton,* a 2007 film from director Tony Gilroy, is set in a reality much like the one Plato presents in "The Allegory of the Cave." The Kenner, Bach, and Ledeen law firm is a financially successful yet underhanded and corrupt workplace in which employees choose to mindlessly follow their greedy superiors and support their irresponsible clients, disregarding any moral or ethical questions. The movie highlights the ascent of Michael Clayton, with the guidance and motivation of his friend and co-worker Arthur, from being an obvious cave dweller—the materialistic, egocentric man that he is at the beginning of the story—to an enlightened soul who is compelled by virtue to do what is right.

2   As Plato explains, a cave dweller only understands the world in physical, material terms, "distracted in the struggle for power" (167), something we definitely notice in Michael's class-conscious and arrogant attitude at the start of the movie. When Michael's son, Henry, talks about his favorite book *Realm and Conquest,* he mentions that within the novel's war-torn environment, it has to be "everyone for themselves" (*Michael Clayton*). Michael quickly laughs, saying that reality is no different. This automatic response shows how deep in the cave Michael really is; for him, the world is a place where one must put self-interest before anything else: a belief shared by all cave dwellers. Throughout the majority of the movie, we see Michael focus all of his efforts on his duties as a fixer—doing under-the-table deals to cover up the illegal and embarrassing actions of the firm's wealthy clients—and as a failed restaurant owner, but we never see him concentrate on his duties as a father, son, brother, or friend. The photograph of Henry and Arthur that sits on Michael's desk is significant because it's something personal in an

otherwise sterile office. According to Plato, tangible objects, such as the photograph, will not stand the test of time. Plato believed that ideas are more truly real than physical objects; they transcend time and signify enlightenment. It's clear early in the film that Michael does not understand this concept; he seems to think that a photo can suffice to prove his love. Michael does care deeply for Arthur and Henry, but his actions never convey those feelings. For example, after the outburst in which Arthur calls out U-North's corruption and extricates himself from the case, Michael doesn't defend Arthur or even give him the benefit of the doubt; he simply shakes his head and says that Arthur "wasn't really making much sense," blaming the episode on Arthur failing to take his medication (*Michael Clayton*). At this point, Michael is still very much in his cave, but soon it starts to become clear that Arthur has experienced his own enlightenment and is the only one who can possibly guide Michael into the "heavenly light" of the good and the truth (Plato 167).

3   In this movie, Arthur serves as what Plato would call a liberator because he is the sole reason that Michael begins to look at life from a different perspective. He is the complete opposite of Michael: willing to lose his job, his money, and his reputation in order to stand up for what is morally right. Once he understands the corruption of U-North and the damage they are doing to nature and to human lives, he chooses to stand up for the innocent and for the truth, no matter what the personal repercussions may be. When Arthur first describes the experience of his own enlightenment, we can clearly see his intention to be a liberator as he pleads with Michael to trust that this "is not just madness" (*Michael Clayton*). He is trying to open Michael's eyes to the light, because Arthur now understands that there's a "more real existence," and his duty is to share his realization with others (Plato 162). His job is the hardest within the scope of Plato's allegory, because the liberator always faces intense resistance from the cave dweller, as is very evident in Michael's resistance to Arthur's awakening.

4   The main confrontation between the two characters occurs when Michael visits Arthur in jail. Arthur says desperately that he has "absorbed [the] poison" of the unethical law firm for too long and that he's "not losing" his newfound freedom (*Michael Clayton*). Even though it doesn't seem like Michael understands at the time, everything Arthur says slowly helps Michael open his eyes to the corrupt, material-driven life he's been living. Arthur's influence on Michael is obvious when Michael leaves a voicemail on Arthur's machine admitting that Arthur is in fact right in some ways. Like Plato described, Arthur is unable to "put . . . knowledge into [Michael's] soul," but he can help Michael to eventually turn his soul "into that of being" (165). No matter Michael's response, Arthur refuses to

succumb to the "false notions" of life and tries incessantly to make Michael aware of their harm as well: a valuable characteristic of a virtuous liberator (Plato 163).

5   After Arthur's death at the hands of corporate assassins covering up U-North's corruption, Michael must be responsible for his own journey towards enlightenment and for finishing what Arthur started. Michael starts to discover for himself what Arthur has been saying all along; he's finally starting to see in the light. The initial "bewilderment of the eyes" (Plato 164) that Plato mentions is similar to Michael's confusion when his boss, Marty, states that Arthur's death was a lucky break and when he hears news of the U-North settlement (*Michael Clayton*). The confusion on his face mirrors the confusion of the cave dweller when he has come into the light and is beginning to see the sun—or goodness—for the first time.

6   Michael finally realizes that enlightenment is worth the sacrifice. He chooses to forgo the enormous amount of hush money he is offered by both sides to buy his silence and instead value the universal ideals that should dominate our existence—justice, freedom, love, and equality—just like Plato demands. One of the final tipping points before Michael fully emerges from his cave is during his last talk with Marty. He admits that Arthur wasn't crazy, and he seems shocked by Marty's conscious disregard for virtue. After this interaction, he can see right through the "poisonous" law firm; he can finally see the sun (*Michael Clayton*). When Michael refers to himself as nothing more than "a janitor," like Arthur once said, instead of as a fixer, we see that he has reached enlightenment (*Michael Clayton*). He has given up the title that once ruled his entire life. Soon after, when his car explodes, Michael makes the decision to fake his own death by burning his possessions (including his cell phone and wallet), sacrificing powerful symbols of his materialistic existence. After this moment, as he's running, he is choosing to leave behind his entire past to start making a positive contribution to the true "world of knowledge" that he has recently discovered (Plato 164).

7   If we're not focused on material possessions, it is possible for everyone to be rich: to be "truly rich . . . in virtue and wisdom" (Plato 167). When we all accept this definition of the word "rich" and embody the ideas that it requires of us, we will have reached enlightenment. As Plato says, we are born into this unfortunate, materialistic cave that stifles our growth until someone is able to get through to us and convince us that the real world is worth living in: the world that embraces the universal ideals of living, instead of material gain.

Works Cited

Michael Clayton. Directed by Tony Gilroy. Performances by George Clooney and Tilda Swinton, Castle Rock, 2007.

Plato. "The Allegory of the Cave." *Criteria: 2007–2008 A Journal of First Year Writing*, edited by Mary K. Jackman and Vanessa Hopper, SMU Department of English, 2007, pp. 161–168.

For Consideration:

1. Parmelee opens her essay by challenging the most common usage of the word "rich," and she closes with the argument we might all call ourselves truly rich if we put more effort into virtue and wisdom than into material gain. Write a paragraph in which you explain how Michael's life may improve now that he has stood up for justice rather than remained silent and protected his wealth. Draw your conclusions based on evidence about his character that you can glean from this essay. If you've seen the film, your response should be more detailed and specific.

2. Have you read Plato's "Allegory of the Cave"? If so, does your memory of that text align with Parmelee's application? Explain your answer. If you have not read Plato's "Allegory of the Cave," what is your understanding of philosophical idealism based on this essay?

3. Think of one movie or television show you have seen that addresses questions of business ethics as a central theme. Summarize the plot and explain how that particular movie or show addresses the theme. Is it a cautionary tale? More of a documentary style? Does it glorify business corruption or cast it in a negative light? Explain.

This writer argues for the inclusion of the 2008 film The Duchess *in the SMU first-year Honors Program DISC curriculum, emphasizing how it would enhance the understanding of already required texts as well as what it offers that none of the other texts currently contribute.*

Identity as a Political Machine:
Expressing Humanity in Times of Strife
Marina Leventis

1   History provides enriching context for understanding the greatest struggles of the 21st century. One issue that lingers as a relic of a more oppressive time is society's views and treatment of women relative to men. Keira Knightley's portrayal of the famed Duchess of Devonshire, Georgiana Cavendish, brings a touchingly human element to the discussion of the hypocritical, rigid, and material nature of the British aristocracy. *The Duchess*, set in the 18th century and based in fact, is valuable to a discussion of ethical importance as it represents divisions across gender lines in a way that addresses the role of public perception in relationships, as well as how one can bend society's rules while simultaneously succumbing to them. Without the inclusion of *The Duchess* in the curriculum, Honors Discernment and Discourse students will miss out on a historical understanding of how gender expectations have negatively influenced and inhibited the actions of individuals across the fabric of time, and how those issues have evolved to affect humanity today.

2   Fashion is an art form that has allowed individuals to express themselves for millennia; however, fashion can also be a means of achieving greater ideals. Georgiana Cavendish began her venture into the world of outrageous, avant-garde fashion with an understanding that her status as the Duchess of Devonshire was one that necessitated understanding her position in the public eye. When the duchess attended a ceremonial play in Bath, she introduced herself to the audience with confidence, knowing that the designs she had worn to the play would be worn by the public the next day. Venessa Lau, a journalist who studies the effects of style in media culture, recounts Georgiana's fashion choices as critical because Georgiana used her style to draw attention to political issues. For example, she donned large wigs and headdresses with specific attention to color, often blue and cream, to signify her support of the Whig party. As a notable public figure, Georgiana consciously used the attention she was guaranteed as the wife of a powerful noble in order to draw focus to her social issues of choice. Her employment

of colors and fabrics in a way that promoted the values of the Whigs to some extent politicized popular culture (Lau). While other works we have studied this year, like *The French Lieutenant's Woman,* also emphasize how gender can impact one's place in society, and while both Ernestina and Sarah represent feminism in their own right, *The French Lieutenant's Woman* is ultimately the story of Charles Smithson and a world seen through a man's eyes. The trend of women considering clothes as consciously meaningful signifiers originated with women like Georgiana, who used fashion not only as a means of expressing mood or personal style—like Ernestina in *The French Lieutenant's Woman*—but also to comment on social and political issues. Without having the insight into the world of fashion that *The Duchess* presents through a woman's eyes, the honors curriculum lacks depth in exploring how femininity itself can be used not only as an extension of identity, but also as a critical means of activism.

3   As fashion was an avenue to activism for Georgiana, Georgiana's fashion was readily criticized by her opposition. In the midst of her love affair in Bath with Charles Grey, Georgiana showed him a political cartoon depicting her in an embrace with a butcher while others gather around to show their support. Charles jokingly asks her if using fashion is an admissible way of gaining voters for the Whig party, clearly mocking the intention of the cartoon to undermine Georgiana's use of style as a political tool. As Dr. Amelia Rauser, a professor of Art History at the College of Franklin and Marshall explains, this scene in the film serves an accurate historical purpose as her fashion was seen by critics as too far removed from the expectations of women at the time, and as reflecting a declining morality and virtue amongst British women as a whole. Commentator William Combe went so far as to say her style of dress endangered the health of Great Britain as a nation and would lead to a rise in political tyranny due to female error. As Rauser and Combe attest, the contrast between the duchess and the butcher in the political comic interprets Georgiana's femininity as a threat to the masculine patriarchy that men like William Combe believed was superior (Rauser 30). Georgiana's critics are just as important to the message of political activism as is her fashion. The Duchess of Devonshire's determination to use her femininity —in the form of fashion—to reflect and influence politics clashed with the conservative tendency to preserve male dominance; this represents a vital facet of the feminist struggle that deserves to be examined.

4   While Virginia Woolf's *A Room of One's Own*—required reading this year in Honors Discernment and Discourse—attempts to address gender differences in the context of fiction, *The Duchess* adds the historical context that Woolf's work is largely missing. The addition of this film would supplement an honors student's

understanding of how gender expectations can influence behavior. *The Duchess* takes Woolf's argument to the next level by emphasizing *how* women can use systemic oppression to their advantage. If women are expected to focus on their appearance, women can adapt that expectation to suit their own interests. Rather than merely exemplifying that the patriarchy historically restricted the freedom of females in art, politics, and culture, *The Duchess* redefines femininity. Instead of demonstrating expectations of women as merely constraining, in this film we see a woman being unapologetically feminine yet still asserting the force of her personality and intelligent perspective in a society dominated by males. Her determination and ruthlessness make her difficult to ignore, so much so that other men—like statesman Charles Fox—view her more as a peer and less like a subordinate. *The Duchess* presents an outlook on female agency that no other text currently in the honors curriculum provides in an example of a woman—an oppressed individual—who finds ways to use her voice within the confines of the rules of society. It is fundamental that students learn that in being most true to themselves they can make the largest impact on the world, and that they might be able to do this by still playing within society's rules.

5   Gender plays an important role in the construction of family in how love and sex are viewed, shaped, and permitted. In Georgiana's time and for a woman of her aristocratic position, her obligation to her husband was not to be a loving wife, but to give him a male heir. Despite Georgiana's best attempts to win the affections of the duke, it is made clear in the film that she is valued by him only for her ability to produce a male child. The lack of emotional intimacy between William Cavendish and his wife demonstrated from the beginning, on their wedding day, when he enters her bed chambers, orders for scissors to be sent, and cuts her out of her dress without so much as blinking (Lau). For the duke, marriage is simply going through the motions of sex to conceive a boy, and it does not include emotional components like love, trust, and partnership. This is evident in the duke's anger at Georgiana upon discovering her romantic affair with Charles Grey after which he rapes her, despite having a mistress of his own. The duke's coldness toward his wife escalated to violence upon her realization of true love, as if to suggest that she doesn't deserve happiness. He perceives his own wife as a sub-human object that exists for one purpose only.

6   After the birth of their son, William Cavendish is still unwilling to allow Georgiana the same happiness he experiences with his mistress, Bess. The duke's hypocrisy demonstrates the paradigm of upper class love and marriage in 18th century Britain. The duke may keep a mistress for his own pleasure, but Georgiana exists only for *him*, and he has no obligation to her as a human being

with emotions, needs, and desires. His treatment of women as commodities is not foreign even in today's society: many men believe that they are owed a date or a phone number from a woman in return for a single compliment. The duke believes that his legal contract with Georgiana and her obligation to produce an heir gives him free reign over her body. William is not envious of Georgiana's affection for Charles Grey, nor is he hurt by it. Instead, he is concerned about the public implications on his masculine status. Men were expected to dominate and control their women, who were to be passive and submissive to their husbands. This is especially challenging for the duke when his own popularity becomes largely dependent on Georgiana's own, as she becomes increasingly interesting to the public; he becomes territorially threatened because he views Georgiana as his property. Georgiana is not allowed to express any opinion about the duke's relationship with Bess because as a woman, she is entitled to nothing—even emotions. This aspect of the film would add resonance to the required viewing of the documentary *The Hunting Ground*, which addresses sexual violence on college campuses by boldly exposing the ugly reality that the potential for abuse and commodification does not end after graduation, nor it does not end with the termination of a relationship, and may not end even at the doorstep of a woman's own home. Understanding the social changes that have—and have not—occurred over time with respect to relationships can help honors students understand not only that trust, love, compatibility, and equality are relatively new concepts in marriage, but also why gender imbalances and the objectification of women in relationships still occurs.

7   There is a chilling insidiousness in the Duke's treatment of Georgiana. William Cavendish is so cold to his wife that it renders her completely vulnerable in a number of ways. The duke is only interested in Georgiana when he feels his dog has escaped the leash; his treatment of her is destructive, unjust, and damaging to her psyche. Georgiana turns to poker and drinking as a means of coping with her extreme isolation in the duke's estate, and she reaches a breaking point after he rapes her. Georgiana begins attempting to suppress her own humanity as reaction to the duke's violation of her, and this is notable in her attire. Georgiana, for the first half of the film, wears loose necklaces as a symbol of her freedom. This is particularly notable in her excursions with Charles Grey, who truly loves and admires her and whom she loves in return. After she is sexually violated by William, she begins to wear tightly-wound velvet bands around her neck, as if to demonstrate her suffocation to the rest of the world (Lau). For a woman as loved by so many and as seemingly powerful as Georgiana to be neglected and ultimately abused signals a greater message that would be integral in the honors

curriculum. Domestic violence is not an issue that has gone away since the feminist revolution; it is highly mutable and has adapted itself to the present day. Many men marry women that they view as beneath them, and use their wealth and power as a mechanism to threaten, abuse, and contain their wives. Men can be victims of domestic abuse as well; however, the stigma associated with that of "trophy wives" is more advantageous and common in what is still a male-dominated community where victimizing females remains common.

8 First year students are in a unique position where they are beginning to learn first hand the trials of adulthood. For the first time, we are being educated in issues beyond what is politically correct and beyond what parents may want us to know. Understanding the dangers of sexuality and relationships is critical in order to understand how to preserve and protect the fundamental human rights we all possess. No other work in the curriculum currently offers such a blatant, relatable, and deeply emotional depiction of issues like marital rape and unloving, abusive relationships to the degree that *The Duchess* does.

9 Although Georgiana begins the film as a seventeen-year-old allowed to run freely with friends, she ends the film a stoic, seasoned adult whose only occasional pleasure in life comes from her children. Georgian's friend, Bess, becomes the duke's mistress, and Georgiana struggles to understand Bess's initial betrayal of her friendship; however, she later begins to understand that Bess acts as she does because she would do anything for her own children, no matter the cost. William forces Georgiana to choose a life of love with Charles Grey, and the right to raise her children, whom he will deny her access to if she doesn't behave according to his will. Despite Georgiana's initial refusal to cooperate with the duke's terms to either leave with Charles and never see her children again or give Charles up, she caves in and elects to stay and be a mother rather than abandon her children. Even in her fierce devotion to her children, Georgiana is still forced to give up her illegitimate daughter, Eliza, to the Grey house. This also demonstrates the clear hypocrisy in societal expectations for women: Georgiana was expected to raise the Duke's illegitimate daughter, Charlotte, as her own. Georgiana's loyalty to her children over her lover is admirable, yet it is a choice she would have never had to make if she had been a man.

10 Dr. Daniel Robinson, recipient of the American Psychological Association's Lifetime Achievement Award, argues that Georgiana's choice is questionable with respect to the rest of her story. He asserts that although she is an emblem

of feminism, her choice to remain tethered to motherhood serves as a potential contradiction as "Georgiana is and was realized in her maternity. Given her aristocratic status, the political implications of stereotyping points ironically to an unintentional reification of primogeniture" (Robinson 197). This is to say that Georgiana, despite her revolutionary moments in breaking female silence in politics, succumbs to what society has designated her to be as a person valuable only as a mother, and particularly, one who has borne a son. I disagree. Georgiana's choice to remain a mother actually serves to challenge the idea that women had duties only to their children, as she *was* given the choice to leave them. Rather than use force to ensure Georgiana fulfilled her maternal duties, the duke allows Georgiana to pick her own fate. This does not at all undermine Georgiana's activism; in a way, through having become such a powerful and public entity, she has forced the duke to allow her to choose her own life. Secondly, she elects to remain the duchess without sacrificing her celebrity platform or any of the power she held before her affair with Charles Grey.

11   Individuality is key in combating issues that divide us as well as in bolstering elements of our own humanity. *The Duchess* is a historical reminder that all people are as capable of rising above as they are of succumbing to adversity. It also proves that those at the "top" are not untouchable or perfect, just as those at the "bottom" are not without worth and potential. Georgiana Cavendish is an important figure that most college students have probably never heard of; however, her story would resonate within us all because her struggles relate to the struggles we experience today. No other aspect of the honors DISC curriculum addresses issues like marital rape and abusive relationships: these are crises that could happen to any one of us, and it's important to see the signs to avoid them as well as to not devolve into people like William Cavendish ourselves. Georgiana is a revolutionary in her own right. She proved herself to be timeless and is immortalized in Keira Knightley's poignant portrayal. Her story teaches what it means to preserve and express our humanity in times of oppression and in times of liberation. Georgiana shows us that we hold power within ourselves, and that power in our identity can be unleashed in many ways and become forces to be reckoned with. By hearing Georgiana's voice almost three hundred years after her life, we are reminded to use our own. The University Honors Program curriculum has a pedagogical obligation to expose students to the realities of the world, to the ethical codes that we can subscribe to, and above all, to learn how to express and accept our humanity at its most fundamental level.

Annotated Works Cited

The Duchess. Directed by Saul Dibb. Performances by Keira Knightley and Ralph Fiennes, Qwerty Films, 2008, DVD.

Lau, Venessa. "Duchess Treat: Move Aside, Marie Antoinette, and Make Way for the Enchanting Georgiana." *W*, Sept. 2008, www.wmagazine.com/story/georgiana-cavendish.

This source is part of an analysis of fashion in media done by Venessa Lau, a fashion journalist, in an attempt to explain how style can contribute to identity and to greater forms of expression. In her review of the film's fashions, Lau uses her own research on the Duchess Georgiana for historical context, an interview with the Academy Award winning costume design cast from the film, and specific scenes from the movie in order to point out critical elements of fashion. Lau notes that "in the film [Georgiana's] style is essential to her story—one rich with scandal, politics (she actively campaigned for the Whig party) and steamy sex (illicit affairs, ménages a trois)." She then carefully selects fabrics, jewelry, and structure of dress in order to illustrate the progression of Georgiana in activism, her freedom with Charles Grey, and her confinement by the duke.

This piece was used throughout my own paper in order to add a more specific eye to the details of the film. My original analysis was much more conceptual: Georgiana did wear outrageous fashion, but Lau's analysis adds the far more relevant context as to why the duchess dressed the way she did. Without the integration of Lau's commentary in my work, I would have neglected a critical element of Georgiana's identity, as well as one of the primary techniques the filmmaker used to tell Georgiana's story.

Rauser, Amelia. "The Butcher-Kissing Duchess of Devonshire: Between Caricature and Allegory in 1784." *The Johns Hopkins University Press: Eighteenth-Century Studies*, Vol. 36, No. 1, Fall 2002, pp. 23–46. *JSTOR,* www.jstor.org/stable/30053337.

Dr. Rauser is the most important source in this paper in terms of verifying the history of the film in regard to Georgiana's activism. While the film demonstrates Georgiana is heavily admired by the public, it does fall short in reminding its audience that Georgiana was not loved across the board. Dr. Rauser rectifies this by analyzing political caricatures; she examines the actual cartoon that inspired the scene between Georgiana and Charles Grey in Bath, and utilizes both historical and artistic context to explain the nature of Georgiana's perception by the public. She notes that Georgiana's outrageous fashion was seen as unladylike by many and by some as an attack against Great Britain. Amelia Rauser is perhaps the most dedicated author in my three sources and the most highly qualified. She has served as a professor of Art History for much of her adult life and has specialized in historical British political cartoons, going so far as to publish an entire book-length study on them. This source was critical in discussing the gender imbalance and negative public perception points I addressed in my paper.

Robinson, Daniel. "The Duchess, Mary Robinson, and Georgiana's Social Network." *The Wordsworth Circle*, Vol. 42, No. 3, Summer 2011, pp. 193–197, *JSTOR*, www.jstor.org/stable/24043147.

Dr. Robinson's work examines *The Duchess* across Georgiana's history as well as other references in popular culture—in particular, the works of poet Mary Robinson. Dr. Robinson as a historical psychologist delves deeply into Georgiana's mindset and emotions as a mother, activist, and tortured wife. He explains that Georgiana's willingness to befriend Bess despite her infidelity is consistent with her status as the duke's objectified wife, and that her choice to put her children first is a product of her obligation of the time. In essence, Dr. Robinson argues that while Georgiana is progressive and ahead of her time, there are potential drawbacks to the idea of her as a revolutionary. In fact, while the film makes a major issue of Georgiana nursing her children rather than using a wet nurse, her own mother, Lady Spencer, did so as well. Thus, Georgiana, in Dr. Robinson's eyes, is relegated to less of what we might think of as an anomaly and more of a novelty.

I have used this source for a point of refutation in my paper. Dr. Robinson presents Georgiana as having what is an impossible choice, but it is a choice nonetheless. Georgiana's willingness to give up the love of her life and later their child in order to raise her other children is absolutely not out of feelings of obligation, it is out of the immense devotion and love she feels for them. That, to me, represents Georgiana's strength, not weakness. Dr. Robinson provides an otherwise resourceful account of the historical context and personal motivations for Georgiana's actions in the film that are also important in the writing of this paper. In order to best understand why Georgiana acted the way she did, and in order to understand the choices she made, I often referred to Dr. Robinson as a source for broader understanding as I developed my thesis. My use of Dr. Robinson's work in the paper influenced what I think to be its strongest point—that Georgiana was successful in being a strong woman in a man's world.

For Consideration:

1. Think back to a class that you've taken—here at SMU or even in high school—that you think would've benefitted from the inclusion of a certain text. Based on the techniques this student writer used, make your own argument directed to the faculty or professor of that particular class.

2. What do you feel was Leventis's most convincing point in support of her thesis? Explain your answer. If one point could've been given more attention, which one would you suggest? What kind of additional support or explanation would you like to see? Be specific.

3. Leventis points out, across the historical figure of the Duchess of Devonshire, that fashion can be a way to make statements about serious issues—like one's political beliefs—while still playing within "society's rules." Have you ever used fashion in this way? Do you know others who have—people you've encountered in your own life, characters in movies or on shows, or celebrities? List as many examples as you can and, when you and your neighbor are finished, compare lists and see what conclusions you can draw.

Virginia Woolf's A Room of One's Own *was originally delivered as lectures on women's rights at a women's college in England in 1929. The following three students were tasked with arguing which of the first three chapters would've been most likely to appeal to male readers of the period, as if a London newspaper had offered to publish one chapter specifically with that goal in mind. Each student makes a good argument for a different chapter. Discussion questions for these essays follow the third essay.*

A Beginner's Guide to Feminism
Samantha Hites

1   The first step in convincing people to change is giving them a justified reason why they should. The first chapter of *A Room of One's Own* places an emphasis on the unfavorable life of women in the 1920s as a result of the gender-role paradigm in a way that does not place blame or spotlight the iniquities of men; rather, chapter one educates and rationalizes a paradigm shift. Through universal analogies and emotional, potent speech, Woolf critiques the paradigm instead of men themselves. This temperate chapter would be received more positively than chapter two or three by a 1920s man who had likely never before experienced feminist literature.

2   According to Woolf, men and women possess an irrefutable, metaphysical similarity. Her brilliant metaphor of the lamp "halfway down the spine, which is the seat of one's soul" (11) and which is lit when one experiences pleasure and its attribution to material items such as food is a universal sentiment that would have undoubtedly piqued the interest of a 1920s man. Subsequently, he would have realized that Woolf, a *female* author, had not only experienced the same feelings of pleasure as him, which would equalize men and women, but she was also capable of verbalizing it in a poetic and evocative manner. This insinuates that not only was she akin to him in emotion, but also in intelligence. If he were humane to even a small degree, he would feel a twinge of similarity between the two sexes; further, it would be difficult for him to sincerely believe an intelligent individual, who was capable of the same emotions as himself, deserved "poverty and insecurity" (24). The concept of the lamp discretely influences the male reader by allowing him to authenticate the existence of an emotional similarity between the sexes in his own mind.

3   Woolf strengthens her argument by contrasting the glamorous luncheon and lackluster dinner to represent the flawed gender-role paradigm. The bland food

and reserved atmosphere at Fernham, the women's college, are a stark contrast to the delicious food and lively conversation at the men's hall in Oxbridge. This illustrates the inferiority of the women's university, not because its attendants were inferior, but because it was poorly funded. Because pennilessness is the cause of an unsatisfactory meal and "[o]ne cannot think well, love well, sleep well, if one has not dined well" (18), a 1920s man who may not have experienced impecuniousness would still consider the "effect poverty has on the mind" (24) after reading the dining scenes. Woolf created an analogy for inequality via these dining situations to portray the disparity between the sexes in an accessible, temperate way. The man would be more willing analyze the disparity in this manner rather than personally and subjectively; the analogy allows the man to conclude that women were victims of the financial paradigm instead of by an individual man such as himself.

4   Men were aware of women's societal restrictions, but because men benefitted from the paradigm, they were oblivious to the notion that women felt trapped inside it. The declaration that "it [was] worse perhaps to be locked in" (24) is of vital importance. Women were displeased with their everyday restrictions, and they were dissatisfied with their predetermined role in society. It would have been important that a man understood that women were not angered by the freedom the opposite sex possessed, but that rather by their own inability to access the same freedom. The way Woolf blames the societal paradigm for the unfair treatment of women instead of blaming men directly would've made her argument less intimidating: it is clear that women do not want to take away men's power, they simply want the same opportunities to live up to their potential and live their own choices. Her decision in this chapter not to focus on misogyny and masculine insecurity as the underlying causes of women's distress (because they were, indeed, among the reasons for the gender role restrictions) was an ingenious way to declare the existence of a social problem while keeping men interested and pleased with her writing.

5   The most influential aspect of chapter one is Woolf's impassioned monologue about the lack of inheritance left by maternal ancestors. The way Woolf crafts this section underlines male privileges, such as the ability to have an educated conversation about sciences, by lamenting that she cannot partake in these luxuries. A man would have been likely to read this monologue and recognize his freedom to do everything she mentions; then, when Woolf explains that those things are only possible with money and reminds her reader that women were forbidden to have fortunes of their own, the man would come to an epiphany. He would surely recognize the correlation between finances and freedom, and he would realize that

feminism is not focused on the resentment of men; rather, feminism is focused on the paradigm, the discrepancy between the financial rights of the sexes, and the subsequent consequences of them.

6   The intention of this essay is not to say we must coddle men and, for the sake of their egos, tell them only what they want to hear. It is imperative, further along in the process of converting a man to a feminist, that we explain the truth to him, however harsh it may be. However, for a 1920s man who had never considered feminism or its motives, picking apart his psychology would be the quickest way to deter him. No man would want to read or accept a text that aggrieves him or inspires guilt, so chapter one is unquestionably the best candidate for a beginner's guide to feminism.

Works Cited

Woolf, Virginia. *A Room of One's Own*. Harcourt Brace & Company, 1989.

Twentieth Century Women: By Men, for Men
Shara Jeyarajah

1. Each day in the early 1900s, men spanning across ages and classes became equals for a moment as they sat down to enjoy the newspaper. Little did they know that during that daily ritual, the pages would deepen the separation between the sexes. In the second chapter of *A Room of One's Own*, Virginia Woolf dissected the root of men's trivializing of women in their written works in an engaging narrative format; her argument detailing the anger that perpetuated the patriarchy and addressing the deeper grievances of both sexes would make the best appeal for gender equality to the male newspaper reader in 1929.

2. Woolf expressed the truths she drew from her research on gender inequality in the form of a personal narrative. Seeking insight from "the learned and the unprejudiced," the author searched for the evolution of sexism at the British Museum (Woolf 25). She soon noticed a pattern of reductive treatment towards women in empirical texts. Some professors found women wise, but others marked them as foolish; some worshipped women as goddesses, while others deemed them subhuman. Educated men throughout history authored these textbooks based not on objective evidence, but reductive preconceptions developed over the course of generations. Woolf found neither fact nor truth in authors' conflicting portrayals. Interestingly, she doesn't hide under the facade of objectivity that other scholars did when she delivers her findings on the systemic root of sexism. On the contrary, she notes the ebb and flow of her emotions in light of uncovering these new perspectives. If Woolf attempted to put forth her argument in dry factual terms, male readers would reject her grievances regarding the mistreatment of women by male writers as easily as Woolf rejected the textbook authors' skewed messages. The subjective nature of Woolf's depictions suggests that her account contains "more truth than fact" (Woolf 4). Thus, as one would contemplate the values proposed in fictional literature, newspaper readers would be encouraged to decipher the truth in Woolf's narrative for themselves.

3. What motivated textbook authors to write such reductive rhetoric about women? While contemplating this question, the hypothetical researcher in the library—a technically fictional character who is clearly meant to represent Woolf—absentmindedly marred her notes with a sketch of an imaginary man, Professor von Ex, who published a book about women's inherent inferiority, a subject as wretched as the appearance she gives him in her drawing. The same

way learned men described women based on their own unsympathetic projections rather than her character, the speaker herself fell into the trap of lumping textbook authors' complex array of perceptions and experiences into an oversimplified scribble. She admits that "the sketch of the angry professor had been made in anger" (Woolf 31). In allowing her pen to submit to her unconscious emotions, Woolf better understood male authors' depictions of women as a product of an underlying "anger disguised and complex, not anger simple and open" (Woolf 32). Newspaper readers could not fault Woolf for regarding the opposite sex from a sanctimonious position, as she submitted to the same emotional charge as her counterparts. In addition, she defined the anger in human terms—a condition both sexes fall prey to—allowing the reader to consider to what degree he empathizes with the authors' rancor.

4   Woolf arrived at the conclusion that angry men were "concerned not with [women's] inferiority, but with [their] own superiority" (Woolf 34). Men embraced their dominance with a constant fear of subversion from the lesser group. Thus, they promoted the discrepancy between genders at every opportunity: in academia, media, the workforce, and politics. Fathers raised their daughters on the belief that their sole objectives in life were acquiring and pleasing a suitable husband. Women were expected to serve "as looking-glasses . . . reflecting the figure of man at twice its natural size" (Woolf 35). Though her claims could initially alienate her readers, she admitted that even men face hardships due to their gender. In some ways, men were also victims of a sexist system, tasked with the burden of attaining status and wealth for their whole family. She deflected blame from the male gender to greater societal pressure, as "it was absurd to blame any class or any sex, as a whole" (Woolf 38). In doing so, Woolf departed from an accusatory tone, allowing male readers to approach her claims with reception rather than a feeling of persecution. Woolf granted that her reader may be a good husband, father, and son in private, but his only hope of not collapsing under systemic pressures is by buying into and perpetuating the illusion of the looking-glass. Woolf even relented that, to a certain extent, womanhood was a "protected occupation," as the most violent and physical jobs were reserved for their counterparts (Woolf 40). Putting the roots of sexism in explicit terms would've forced male readers of the period to consider their own role in perpetuating a cycle that leaves both sides disadvantaged.

5   The common newspaper reader in 1929 might have perceived Woolf's claims to be a product of subjectivity or perhaps an engaging fiction. However, the male

readers affected by the calls for gender equality could examine their own periodical to confirm bias against women in the lack of diversity in the headlines and bylines alike. The second chapter of *A Room of One's Own* addresses inequalities in a way that only reinforced the need to provide a platform for those whose voices are the most suppressed. Woolf, combining the intrigue of fiction with compelling rhetoric for women's rights, is the perfect mouthpiece.

Works Cited

Woolf, Virginia. *A Room of One's Own.* Harcourt Brace & Company, 1989.

Read All about It!
Chapter Three of *A Room of One's Own* as Required Reading for Men

Maria Katsulos

1   No matter the time period, feminism of the sort Virginia Woolf espouses in *A Room of One's Own* (that is to say, unabashed and overt) must be tailored depending on the audience. The young women for whom Woolf composed her lectures reacted much differently than male students from Woolf's imagined Oxbridge might have. As the privileged members of society, especially in Woolf's topics of education and economy, men of the time could not so easily understand Woolf's point of view as a woman. In reading Chapter Three of *A Room of One's Own* in a 1929 newspaper, men would've seen women's real struggles through the lens of fiction and actually related to them because of their own precarious place in a bourgeois society.

2   Especially in a field as cloistered as education, many men in 1929 were unaware of, or unwilling to open their eyes to, the struggles women of the time faced. Even if they seemed to be well-off, women struggled economically because they were barred from premier educational institutions and forced into gendered roles of marriage and motherhood. The true issue lay in the fact that women were not mistresses of their own fates. Any money a woman had to her name was controlled by her father or husband. While the lack of choice in and control of their lives seemed to be exclusive to women, in reality, a bourgeois system steals everyone's freedom. No matter their social class, people were often stuck in their caste and the expectations that came along with it. The profession of writing, which accepted any man, had long remained off-limits to women. Women's attempts at the craft were greeted with "not indifference but hostility" (52). Women were not allowed to wield the pen, so their representation in fiction was crafted by men who did not truly understand or accurately represent their experience.

3   Ironically, though few real-life women managed to publish fiction, men wrote female characters with strength they were not permitted in reality. Drawing upon well-known characters such as Lady Macbeth and Cleopatra, Woolf provides examples of powerful literary women that any educated man in 1929 would be familiar with. These women were nowhere to be found in real life, though; even though women in books could do anything a man could and be recognized for her power, "practically she is completely insignificant" (43). Not only that, but it was a rare, fairly egotistical woman who would describe herself or write her own story

in the nature of Lady Macbeth or Cleopatra. The stories men read about women weren't about women at all—they were just men's ideals of women, which was usually a bolstering figure to a man like Macbeth or Mark Antony. Yet this was not a cultural symptom limited to differences in gender; within bourgeois society, upper-class writers often wrote stories of those blissfully happy while living in poverty. False representation of the oppressed is just one way an oppressor stays in power.

4   Thus, Woolf's biography of the hypothetical Judith Shakespeare is really a powerful metaphor representing the issue of women in fiction. Woolf's shared experiences with Judith form a story much more genuine than any man's creation of a fictional female could be. Like so many other real-life women, Judith never got to write her own story, which is why women are "all but absent from history" when one attempts to research the lives of women prior to the 20th century (43). Judith's story of trying to move up in the world and then failing was, unfortunately, not at all uncommon—among both men and women. Members of the lower class had no control over how their stories were told; much like the library where Woolf researched was devoid of books by women, there was a similar dearth of books by the poor. Judith's story shows that a bourgeois system is the great equalizer between genders. Men of the proletariat could immediately associate with Judith's story, having been kept out of certain professions and positions as well. Until people can see themselves in others' shoes, it is impossible for them to truly relate to others' struggles. Like Judith, many men in a bourgeois society wanted more for themselves than the hand birth had dealt them, but society dictated that social status was as unchangeable as gender. Though Judith's tale had an unhappy ending, her significant role in Woolf's story should have inspired both men and women to advocate for total equality.

5   The privileged members of any system are reluctant to hear the stories of those they oppress for fear of sympathizing too deeply with them. Whether those members are men realizing the plights of women or the wealthy becoming aware of the impoverished, those on top of the social ladder are loathe to release their grip on it by hearing out the other side. In Chapter Three of *A Room of One's Own*, Woolf makes the issue of women in fiction—basically, that there are no women in fiction—too vibrant to ignore. Men in 1929 reading their daily paper and coming across this chapter would have a brand-new perspective on women's issues, presented, finally, by a woman. Nearly a century later, men in 2018 could benefit from the same treatment. How many men would have the same opinions on women's issues if they had to suffer the same constant indignities?

6 The kind of educational and economic equity Woolf advocated for in 1929 might be different from the kind feminists fight for today, but the fact remains that to solve women's issues, they have to become men's issues as well. Men don't need to join women on the lower steps of a ladder. The goal is to bring the marginalized—women, the proletariat, or any other oppressed group—up to the level of the oppressors, and to remove the distinction between the two. Magnifying voices that may have been ignored in the past will achieve that goal, either in 1929 or 2018.

Works Cited

Woolf, Virginia. *A Room of One's Own*. Harcourt Brace & Company, 1989.

For Consideration:

1. Each writer argued for the publication of a different chapter. Which do you feel made the most convincing argument? As you determine your choice, consider not only the points made by that author, but also the delivery of ideas: strength of title, introduction, conclusion, organization, use of supporting examples and quotes, and so forth.

2. In order to effectively argue not just in general favor of one chapter, but for the effectiveness that a chapter would have in reaching a very specific audience in a specific time and place in history, what sorts of considerations would these student writers have had as they brainstormed ideas for this essay?

3. These chapters of Woolf's *A Room of One's Own* are not very long. Locate any one of the three chapters online—perhaps the one you found to be the most intriguing, based on the author's argument—and read it for yourself. Then, write a response in which you critique or reinforce the student author's arguments with your own carefully considered insights and examples.

This poignant essay demonstrates the value of literary analysis, as it addresses in critical terms the vital issues of art's function in our development as individual humans and its power to not only inspire us but to shape society on many levels.

The Importance of Art and Elisabeth Demand in *Autumn*

Sydney Maddox

1   Noted twentieth-century Marxist author and art critic Ernst Fischer once said, "In a decaying society, art, if it is truthful, must also reflect decay. And unless it wants to break faith with its social function, art must show the world as changeable. And help to change it" (Fischer 15), which is to say that art shapes the world by expressing the thoughts and ideas of societies and can bring about change within a society. Because the meaning of art is subject to interpretation, it can evoke both positive and negative reactions depending upon the audience. In Ali Smith's *Autumn*, a novel about the relationship between young Elisabeth Demand and her neighbor, Daniel Gluck, seventy years her elder, art is frequently discussed to encourage exploration of different perspectives. It is art that breathes Elisabeth back to life after ten years away from her dissertation research and from Daniel, and that drives her to return to living with her mother and visiting Daniel who is now in the hospital. It may seem like Daniel and Elisabeth frequently discuss and care about art with significant but infrequent effects on their lives. However, through Daniel's efforts to teach Elizabeth to think beyond herself by using art, the change in the knowledge and recognition of Pauline Boty's work to being viewed as valuable, and the time Elisabeth spends experiencing art around her and sharing it, art is shown to have a profound and multi-faceted impact on Elisabeth and those around her. Through its effects on Elisabeth and her community, art enables Elisabeth's community to move towards change.

2   In an effort to teach Elisabeth to think more about the world around her, Daniel describes art to Elisabeth in a way that pushes her to see the world differently. Daniel has Elisabeth close her eyes and imagine a painting, describing the physicality of it to her to encourage her to realize there is more than superficial beauty within art: "[T]here's some pink lacy stuff, by which I mean actual material, real lace, stuck on to the picture in a couple of places, up near the top, then further down towards the middle too" (Smith 74). This description of the material prompts Elisabeth to look past the superficial qualities to find meaning and

expression. The pink lace represents females in the work. The idea of the lace as a layer on top of the art represents the meaning that is found when Elisabeth looks deeper into the many ideas within a piece of art. This translates later in Elisabeth's life to her studies of art, and particularly her research on British Pop artist Pauline Boty, whose art is very forward-thinking on social issues such as women's rights. The gendered pink lace in the art Daniel describes symbolizes Boty's push to use female stereotypes to counter male privilege. Elisabeth becomes a proponent of these feminist ideas and learns from Daniel to oppose the oppression of those who have less power. Daniel's efforts to use art in teaching Elisabeth cause her to think differently and find meaning in art and the world around her.

3   Daniel describes different works of art to Elisabeth in an effort to teach her to think beyond herself. Studio artist Olafur Eliasson writes to promote the belief that art can turn thinking into doing: "I believe that one of the major responsibilities of artists—and the idea that artists have responsibilities may come as a surprise to some—is to help people not only get to know and understand something with their minds but also to feel it emotionally and physically" (Eliasson). The concepts of understanding, emotion, and physicality are used as rhetorical devices by Daniel in his lessons for Elisabeth. By encouraging her to understand that there is deeper meaning within art beyond superficial beauty, to feel that art can cause emotional sensations within the self that encourage exploring different perspectives, and to know that art is physical and visceral, Daniel teaches Elisabeth to find her most fully human self. When Elisabeth begins to fully realize herself through Daniel's art, she becomes an activist in the community. At a young age, Elisabeth goes home to share her newly developed sense of art with her mother to give her mom the same feeling that she received while pondering the art. This shows how deeply this interaction with art has affected Elisabeth, and it is only the first interaction of many. Elisabeth's emotional and physical responses illuminate art's importance and impacts her future by leading her into an education, and later a career, in the arts.

4   When Elisabeth takes interest in Pauline Boty and chooses to research her, it leads to a change in the recognition and reception of Boty's work. Elisabeth is interested in the fact that Boty is a female British Pop artist, and her male professor, who does not recognize nor find value in Boty's work, has told her that "categorically there had never been such a thing as a female British Pop artist, not one of any worth, which is why there were none recorded as more than footnotes in British Pop Art history" (Smith 150). While her professor does not recognize Boty's work nor view it as capable of causing change, Elisabeth values Boty's feminist work and seeks to dismantle this male opposition. As her research of Boty's

work progresses, Elisabeth becomes more aware of the world around her as do the other women in her life. For example, Elisabeth's mother is affected by the research, taking an interest in antiques and educating herself on history. Antiques are also a form of art, and Elisabeth's own research of art inspires her mom to not only educate herself on the world around her but also on art and culture.

5   Elisabeth chooses to write about Pauline Boty for her dissertation, and as she further explores Boty's life and work, she realizes the importance of her struggle to be recognized and appreciated. Kalliopi Minioudaki, feminist historian of modern and contemporary art, describes Pauline Boty's feminist pop art, acknowledging the highly sexualized and extremely feminist side of Boty's art, and recognizes "the feminist potential of the pin-up as the popular culture's genre of sexually aware women, a view that does not necessarily concur with its contemporaneous manifestations in popular magazines like *Playboy* but does . . . echo the genre's feminist history and its empowering potential for women artists" (Minioudaki 417). Boty's sexualized and feminist work makes viewers uncomfortable and therefore critical of her work instead of appreciative. When Elisabeth's choice to research Pauline Boty is met with male distaste for the feminist work, she chooses to continue her research with another advisor, rather than accept the gender privileging view of the academic who derides Boty's art. In Elisabeth's exploration of Boty's work, she finds appreciation and purpose in her own life and strives to share Boty's work with those around her, affecting their perspectives on feminist art. Elisabeth's research proves the value and importance of the work of Boty, and inspires her mother, the most important female figure in her life, to become more worldly and open to progressive ideas. Boty's work causes a change in Elisabeth, as well as the female characters in the novel, by building the strength of women's voices.

6   Pauline Boty's art inspires Elisabeth to return to living her life at her full potential, just as Daniel has worked to teach her through her childhood. Elisabeth sees Boty's work in a catalogue after putting away her research for ten years, and she finds inspiration and a reminder of why she began her research on Boty as she "opened the Boty catalogue again and flicked through it. The wild bright colors came off the page at her as she did" (Smith 225). The bright colors remind Elisabeth of why she was attracted to Boty's work. It is bold, lively, and liberal. Bright colors were abnormal in the art of Boty's time, and she was the first female artist to begin working outside of the status quo for artists in her time. The bright colors are a literal and visual entreaty to Elisabeth to live a full, bright, colorful life, rather than to continue living the life of a recluse. Elisabeth had strayed from Daniel and from her research to truly do absolutely nothing, and Boty's work

calls her to return to making something of her life and inspiring those around her through her own original work.

7   The frequency with which Smith uses Pauline Boty's art in the novel reveals a deeper meaning within the art which impacts Elisabeth's life. In an interview by Karl Anderson, Ali Smith discussed her own inspiration by the bold and lively work of Pauline Boty: "I happened on a Boty picture, so full of brightness and vivacity, and then learned her life circumstances, and looked at more and more of her extraordinary and vital work, and saw how she went about demolishing the borders and divisions and given limitations for a young woman of her time." Boty's feminist work, "full of brightness and vivacity," resonates deeply within Elisabeth and brings her back to life. When Elisabeth realizes that Daniel will never love her in a romantic way, she shuts down and strays from both her art and her relationship. It is only recognizing the beauty and meaning in the world around her that reminds her of the Boty research and of Daniel, which brings her back into his life once more. Boty's art sparks a light within Elisabeth because she has grown up to find importance in the seemingly unimportant, which is how many view Boty's art when Elisabeth first discovers it. Elisabeth, like Smith, finds empowerment for herself in the boundary-breaking work of Boty and is inspired to be a forward-thinking woman.

8   When Boty's work brings back Elisabeth's will to live her life fully, she experiences the concept of retreat and return, coming back from her time alone into life with a new perspective. Dr. Astrid Bracke writes for the *Oxford Handbook of Ecocriticism* on this concept that "the desire to retreat or escape to an untouched or unspoilt natural place is always countered by the necessity of return to a less-than-ideal space" (Bracke 435). Elisabeth retreats for several years, not working on her research nor connecting with any of her family, but experiences return when Boty's work reminds her of the importance of living a full life. Elisabeth retreats to a place of solitude to take time away from the difficulties she is facing in her life. It is less than desirable for Elisabeth to return to a community facing such political and moral conflict, yet her work contributes to the fight against this conflict and has the power to make people experience a different perspective on these issues. When she does return, she returns with a new vigor and the realization that her retreat was an escape from her problems rather than a solution to them. Elisabeth's experience of retreat and return helps her to fully realize her value and purpose in her life, as well as how to live a full life.

9   Throughout Elisabeth's life, art is extremely prevalent in her upbringing and in her community. When on a walk to see her mom, Elisabeth passes a home which xenophobic vandals have presumed to be the home of immigrants that "has

been painted over with black paint and the words GO HOME" (Smith 53) sending a message of hate towards immigrants. The words are pushing for a negative change, for immigrants to leave, because to this artist, they do not belong in this society. People pass by and look away, ignoring this artistic expression, because they are discomforted by it as it is reflective of society's views on immigration and feelings towards immigrants. This art is non-traditional and considered to be street art rather than professional art, and as such is reflective of negative ideals and lacks meaning. When art is no longer made to be appreciated and supportive of a society moving forward, it begins to function as an outlet for the dissenting opinions of a society and reflects the ideals of a decaying society that hinder progress. Rather than being provocative of change in society, this negative art is a reflection of a negative society, in a time of unhappiness and detachment. Art serves as a reminder that there are controversial issues and problems within society, and as a catalyst to promote change.

10   Art causes society to be forward thinking and often to disrupt the status quo, which Elisabeth becomes a strong proponent of doing. Many years later, after the "GO HOME" painting on the house has left its mark on Elisabeth, she walks past the home again and sees "in varying bright colors, WE ARE ALREADY HOME THANK YOU" (Smith 138). The bright colors against the original black colors show a contrast between the dark and disheartening message and the new opposing message that is fighting back regarding immigration. This art becomes more "professional" and less "street" because it is less reflective of decay and more reflective of a progressive and restorative society. When Elisabeth sees the new message on the house, she feels happiness for the first time in a while, realizing that she is not alone in wanting society to move forward. She sees through the artwork that restoration is occurring, and those around her are becoming more accepting of progressive social ideals. Elisabeth's interaction with this art causes her to realize that she is not alone, and that those around her are capable of change.

11   Art, as a means to fight oppression, helps Elisabeth find herself. When she sees the bright-colored words of opposition painted on the immigrant home, Elisabeth feels like she is herself for the first time in a while. During his residency at MIT, artist B. Stephen Carpenter discussed how art can disrupt oppression, particularly the idea of how "the act of teaching—in addition to the practice of creating art—can be directed at disrupting systemic oppression" (Dobkin). Elisabeth experiences this first hand through Daniel teaching her to see the meaning and emotion behind art, and to see it as a means of expressing ideas rather than just superficial qualities. She also creates her own art through her research—it's own art form—which leads her to become a more active and aware member of society.

Upon realizing the power of art and finding that power within herself, Elisabeth becomes more self-aware and active in her life.

Art has a significant impact on the life of Elisabeth and those around her, and through them causes society to progress. Elisabeth is taught by Daniel to not only appreciate art, but to look deeper to find meaning in artistic expression. Every painting tells a story and shares a message with those who view it. She also learns to fully realize herself through Daniel's use of rhetoric within his lessons on art. Through researching the life and work of Pauline Boty, Elisabeth becomes a more active and involved citizen who cares about the world around her and has an influence on it. Boty's feminist work shows the empowerment of women and leads Elisabeth to think about oppressed communities and become involved in acting against oppression. She also causes the criticism of Boty's work to shift from negative—as her dissertation professor saw it—to positive and recognized as valuable. The emphasis on art throughout Elisabeth's life and within her community shows the importance of art in society. Art causes change in Elisabeth's life, but also in the lives of those around her. The art within the novel is meaningful and powerful, and effects the opinions and perspectives of those who view it. Art is a powerful means of implementing change and empowering societies to advance.

Works Cited

Bracke, Astrid. "The Contemporary English Novel and Its Challenges to Ecocriticism." *The Oxford Handbook of Ecocriticism*, edited by Greg Garrard, Oxford University Press, 2014, pp. 423–440.

Dobkin, Sydney et al., "Using Art to Disrupt Systems of Oppression." *MIT News*, news.mit.edu/2017/stephen-carpenter-using-art-disrupt-systems-oppression-1115.

Eliasson, Olafur. "Why Art Has the Power to Change the World." *World Economic Forum*, www.weforum.org/agenda/2016/01/why-art-has-the-power-to-change-the-world.

Fischer, Ernst. *The Necessity of Art*. Penguin, 2010.

Kalliopi, Minioudaki. "Pop's Ladies and Bad Girls: Axell, Pauline Boty and Rosalyn Drexler." *Oxford Art Journal*, vol. 30, no. 3, 2007, pp. 404–430. *JSTOR*, jstor.org/stable/4500072.

Smith, Ali. *Autumn*. Pantheon Books, 2017.

---. Interview by Eric Karl Anderson. "Ali Smith on Autumn, Brexit, and the shortness of life." *Penguin*, 12 October 2016, www.penguin.co.uk/articles/2016/ali-smith-on-autumn/.

For Consideration:

1. Go online and look up artist Pauline Boty. Get some information about her background and her career, and look at some of her artwork. How does your exposure to Boty inform your understanding of Maddox's points about Elisabeth's evolution? How does Ali Smith's, the author of *Autumn*, choice to use a real artist as inspiration for a fictional character affect how a reader might experience the novel?

2. Revisit Maddox's opening quote from Ernst Fischer in the introduction. Explain your understanding of his use of the word "decay." What does it imply? Give examples from actual art that you're familiar with, and be sure to consider all kinds of media, including songs, photography, paintings, sculpture, and architecture.

3. Maddox and Smith agree that art has the power to influence the trajectories of individual lives, and to both reflect and influence culture. Do you agree? Why or why not? Build your response with attention to rhetorical integrity, consciously employing logos and ethos, and possibly pathos if you wish.

Using Edward Albee's play, The American Dream, *Maddox investigates the characters' "American Dream" and how it compares to the phrase's original definition. Although the play's characters do not emerge in a good light, Maddox concludes that there is hope for American society in general.*

The Damaging Effects of Materialism
Mary-Wesley Maddox

1   The term "the American dream" was first coined by James Truslow Adams in 1931 in his "Epilogue" to *The Epic of America*. He developed the concept during a unique transitional period in America following the opulent Roaring Twenties when the Great Depression was beginning to set in. During his lifetime, Adams saw America grow exponentially and, in his view, "slip a long way backwards" (416). Adams' ideas about the regression of the American dream can be observed in Edward Albee's bizarre play *The American Dream*. The play was written in 1959, and it showcases a dysfunctional family that has become possessed by the idea of wealth and looks to the point that they are morally corrupt. Mommy and Daddy's desire for a child in *The American Dream* displays how their life is ruled by their "American dream," which is defined by Adams as a warped idea that one's success is defined by his material possessions which leads to rampant consumerism and conformity.

2   The concept of the American dream is the principle that a person who comes from nothing can reach a high point of success, but throughout history the dream has transformed into a need for accumulating excessive wealth and extravagant possessions to define one's worth. Adams defines the American dream as "that dream of a land in which life should be better and richer and fuller for every man, with opportunity for each according to his ability or achievement," which outlines how the dream was perceived in its humble beginnings when America was still expanding (404). However, he makes the argument that the dream has become wrapped up in materialism and people view success as being marked by items that they acquire rather than making a difference on the world. This "post-war materialism," as he calls it, was born out of a period of sacrificing for the war and was displayed during the lavish 1920s.

3   The materialism that Adams criticizes is also discussed in Albee's play *The American Dream* through the nature of Mommy and Daddy's marriage. Mommy is obsessed with wealth, despite not having a job, telling Daddy, "I have a right to all your money when you die" (Albee 14). She does not see the value in hard

work to obtain money but instead focuses on her entitlement to her husband's money and what she can buy with it. Mommy's characteristics comment on the declining importance that Americans place on being honest and working hard. The pursuit of new clothes, cars, and houses has outweighed the need for financial security and an overall rich life, and it has spiraled out of control. American society is all about looks, which Albee expresses through Mommy's extended rant about the "lovely little hat" and her pursuit of satisfaction (10). Mommy gets into an argument over the hat's color because the chairman of the women's club made a comment, showing how she is obsessed with what others think about her and determined to receive "satisfaction" in life, even if it is fabricated in her mind (Albee 11). Albee's portrayal of Mommy reveals that a fixation on what one wears or buys eliminates the original American dream in which everyone has equal opportunity for success.

4   Mommy and Daddy display how the "American dream" has a deeper effect on human nature in general that, if left unchecked, will influence generations in the future. They have developed a consumerist mindset that Adams explains in *Epic of America,* as he states that "mass consumption [means] a distinct lowering in the quality of [one's] thought and expression" (409). In a country defined by consumerism in a capitalist system, there is more value placed on having expensive items to fit in than on being original. Mommy and Daddy in *The American Dream* focus on how things look on the outside, both with their treatment of Grandma and their child. To them, Grandma is a burden and they often shrug off what she says and does. When she presents them with several boxes, Daddy comments on "how nicely [Grandma] wrapped [her] boxes" and Mommy agrees, but they refuse to see the contents inside (Albee 13). Later in the play it is revealed that Grandma's boxes contain miscellaneous and generally worthless items, but they all have significance to Grandma. Mommy and Daddy's refusal to entertain her and see what is inside the boxes conveys their lack of consideration for her as a person and for people in general. Their focus on a need for satisfaction through material items runs deeper and causes them to treat Grandma and each other poorly, and their conscience overall has become desensitized to their own corruption. The materialism in *The American Dream* has led the family to become debased, which is reflected in their treatment of one another and the treatment of their child. Albee argues that their virtue has been violated by a capitalist society, and this supports Adams' view on how consumerism changes people for the worse.

5   Adams presents the idea that part of the new American dream is morally corrupt based on the focus on materialism, and Mommy and Daddy in the play

embody this mindset when they receive their adopted child. They see the child as another thing to buy, which shows that they have adopted the consumerist mindset that Adams mentions in his work. Adams comments on how the business leaders of the world encourage high-earning men to "increas[e] [their] powers as a 'consumer'" while they get trapped in a cycle of earning more just to spend more (407). The nature of the wage-earning system entraps workers because they are not influenced to relax and enjoy their financial security, but rather to purchase more and obtain certain societal status symbols that are essentially worthless. Adams argues that in this cycle lies the breakdown of the original American dream. Mommy and Daddy display this behavior throughout the play as they pursue a replacement child to complete their American dream. Albee uses their names to define Mommy and Daddy by their roles as parents, but they fail to be responsible parents when they mutilate their first baby. They view their "bumble of joy" as another thing to be obtained as they try to present themselves as the idyllic American family (Albee 28). Albee presents the situation as two consumers looking to buy a product rather than two loving parents looking for a child, which supports Adams' thought that "mass is going to count for more and the individual less" (410). Grandma later refers to their replacement child as The American Dream, commenting on how Mommy and Daddy see him as their dream, a puzzle piece to complete their perfect family. Mommy and Daddy view the Young Man as a possession they are entitled to and they choose to ignore the sinister truth that their past wrongdoings have destroyed his life. They represent the way that Adams describes Americans through their need for material possessions and quantity valued over quality.

[6] Adams presents the idea that there could be hope in the future for the American dream, stating, "to make the dream come true we must all work together, no longer to build bigger, but to build better" (411). He reiterates the idea that quality must be valued over quantity in order to achieve this. In contrast, *The American Dream* portrays an extreme variation of a family fixated on quantity, and the piece leaves little room for improvement for the characters. Albee's disturbing presentation proclaims the grim ways the American dream can influence a society.

Works Cited

Albee, Edward. *The American Dream*. Dramatists Play Services Inc, 2009.
Truslow Adams, John. *The Epic of America*. Little, Brown and Company, 1931.

For Consideration:

1. Maddox states, "a fixation on what one wears or buys eliminates the original American dream in which everyone has equal opportunity for success." In two or three paragraphs, explain how this "fixation" on materialism runs counter to Adams' original definition of the American Dream that "everyone has equal opportunity for success." Be specific in your use of examples and details to support your views.

2. In her conclusion, Maddox states that Adams' view of the American Dream gives American society hope whereas the family portrayed in Albee's play illustrates how the American Dream can twist it. Reflect on your own knowledge of and experiences with American society. In a thesis-driven essay of your own, explain which of these two outcomes you see the most likely regarding the American Dream today.

3. Maddox's essay points out that "the wage-earning system entraps workers." Rather than being encouraged to enjoy the life their financial stability can afford them, Americans are persuaded to purchase more material goods to achieve a particular social status. In three or four paragraphs, explain in detail how you believe this cycle works and why it would be counter to what Maddox tells us is Adams' definition of the American Dream.

After viewing the 1947 film Gentleman's Agreement, *first-year student Zoe Kerr finds parallels between the anti-Semitism the movie explores and the Hollywood sexism of the 2010s. Explaining that most people live in ignorance about problems they themselves don't suffer from, Kerr focuses on the importance of being informed.*

Now Let's Get Information: An Examination of the Socio-Political Parallels between *Gentleman's Agreement* and the Time's Up Movement
Zoe Kerr

1   In 2017, world-renowned producer and studio-mogul Harvey Weinstein was revealed to be a serial sexual predator, coercing unsuspecting women into committing sexual acts with him under the guise of meeting at his hotel to discuss casting opportunities in his films. What followed this revelation was shocking. Dozens of women across the entertainment industry came forward and explained that these heinous crimes have been happening for decades since his career began. People began to wonder how such a widespread problem could go unacknowledged in an industry that prides itself on profiting off controversy. It is easy to see how this thought parallels the 1947 drama *Gentleman's Agreement*. A similar question is even posed in an early scene by one of the main characters, John Minify, the editor of a magazine.

2   When confronted by management about how an article about a controversial subject like anti-Semitism would come across to their magazine's readership, Mr. Minify answered, "Sure, pretend it doesn't exist and add to the conspiracy of silence" (*Gentleman's Agreement* 00:35:52–00:35:55). This concept of a conspiracy of silence, a void where all concerns or moral questions are pushed aside for complacency, is startlingly similar to Hollywood before justice was sought for and by Weinstein's victims. While it is difficult to overcome past injustices and progress, movements like #MeToo and the Time's Up Initiative help eradicate the conspiracy of silence quickly and with great efficacy.

3   Launching countermeasures against assault and sexism in general is a difficult task when half the population does not seem to realize the issue of sexual coercion not only exists—but that it is widespread and pervasive across many different industries. Thankfully, with tools like Facebook and Twitter at their disposal, activists can spread information in seconds, prompting radical change in

a matter of days. In *Gentleman's Agreement*, the main character, Philip, is tasked with exposing anti-Semitism in New York using the much slower method of investigative journalism. He goes undercover as a Jewish man, presenting himself as Philip Greenburg to new co-workers and acquaintances. After extensive research he realizes that anti-Semitism is a thriving prejudice among people of all backgrounds, even his well-to-do fiancée, Elaine.

4   This film demonstrates the true problem with anti-Semitism that can also be applied to sexism: Most of the people unaffected by it do not know it exists as a problem, or do not believe it is as bad as the marginalized group says it is. Ideally, the public would believe a single person who comes forward with evidence proving their experiences of prejudice by another person, but sometimes it takes a lot of documented examples of anti-Semitism like in *Gentleman's Agreement*, or in the case of the #MeToo movement, thousands of individuals confirming that, yes, sexism is a problem. This mass awareness created enormous change in Hollywood. In fewer than six months, over twenty predators were exposed, leading to new mandates preventing such crimes from happening again. Imagine what would have happened and what life as a woman would be like now had the world believed these women from the beginning.

5   However, there is a solution to this disbelief of victims and it is examined thoroughly by Philip in *Gentleman's Agreement*. He realizes early on in his investigation that contributing to the cause is as simple as asking the right questions. With guidance from Mr. Minify, these questions, though oftentimes difficult to ask, led to some shocking realizations for himself and other people.

6   As previously mentioned, Philip's fiancée, Elaine, presents herself as being an equality-driven activist but later reveals herself to be a complacent micro-aggressor who sees the error of her ways only when she is confronted by Philip's Jewish friend, Dave Goldman. Dave gently points out that her acceptance of the conspiracy of silence as being terrible but unchangeable enables the people around her to accept and even enjoy their prejudices. She sees the error of her ways and vows never to be contented with her own involvement in such wrongdoings again.

7   This questioning is crucial in modern examples of sexism such as the Chicago movement, Not in Our House. Not in Our House began as a grassroots campaign for sexual assault awareness after a renowned local theatre closed because of the abusive acts of its founder and lead company member toward his young female co-stars. It began with a public question from one of his victims of whether such treatment was truly acceptable, and why there weren't measures in place to prevent assault happening in the first place. What followed was an incredible journey wherein a new Code of Conduct was proposed to non-union theatre companies,

following a three-step process of escalation that would guarantee awareness of the problem at every level of authority within the company. This Code of Conduct has swept the nation, with companies all over pledging their responsibility in ensuring the safety and comfort of their actors. Independent companies in Dallas have sworn their allegiance to this Code, too.

8   Though the world is different from the time of *Gentleman's Agreement*, there is the possibility of achieving lasting change through similar means to Philip and Mr. Minify. All it takes is acknowledging a problem, questioning, and rebuilding the system that allowed the problem to grow, and promising never to allow the conspiracy of silence to reign again.

Works Cited

Gentleman's Agreement. Directed by Elia Kazan, performances by Gregory Peck, Dorothy McGuire, John Garfield, and Celeste Holm, Twentieth Century Fox, 1947.

For Consideration:

1. Kerr creates a parallel between the anti-Semitism of the 1940s as depicted in the 1947 film *Gentleman's Agreement* and the sexism and sexual harassment in Hollywood that came to light in 2018. Is this a valid parallel? If it is, upon what important concept does the similarity lie? If it is not, why not? Remember to give examples from Kerr's text to support your claims.

2. Kerr refers to Elaine (the fiancée of *Gentleman's Agreement*'s protagonist) as a "micro-aggressor." If you are not familiar with this term, look it up. Then, explain in two or three paragraphs how micro-aggressions can perpetuate racism, sexism, or other prejudices.

3. Kerr states, "Most of the people unaffected by it [sexism] do not know it exists as a problem, or do not believe it is as bad as the marginalized group says it is." Although Kerr is referring to sexism, her essay makes it plain that this is true of other forms of prejudice and discrimination. Do some brief research on the Internet and find examples of other examples of prejudice and discrimination that occurred in American history but were not acknowledged at the time. How are they similar? How are they different?

4. The main title to Kerr's essay is "Now Let's Get Information." In two or three paragraphs, explain how her title reflects one of the essay's central points.

A veteran and single father, John Berry finds new and personal meaning in a classic Hemingway short story. His view on Hemingway's character Harold Krebs sheds light on the difficulties combat veterans have integrating into the society they left behind.

The Last Refuge of the Soldier
John Berry

1   In Harold Krebs, I found a friend. Ernest Hemingway's protagonist in "Soldier's Home" has it all, the numbness towards the trappings of daily life, the dissonance of the inhospitableness of polite society, and the inability to relate that to anyone. Harold Krebs is not a broken man. The war has not made him utterly unable to contribute to society, but it has opened his eyes to how much of society is manufactured for and by busybodies. Even the other soldiers, who have taken to reintegration with fantastical war stories have turned their backs on his disassociation. Harold comes home from the war with a new set of priorities, ones which his family can not relate to, and out of selflessness sets those aside to make the people around him happy.

2   In combat, a man points a gun at another man, and it's a race to pull the trigger. Luck, skill, and speed determine the winner. A mustard gas bombardment lands in your trench, and it's a race to get your gas mask on. Speed, equipment, and preparedness determine the winner. In town, Sally doesn't say good morning to Susie in the right tone, and the next thing you know you're barred from talking to your buddy because so-and-so did you-know-what to whomever. The winner is whoever can be petty enough for the longest and offer the most salacious gossip. Harold Krebs returns from the honesty of man-to-man combat to the complex social networks that inhabit his town. No longer is there a clear right or wrong, no great evil that needs defeating, nor some actual purpose to the expenditure of energy other than "contributing" to a society that is built upon the lies of language. It's not that he hates the people around him, and "he would have liked a girl if she had come to him and not wanted to talk" (Hemingway 226). He just doesn't want to deal with the deceitful and utterly pointless verbal combat that requires a thesaurus to figure out which way someone takes something you say.

3   Krebs' relation to his family is more complex. He understands their needs but sees them valuing the same trivialities as everyone else. The lies hurt him; he hates having to tell them and trying to live them. He wants to be honest with his family; he wants to tell them that their values are pointless and shallow to him, but he

can't do this without hurting them. He values honest physical prowess over the deceitful and weak words that make up so much of his daily life. He tries to value what his family finds important, but they wrap up so much of their values in societal pressures, which have no effect on him. Harold's mother wants him to find a nice girl, not because she'll take care of him and sit silently with him, but because Charley Simmons is going to be married soon. Harold's father wants him to get a job and start working not because he could use his energy to create something, but because Charley Simmons is out there being "a credit to the community" (Hemingway 229). This moment pushes Harold to admit to his mother that he doesn't value the same things as they do, which drives her to tears, but not because she realizes her son has lost his innocence during some of the bloodiest battles of World War I, but because he's not conforming to her social worldview. His family has basically abandoned any attempt at understanding his struggles during which, "he had been badly, sickeningly frightened all the time" (Hemingway 225). They only want to hear sanitized war stories of American heroes defeating the evil German Empire, not the tragedy that is everyday life on the battlefield.

4   Krebs knows they raised him, he knows they care for him, and so he doesn't want to hurt them. He wants to live a life free from the lies of society but doing so will hurt his mother and his sister. He knows that what he has seen is just about the worst humanity can offer, but he doesn't want that reality for them. He wants them to be happy, to be content living a life in which the worst they do is lie and bicker, not kill and maim.

5   His father, a man, should be the one he can admit his pain to, but his father is caught up in the same societal pressure of contributing to a society that will happily send millions of its youth to death and concerned about Harold's ambition instead of his mental well-being. "There would be one more scene maybe before he got away," Krebs reflects, and Hemingway leaves this vague for a reason (231). This is Harold's private thought and can relate to many possibilities. Perhaps the final scene is Harold leaving town, and 100 years ago, it was much easier to lose contact over time. Write the occasional letter, perhaps packed full of lies, and the family can be happy without him around. Maybe, he's simply going to wait until his mother passes away, keeping up the lies until then. His sister will hopefully be old enough to understand by that time. He won't go to his father's office because that's just going to be a fight with more words, but he will go to cheer on his sister's indoor baseball team before skipping town to find his peaceful silence.

6   Harold Krebs is not alone, nor is he irreparably broken by the things he's seen and done. Service members have been bearing these weights since war first was waged. Some can find solace in the society they protect, some in blind patriotism,

and some just relish the thrill of combat, but not all can. Research into the mental health of service members often deals only with the most hurt or disabled veterans, but those whose worldviews have been changed so massively from their society's or local culture can find themselves feeling like aliens in their hometowns. Without social structure of some kind, as when Harold "met another man who had really been a soldier" (Hemingway 225), reintegration becomes nearly impossible. Harold must choose between lying about everything that he has seen and what it has turned him into to placate the busybodies or admitting it and becoming a social pariah for talking about the nasty business that war is.

7   "Soldier's Home" is an excellent introduction to the complexities of war because it doesn't deal with the glamourous side of war, the heroic acts that brave men do to defeat evil, nor does it deal with the horribly broken and disfigured faces of those devastated by war and failed by the country they fought for. "Soldier's Home" simply deals with what people culturally and personally value and how the two may clash. Students are often presented with the extreme stories, extremely good, or extremely bad, but seldom are readers exposed to the disenfranchised, dejected, or disillusioned faces of those who survived combat and returned to find people bickering over shades of white paint on their fences.

Works Cited

Hemingway, Ernest. "Soldier's Home." *The American Short Story*, edited by Calvin Skaggs, Dell, 1977, *Internet Archive*, archive.org/details/americanshortsto00skag, pp. 224–231.

For Consideration:

1. Second person *you* is not often found in academic writing (and some professors actively dissuade students from using it). What is the effect of Berry's use of *you* in paragraph 2? Would the paragraph be as effective without it? Why?

2. As a veteran himself, Berry has credibility in the topic he chose to write about. In what ways does he establish his credibility in his essay without outright announcing he has been in active combat? Are these methods effective? Why or why not?

3. What is the tone of Berry's essay? Give specific examples from the essay to support your answer.

The following two essays take opposite points of view on the 2007 film Into the Wild. *Using the works of Emerson and Thoreau, Christopher Wood and Aja Tom analyze the film's protagonist and come to two very different conclusions regarding the value of his experiences and subsequent death.*

Another Dead Fool: The Value of Christopher's Journey in *Into the Wild*
Christopher Wood

[1] American culture has largely been dictated by the pioneer spirit. Transcendentalism, a philosophical and literary movement prominent in the United States during the mid-19th century, was based on principles embodied by early American pioneers: individualism, aversion to societal pressure, and a close connection between humanity and nature. Although these ideals do still hold some value, they may seem naive to a modern audience. Regardless, transcendentalism is still frequently reflected in today's media. In the film *Into the Wild*, Christopher McCandless, a young man freshly graduated from Emory, embarks on a journey to pursue his transcendentalist ideals in a pioneer-esque lifestyle in Alaska. Christopher's inability to learn from the experiences he has along the way robs his journey of the value it could have had and ultimately leads to his death.

[2] In the film, Christopher McCandless decides to abandon his trajectory of attending graduate school and instead pursue his vision of a lifestyle mirroring transcendentalist ideals, renaming himself "Alexander Supertramp" as the beginning of a new life. Christopher had grown up in a household characterized by deception and conflict, and the film characterizes this choice as an understandable, albeit knee-jerk, reaction to his upbringing. He meets a number of different people along the way, including Wayne, a grain-elevator operator who gives him a short-term job, Rainey and Jan, two other wanderers, a young camp singer named Tracy who falls in love with him, and Ron Franz, an old leatherworker who offers to adopt Chris. Once he finally arrives in Alaska, he finds that he is not as capable of adapting to the wilderness as he had expected, and he starves to death. Christopher's failure to recognize the lessons given to him by both the people he meets and his own experiences led to his gruesome downfall.

[3] McCandless specifically cites the ideas of transcendentalist writers Henry David Thoreau and Ralph Waldo Emerson as the inspiration for his journey,

specifically Thoreau's own experience with a minimalist lifestyle in *Walden* and Emerson's theories on the corrupting influence of society. Ultimately, however, McCandless displays a very surface-level understanding of these works. While Emerson did spend a lot of ink denouncing society, he also spent time talking about traveling: "He who travels to be amused, or to get somewhat which he does not carry, travels away from himself, and grows old even in youth among old things." Ironically, this is exactly what Christopher is doing; he is traveling to escape his troubled upbringing and to "kill the false being within" (*Into the Wild* 12:35–12:39). Emerson underwent a similar journey, and found its promise of freedom to be a hollow one: "I dream that at Naples, at Rome, I can be intoxicated with beauty, and lose my sadness . . . [but] there beside me is the stern fact, the sad self, unrelenting, identical, that I fled from . . . My giant goes with me wherever I go." Both Emerson and McCandless attempt to use their travels as a means to escape their emotional scars (characterized as a "false being" and "giant," respectively), but neither was able to succeed. One realized this and returned to become one of the most revered writers in American history. The other did not and died alone in the Alaskan wilderness.

4   Christopher also seems to have adopted the transcendentalists' romanticized view of nature, describing his intentions as, "I'm gonna be all the way out there . . . just on my own. You know, no watch, no map, no axe, no nothing . . . just be out there in it. You know, big mountains, rivers, sky, game, just be out there in it, you know, in the *wild*." (*Into the Wild* 46:07–46:31) Any outdoorsman would know that this kind of unpreparedness in the wilderness is akin to suicide, but Christopher's experience with outdoor living is limited, and his naivety leads him to react dismissively to people who try to warn him. Not even the experience of a flash flood disabling his car or almost being killed trying to kayak through rapids seems to dampen his confidence in nature's benevolence.

5   When he finally does arrive in Alaska, his idealistic view of nature is quickly shattered, and he finds that he is badly unprepared for the pioneer lifestyle he had envisioned for himself, but when he tries to leave he finds that the river he crossed on the way in has become impassable due to glacial melt. The film depicts Christopher's death as the result of mistaking wild potato seeds with those of the poisonous wild sweet pea, poetically beginning his journey with deception from his family, and ending it with deception from nature. In reality, the circumstances of McCandless' death are debated, but none of the prevailing theories are complimentary to his ability or intellect. Christopher's romanticized view of nature impaired his judgment and led him to ignore the warning signs of nature's callousness until it was too late.

6   Another motivator for Christopher's quest is his disgust with society, and many of the lessons presented to him on his journey have to do with this. "I don't understand why people, why [everyone] is so bad to each other so often," he says, "It doesn't make sense to me. Judgment, control, all that, the whole spectrum" (*Into the Wild* 47:03–47:16). In this, Christopher is once again taking inspiration from transcendentalist philosophy, which states that while people are inherently good, society is a corrupting force. However, Christopher's experience seems to subvert this expectation, even if he doesn't realize it. Contrary to being "so bad to each other so often," the people he meets on his journey are more than willing to help him (excepting an encounter with a railroad bull), even when they know he is marching to his death. None of the other wanderers he meets pursue solitude, at least not as fanatically as Christopher does; they are always open to fellowship with others. Meanwhile the most miserable person Christopher meets, Ron Franz, is alone and detached from society, even while living in it. In the end, Christopher realizes his mistake, but it comes too late to save him.

7   Perhaps the most tragic part of Christopher McCandless' story is how much potential his adventure had. If the circumstances had changed, or if Christopher was more receptive to the experience, his journey could have been an inspiring story of self-discovery rather than an elaborate suicide. Instead, Christopher's resentment towards society and especially his family led him to ignore the lessons others tried to teach him. Ron Franz seemed to sense this, telling Christopher, "When you forgive, you love, and when you love, God's light shines down on you" (*Into the Wild* 2:03:37–2:03:52). Perhaps if Christopher had taken Ron's words to heart and had learned to forgive his family and the world, he could have averted his death. Nevertheless, his caustic unforgiveness continued to eat away at his soul, closing his mind to the warnings of others and destroying any value his journey may otherwise have possessed.

Works Cited

Emerson, Ralph W. "Self-Reliance." *Essays. Project Gutenberg,* 2005. www.gutenberg.org/files/16643/16643-h/16643-h.htm#SELF-RELIANCE. Accessed 25 Oct. 2018.

Into the Wild. Directed by Sean Penn, performances by Emile Hirsch and Vince Vaughn, Paramount Vantage, 2007.

For Consideration:

1. Wood gives multiple examples from the film as well as comparisons between the character of Christopher and Emerson's experiences. Do you feel these adequately support Wood's thesis? Why or why not?

2. If you have previously viewed the film *Into the Wild*, explain in two or three paragraphs whether or not you agree with Wood's analysis of Christopher's character. If you have never seen the film, explain if Wood's analysis allows you a good understanding of the character and his actions.

3. Sometimes, writing persuasively is as much about what is *omitted* as what is included. If you haven't done so yet, read Aja Tom's essay "Finding the Value of Life" which follows this one. What does Tom include in her essay that Wood does not? Does this omission strengthen Wood's essay or weaken it? Give specific details and examples to support your claim.

Finding the Value of Life: Sean Penn's *Into the Wild*
Aja Tom

1   Most people feel as though they could not live without society because they are dependent on others for survival and success. However, in the film *Into the Wild*, a young transcendentalist, Christopher McCandless, challenges this idea of our dependence on others in society. He believes that aspects of society, such as money and relationships, are unnecessary and do not lead to survival or success. He values experiences over relationships and material objects because he believes the latter confine people in society and prevent them from being free. If McCandless is bound by a paycheck and relies on others for his own happiness, he would become miserable and would feel imprisoned by these material objects. This intolerable consequence drives McCandless to live in Alaska in order to be free. Ultimately, McCandless dies of starvation in the wild. However, his journey was of great value to him because he fulfilled his dream of being free from society's restrictions and was able to experience nature in its purest form.

2   McCandless does not care about materialism, but instead he values experiences and moments in life. McCandless decides to take a journey to Alaska in order to escape the confines of society and people's dependence on possessions. He strongly believes that experiencing life is more valuable than the number of possessions he owns. For example, when McCandless' parents offer to buy him a new car because they think his is old and needs to be replaced, he is shocked and replies, "A new car? Why would I want a new car? I don't need a new car, I don't want a new car, I don't want anything, these things, things, things" (*Into the Wild* 00:19:55–00:20:11). He does not care about having a brand-new car to show off to the world. He only needs the car to function properly and allow him to travel places and have new experiences. This incident pushes McCandless to pursue his dream of living among nature. He gives away his money, burns his social security card, and leaves his home because he does not care about the physical objects he has in life, but about living life. McCandless does not conform to societal norms of collecting material effects, but instead follows his own path towards Alaska.

3   McCandless not only rejects material objects, but also human relationships. On his journey to Alaska, McCandless meets an older man named Ron Franz. When McCandless is talking to Franz on a hill overlooking the desert, he tells Franz that joy does not come from human relationships but is "in anything we can experience. People just need to change the way they look at those things" (*Into the Wild* 02:02:45–02:02:56). McCandless is passionate about finding joy in experiences. McCandless believes that experiences can change someone's life, unlike

material objects. This belief is the main reason McCandless decides to venture out into the wilderness. His goal is to experience life and nature in its most pure form. He wants to soak up all of life's experiences and be able to learn and grow from them. He also wants to change the way people look at material objects and experiences, and he does this on his journey.

4   Along the way he meets Jan and Rainey, a couple he stays with for a few days. When McCandless and Rainey are talking about Jan and Rainey's relationship, McCandless says, "Some people feel like they don't deserve love. They walk away quietly into empty spaces, trying to close the gaps to the past" (*Into the Wild* 00:33:05–00:33:18). He shares his knowledge and his views on life with them and changes the way Jan and Rainey interact with each other. He helps them see that the most important value in their relationship is love and the experiences that they have with one another. Overall, McCandless' journey is of great value to him because he is able to share some of his transcendentalist ideals, such as independence from society and relationships, with other people. He changes the way that some people look at life and life's experiences. He teaches them to value the moments over the number of possessions one has.

5   McCandless shares similar beliefs to the transcendentalist Henry David Thoreau, who spent over two years living in nature in Concord, Massachusetts. Thoreau strongly believed that society restricted people from fully experiencing life. In his book *Walden*, Thoreau writes, "I did not wish to take the cabin passage, but rather to go before the mast and on the deck of the world" (Thoreau 356). Thoreau uses the cabin as a metaphor for the confinements of society. He does not want to be confined by society's rules and expectations but rather experience life on the deck of the ship and take all of the experiences as they come. McCandless has a similar outlook on life because he does not want to live life below the ship in the cabin but experience life firsthand. They both shared this idea of living life in the moment and connecting with nature. Thoreau writes, "I wanted to live deep and suck out all the marrow of life" (Thoreau 101). He uses marrow as a symbol for something pure and essential to life. To suck out all the marrow means to experience life in its purest form and to absorb all of life's beautiful moments. McCandless lives by this idea and intends to suck out all the marrow of life by travelling to Alaska. He wants the raw and pure experiences that come with living in the wild, such as finding his own food and eating berries straight from nature. He views these experiences as critical to human life and happiness.

6 McCandless' long and heroic journey served a great purpose to him and even though it was a valuable experience for McCandless, many people strongly disagree. When people hear about his journey, they either think of him as a hero or a reckless fool for trying to live alone in the Alaskan wilderness. Critics believe that the book and movie about McCandless' journey simply transform him from a foolish, young kid into a hero who died tragically. They believe that McCandless' journey was foolish because he was inexperienced and acted irrationally. For example, he kills a moose and does not properly clean it. The moose gets infected with maggots and is no longer edible. McCandless does not have experience with cleaning fresh meat. This inexperience costs him a month's worth of meat and contributes to his starvation. McCandless ultimately dies of starvation and poison from wild berries. His death is another reason why critics believe that his journey is inconsequential. His death could have been prevented if he did not travel alone to Alaska. Many critics believe that his journey was insignificant because of the carefree nature that led to his death. McCandless followed his heart instead of listening to logic and reason. Even though many critics believe that his journey was worthless, it was very valuable to him and to others because he was able to fulfill his dream of experiencing nature and pure freedom from society. He followed his dreams and was able to make himself happy without human relationships, money, or other material objects.

7 Christopher McCandless set out on his brave journey into the Alaskan wilderness to free himself of society's boundaries and fulfill his dream of being independent and experiencing raw nature. Ultimately, his journey was a success because he was able to live a happy life, free of any limitations. Even though McCandless died of starvation, he was still able to achieve his goal of total freedom. He set out on this journey to experience life and to live freely, which inspires many people. McCandless' journey is significant to society today because it teaches people that material possessions are not paramount in life, and that experiencing life and living in the moment can lead to pure happiness.

Works Cited

Into the Wild. Directed by Sean Penn, performances by Emile Hirsch and Vince Vaughn, Paramount Vantage, 2007.

Thoreau, Henry David. "Walden." *Walden.org*, https://www.walden.org/work/walden/. Accessed 29 Nov. 2018.

For Consideration:

1. If you haven't already, read Christopher Wood's essay "Another Dead Fool...," which precedes this one. In an essay of your own and using examples from both texts, explain which of the two essays, Wood's or Tom's, presents the most persuasive arguments.

2. Read (or re-read) Christopher Wood's essay "Another Dead Food..." Wood's essay focuses on the benefits that *Christopher* might have reaped from his journey to Alaska in *Into the Wild*. On the other hand, Tom's essay focuses on how Christopher's journey is worthwhile because of what he brings *to others*. In an essay of your own, explain which of these two you believe is what makes a life more worthwhile: learning from one's own experiences or giving others the benefit of your experiences.

3. Tom calls Christopher McCandless "brave" and "heroic" in her essay. After reading both her essay and Christopher Wood's essay "Another Dead Fool...," write your own essay explaining how you see McCandless' decision: was he foolhardy or a brave transcendentalist?

Learning and Reflecting: Education and the College Experience

The following essays offer candid glimpses into student life here at SMU—honest, thoughtful anecdotes that took courage to write, and that may help other students feel less alone as they seek validation and meaning in their journey to become educated, in their search for community, as they face new challenges, as they figure out how a liberal arts education may best benefit them as individuals. Students, faculty, and administrators alike can benefit from the voices of our students as they write about the college experience and lessons they are learning from life: after all, the world is, itself, a classroom—and only by listening and working together can we understand what it means to be human.

Not all journeys are purely physical. In this narrative, Briana Rollins describes the journey she takes as an African American woman through her first semester at SMU. What she experienced gives a different perspective on aspects of SMU student life others might take for granted.

Blazing New Trails: Undertaking Life as a Minority Student[1]

Briana Rollins

1   May 1st, 2014—the date by which I had to make the decision that would drastically alter my life. As the college acceptance letters began rolling in during the spring semester of my senior year in high school, I was finally able to see all of my hard work paying off. When I began to weigh my options, I started to feel apprehensive about my ability to select the college that was the overall best fit for me. As a young African American woman, the dynamics in selecting my ideal college were significantly different from those of the average American student because within the African American community several stigmas are associated with both Historically Black Colleges and Universities (HBCU) and Predominately White Institutions (PWI). The decision between attending a historically black college versus another university weighed heavily on my mind. As well as each school having its own pros and cons, "It is a well-known fact that black students perform better and graduate at higher rates at HBCU's, however PWI's tend to have more economic resources and offer better facilities and amenities" (Robertson). Ultimately, however, my decision was heavily influenced by the financial aid packages offered by each university. After assessing all my options, I made the decision to attend Southern Methodist University. While SMU offered a beautiful campus, small class sizes, state of the art facilities, and an ideal geographic location, only five percent of the total undergraduate population is African American. Academically SMU was the perfect choice; however, I had to sacrifice socially to obtain the education I desire.

2   I spent my summer eagerly preparing for my freshman year of college. I was ready to Pony Up and become a part of the Mustang family. My parents had previously voiced their reservations about SMU; however, they cast their worries aside as we headed to Dallas for my freshman orientation. As I collected my orientation materials, I was a bundle of nerves. The entire process was nerve wrecking because

---

1. This essay first appeared in the 2016–2017 edition of *Criteria*.

I honestly didn't know what to expect. As my family and I found our seats and waited for orientation to begin, we noticed we were the only African Americans in the entire ballroom. It was at this moment that I realized this feeling of being a minority would be my new reality.

3   Throughout the two-day orientation, it became quite clear the SMU campus did not have too many students of color, and I finally understood why my parents had been concerned. As we headed back to Houston, my family openly discussed the lack of diversity on campus. One aspect we discussed was the letter I had received a few weeks prior to orientation from the Connect Mentoring Program. The letter had explained their goal of assisting first year students of color in becoming successful within the SMU community and invited me to participate in their program. Knowing that I would have this support and that of the Office of Multicultural Student Affairs somewhat eased my family's trepidations. In the days leading up to my move-in date, I had to constantly remind myself to think positively and to look forward to starting this new chapter of my life.

4   I viewed attending SMU as an opportunity to step outside my comfort zone. I purposely selected a college none of my high school friends were attending because I wanted to start anew. I wanted to branch out and meet new people and create friendships that would last a lifetime. I didn't know a single soul in Dallas, and as my move-in date quickly approached I began to see leaving my friends and family as more of a mistake than an opportunity. I will never forget the pain that I felt when it came to say goodbye to my family. We had spent all day making trips back and forth from the car, setting up my room. I remember all of us standing in my dorm room, looking around at the finished product. My mom and I kept finding little things here and there to fix because we weren't prepared to say goodbye. I attempted to remain strong; however, when the time came for them actually to leave, I couldn't contain my emotions any longer. My family had always been my source of comfort and security, and it was immensely difficult to see them leave.

5   Words cannot begin to describe the emptiness that overcame me. I was alone in a new city, with no friends, no family, and no idea of what I had gotten myself into. I began my Connect Program two days after my family's departure. I was still extremely homesick and crying myself to sleep each night, but I put on a brave face and was determined to make the most out of this experience. My stomach was full of butterflies; my skin and palms were clammy, and my pulse was through the roof as I walked into Annette Caldwell Simmons Hall to begin my first day as a Connect Mentee. I was delighted to be welcomed with smiling faces and tender hugs. It was also refreshing to see staff and students of color, something that I wasn't exposed to during my AARO orientation.

6   During the three-day program, I was informed about minority student life on the SMU campus. I was like a sponge, absorbing all the knowledge I could from the OMSA staff and my mentor. After having conversations with other mentees and mentors in the program, I realized we were all experiencing the same bouts of homesickness and apprehension, and I wasn't alone. Being an African American at a predominately white institution brings about a unique set of challenges, and the Connect Program was there to assist students like myself overcome these issues. After completing the program, I began to feel as though things were looking up and weren't going to be as bad as I was foreseeing them to be.

7   Before I knew it, it was time for Mustang Corral. I had just finished up with the Connect Program, and now I was headed to Greene River Camp to embark on an SMU tradition. According to the Corral leaders this was going to be an opportunity to bond and connect with my fellow SMU students while also deepening my love for SMU. I had heard mixed reviews about Corral from the Connect mentors, so I was interested to see what I would take from the experience. As we prepared to leave campus, I began to see how easy it was for everyone around me to make friends. I had never had issues reaching out and socializing with others because I have always been a social butterfly. However, I simply felt as though I had nothing in common with the students I had encountered outside the Connect program.

8   Throughout the entire process of leaving the campus, arriving at the Camp, and breaking off into rooming assignments I felt like an outsider looking in, a feeling I wasn't accustomed to. The most upsetting aspect of the Corral experience was the poorly executed diversity talk that was supposed to allow students to see the great deal of diversity present within the class of 2018, when in actuality the class was the furthest thing from diverse. For me personally, Mustang Corral wasn't all it was geared up to be, and I could have done without the experience. Between the Connect Program and Corral, it had been a long week. I was exhausted, and the semester hadn't even started yet; however, I was excited to begin classes and really get immersed in the college lifestyle.

9   With a seventeen-hour course load and a part-time work-study job, I was extremely busy. Despite my hectic schedule, I made an effort to participate in some of the traditional SMU activities, in particular boulevarding. My first boulevard experience could be described as overwhelming at best. I remember walking with a few good friends of mine and being utterly shocked at the lack of diversity present. We felt isolated and unwelcomed. We passed by several sorority and fraternity tents, none of which appeared welcoming to an outside crowd, so we kept walking up and down the boulevard waiting to be awed by this so-called wonderful SMU tradition. My friends and I finally stumbled upon the OMSA tent

and saw some familiar faces. We stayed for a while and chatted with some other friends of ours and then decided to head back to the dorms to wait for the game to start later on that day. Yet again, another traditional SMU experience had not lived up to my expectations.

10   In the week following that Boulevard, the Association of Black Students held a welcome retreat for all of the new members. During this retreat, we had the privilege of meeting the Black Alumni of SMU board leaders. We openly discussed several issues that African American students face here on campus and had really powerful and meaningful conversations. The advice I received from the alumni during that retreat proved to be invaluable and fueled me to get the most out of my education.

11   As a young woman, finding my niche in the SMU community was extremely difficult during my first semester. The transitional period college represents for young adults in which they experience self-discovery and maturation was made all the more difficult because I am a minority. As a student who didn't fit the mold of the typical SMU student, I felt like a recluse. I had zero interest in rushing a sorority, attending formals, going to Home Bar, boulevarding, or any of the other mainstream SMU activities. Thankfully I was able to find several outlets on campus in which to get involved where I honestly felt welcomed and understood.

12   Ethnically diverse college campuses provide students the opportunity to collaborate and study with students from racial groups different from their own. SMU has slowly been attempting to improve diversity issues here on campus; however, with over seventy percent of the student population representing one race, a great deal of work is still to be done. I am often the only student of color in my classes. This presents the burden of me being conscious about everything I say and do because I essentially represent the black community. I personally had never felt this burden to represent my community until I came to SMU.

13   I am proud to be a young woman in today's society, and remaining connected to my heritage is extremely important. However, at times it's hard to display this pride when I feel alienated from the bulk of the student body. There have been several instances, specifically on social media, when fellow members of the SMU family have openly vocalized their distaste for the black women here on campus. An obvious stereotypical image comes to mind when asked the question: What does a typical female SMU student look like? If a young woman doesn't fit this description, myself included, then self-esteem issues can arise. This is why it is so important to have the ability to interact with students who are from the same ethnic background and can relate to the day-to-day issues I face here on campus.

Shortly after meeting with the Black Alumni board leaders, I was inspired to get more involved and really elevate the black community here on campus and, more specifically, uplift the strong and beautiful black women at SMU who often are overlooked and ignored.

14 "Women of color who attend predominately White colleges in the United States live within diverse social worlds," and I can personally attest to this because unlike any other social/racial group on campus, we are "bound by the macrocosm of American-White culture, but also racially identify with a specific sub-culture" (Hesse-Biber 697). Throughout my first two semesters at SMU I found myself in many distinctive yet conflicted roles. It all boils down to the dynamic of being too black for white friends, and too white for black friends. Trying to find an overall balance between these two vastly different cultures is my ultimate goal. My journey of becoming an SMU world changer is still in its infantile stages. I look forward to furthering my education and making the most out of every opportunity. I hope one day to be an inspiration to my family and my community. This journey has been far from easy; however, I can honestly say that I am proud to be a Mustang. Experiencing college as a minority has initiated the process of me becoming the strong and independent woman I was born to be.

Annotated Bibliography

Hesse-Biber, Sharlene, et al. "Racial Identity and Body Image among Black Female College Students Attending Predominately White Colleges." *Sex Roles,* vol. 63, no. 9, 2010, pp. 697–711.

This scholarly article examines the thoughts and feelings of African American women attending predominately white universities throughout the United States. Racial identity and self-esteem in correlation with body image were examined through the interviews of 34 women. The purpose of this study was to see how specific school experiences affected their overall sense of self and body image. One of the most important points made within the article was that "Women of color who attend predominately White college in the United States live within diverse social worlds" (697).

Hesse-Biber's research was effectively used throughout my narrative to support my own personal experiences and claims. This article, unlike my other sources, was from a peer-reviewed journal, which ensures the information is indeed reliable. The information presented came from 34 separate case studies, and the study was conducted using proper scientific investigative methods. Hesse-Biber used "a grounded theory approach to give to these women's subjugated knowledge" which means both deductive and inductive reasoning was used throughout the article (697).

This article supported my underlying purpose in writing my thesis-driven travel narrative. The overall message that I plan to convey to readers is that as an African American woman at a predominately white university, I struggle to maintain my racial identity and self-esteem. Incorporating the experiences from 34 other women, who have experienced similar situations, substantiates my argument and makes the purpose all the more powerful.

Roberson, Susan L., and Michel Butor. "Defining Travel." *Defining Travel: Diverse Visions*, University Press of Mississippi, 2001, pp. xi–xxvi.

In this source Susan Roberson and Michel Butor discuss "the role of travel in the formation of identity" (xii). The two authors work cohesively to explain the effects traveling has on an individual's identity. Within the section entitled "The Alien," Butor begins to explain what it feels like to arrive in a new and unfamiliar place by stating that "the gestures will not be the same: other manners, other laws, other rules . . ." (76). Roberson and Butor set the foundation for discussion about the relationship between a person's physical location and their identity.

Defining Travel set the foundation for all travel narratives. The purpose of this assignment was to analyze our own experiences and reflect on how they shaped our lives. Roberson and Butor's work contains reliable information that assists in making those connections between location, experiences, and self-identity. Their work contains some biased information; however, holistically it provides objective information. The goal of their writing is to connect one's personal experiences with one's identity. When Butor discusses what it feels like to be an outsider or "alien" I couldn't help but make the correlation to the similar feeling students of color on the SMU campus. The manners in which the student interact, talk, and socialize are vastly different from those I am accustomed to. I can't help but feel as though I am sometimes an outsider looking in, which is a central theme present throughout my narrative. This source helped flesh out my topic during my initial brainstorming process.

Robertson, Ray Von. "When White Is Not Always Right: The Experience of Black Students at Predominately White Institutions." *Black Agenda Report*, 13 Dec. 2011. www.blackagendareport.com/content/when-white-not-always-right-experience-black-students-predominantly-white-institutions.

Ray Robertson attempts to answer the question, "Why does such a large proportion, approximately 85% of Black students attend PWIs?" In this article, he examines common beliefs within the African American community about attending college. He claims that there is persistent certainty amongst African Americans that predominately white institutions are "better" than historically black colleges. Robertson goes on to dispel this notion by providing three reasons why "White isn't necessarily right."

This article was extremely interesting because several of Robertson's points are valid. However, this article isn't peer reviewed, which means the information isn't considered as reliable. It is very clear that Ray Robertson has a distinct perspective on the issue, which can be seen through his very creative and catchy title. I purposely selected this article because it addresses everyday issues that plague the African American community.

The fact that Robertson boldly expresses his opinions without the fear of sounding politically incorrect greatly changed my outlook on how to present my narrative to my readers. My goal in my narrative was to speak to my readers wholeheartedly and honestly. Race relations on the SMU campus have always been an issue that many have treaded lightly on; however, to expose the issues, someone has to be bold enough to say honestly what it is like to be black on a campus full of white students and staff. Reading this article made me unapologetic for the manner in which I presented my narrative.

Satrapi, Marjane. *The Complete Persepolis*, Pantheon, 2007.

Satrapi's novel is a memoir of her experiences of growing up in Iran during the Islamic Revolution. Taking place in Tehran, Iran, Marjane Satrapi's story begins with her at the age of 10, when it became mandatory for women to be veiled at all times. From an early age, it was apparent that Marjane had a fiery spirit. Throughout the novel, we see Marjane develop into womanhood in the midst of political and religious turmoil.

Compared to my other sources, the novel most closely correlates with the research presented in Hesse-Biber's research. Satrapi's personal experiences as a woman of color were recorded in her memoir, similar to the case studies of the 34 African American women. The information presented in *The Complete Persepolis* has been deemed reliable. In addition to being a memoir, Satrapi's novel recounts a substantial amount of information surrounding the history of Iran, the Iranian revolution, and the second Iran and Iraq war. This source has bias present, which is to be expected. This is the account of a single woman, so her personal experiences only portray one side of the entire story.

This source was particularly resourceful because Marjane at one point in the novel stated that she is too Iranian in the West and too Western for Iran. Marjane's racial identity struggles are extremely similar to my own. Her memoir helped shaped my narrative and was yet another example of a woman of color struggling to find her place in society. Although the oppressions are different, the battle is still the same. This novel reaffirms the fact that women of color struggle significantly more in society, which is the ultimate message I wish to convey to my readers.

For Consideration:

1. Note that Rollins includes an annotated bibliography with her essay. What differences are there between an annotated bibliography and a works cited page?
2. Explain how Rollins organizes her essay and how that organization emphasizes the argument she is supporting.
3. In what ways might you unconsciously isolate or shun people who you do not feel comfortable around? Who are these people? Why do you behave in such a way?

In this essay, Lauren Alexander reflects on her speech as high school valedictorian on graduation day as the beginning of her journey to understanding what it means to be an educated person, a journey which leads her to this vital observation: "A world in which people stop learning is a world in which people's respect for one another is jeopardized." In the next essay, Alexander addresses the necessity of mutual respect between student and teacher, with a focus on the value of patience when it comes to educating.

Something Permanent[2]
Lauren Alexander

1. One hundred and seven faces. One hundred and seven dreams. One hundred and seven people waiting for me to tell them why their education mattered, why it was worth it, and why they should be motivated to "go do great things." The problem, however, was that I didn't have a clue how to answer any of these questions. Months before my high school graduation, I kept picturing myself standing at the podium with no words to say that would be worth remembering. As I dreamed of that day, I couldn't come up with the perfect pearl of wisdom that I felt pressured to present as valedictorian.

2. During the middle of such a daydream, I was snapped back into reality by the blistering June heat and distinct voice of my principal over the old and crackling sound system. I looked out at the one hundred and seven faces, and, for the first time, they gave me hope. Leaving my scribbled speech outline behind, I walked to the stage, assumed my position behind the podium, and pulled the microphone down to my level. All of a sudden, I knew exactly what I needed to say: "Most graduation speeches focus on how to succeed. And don't get me wrong—I have no doubt that you all have the ability to achieve degrees, success, and fame. But in the end, success measured by a trophy or paycheck will not make you happy. I don't think that's what our education is about."

3. That moment was filled with pure joy, but it wasn't happiness derived from the gold stole around my neck, jingling medals, or diploma that memorialized my grueling hours of studying for the best grade. During that moment, my step towards education was marked not my GPA but by the life lessons I had learned, relationships I had made, and appreciation for others that I had gained. Why should anyone care about becoming an educated person? The answer is simple: the truly educated person has a sense of fulfillment that lasts a lifetime.

---

2. This essay first appeared in the 2016–2017 edition of *Criteria*.

4   I don't think pure luck allowed me to stumble upon this epiphany on that steamy Texas evening. Some magical quality is unmistakably present at a graduation ceremony—an ambiance that encourages self-reflection. This same atmosphere led college teacher and educator Thomas Jones to a huge realization during a speech at his own graduation. While listening to a speaker, Jones was challenged to "reflect on the question 'What is an educated person?'" (11). Jones and I, both perplexed, had the same questions. Is it the person who holds a crisp and carefully placed diploma in an official-looking leather cover? No. This ornamental item serves as a reminder of a student's hard work, but it certainly doesn't have the power to give him an education. Is it maybe someone who speaks at a graduation? At my graduation, the answer was a quick and resounding, "No." Although I had caught a glimpse of what legitimate education looked like, I hardly considered myself the archetypal "educated person."

5   This educated person question has the power to stop someone dead in his tracks. Unfortunately, students who treat school as a dreaded chore or long and lazily completed to-do-list are walking away no more prepared for the real world than before. After tassels are turned on graduation day, these individuals may watch the sunset and wonder, "What's next?" The truth is that they have missed the purpose of education. They are not better thinkers, leaders, problem solvers, innovators, or truth-seekers. They haven't learned from communication and observance, from history and from current events, from success and from failure. They have missed the point.

6   Having some grasp of this question, I believe, is a prerequisite to answering why anyone should care about education. How can a person care about something that she can't even define? That night, it became very clear to me what education is *not*. Education is not just passing a test, class, grade, or even passing on to the next academic institution. Instead, I think true education is what a person misses when she focuses on material success and "drift[s] from one classroom to another, follow[ing] the required paths toward graduation" (Jones 11). Although grades are important and graduation is a necessary milestone, "those who believe in the finish line never get the gold medal; only those who continue running and taking in the view find happiness and success" (Warsop 37). While a person might eventually finish a curriculum or retire from an occupation, the journey towards higher education has no finality and is thus exceedingly more fulfilling.

7   True education is the art class that the typical student refuses to take because it might hurt her GPA, the book that she never thought she would read, or the conversation about subject matter that is completely out of her comfort zone. Education is forming opinions and expressing them. Education is learning from

the diversity and wisdom others have to offer. Education is the "lifelong process of learning, study, reflection, experience, and action—not just four years of classes" (Jones 11). The journey toward true education includes the process of becoming a better member of society, not simply accumulating a better grade average.

8   This concept of education becomes clear in the film *Higher Learning*. During the beginning of this movie, Malik views himself as a "thoroughbred" being used by the track department at Columbus University. He feels completely bogged down by the combination of studying and athletics, and he fails to see the greater picture. Obviously, his shallow understanding of an education leads to a lack of satisfaction. With his heart in neither track nor his studies, Malik successfully personifies the typical student that Jones speaks of—one who manages to get by, but not to learn.

9   While Jones regrets not spending his time in college with the "educated person" question in mind, Malik's ignorance affects him on an even larger scale. Malik has an extreme lack of knowledge pertaining to cultural diversity "in the context of life outside the classroom" (Jones 12), and he often resorts to violence. Had this not been the case, Malik may have helped resolve the racial tension at his university instead of becoming a victim of the violence that eventually resulted in the murder of his girlfriend Déjà by a white supremacist. His reaction to this horrific event seems to answer Jones' question about whether pondering the meaning of education sooner would have affected the outcome of events. Malik eventually learns to do more than just try to get by; he takes the advice of an older friend, Fudge, to study "for [himself] and not for some damn class" (*Higher Learning*). Additionally, he runs the track alone and takes initiative in his athletic life because he actually wants to, not just to produce a check.

10   As Malik mourns after the eye-opening murder of his girlfriend, he meets Kristen for the first time, and he finally faces the ignorance that fueled violence. As both students stand at Déjà's memorial, regret overcomes Kristen because she feels as if she is responsible for the shooting. Awkward at first and struggling to overcome his own self-righteousness and stereotypes, Malik reaches out to Kristen and comforts her during her despair. Because of the connection the two establish, this scene beautifully demonstrates authentic education—the kind that obliterates ignorance and social barriers, allowing two people from different walks of life to come together. Malik and Kristen begin to care about obtaining this sort of education, as should all students. Not only does education bring purpose and joy to one's life, as demonstrated by the film, but it also ensures that tragedies such as the murders in *Higher Learning* do not occur. A world in which people stop learning

is a world in which people's respect for one another is jeopardized, and this is certainly a reality that no one wants to face.

11   As I remember those one hundred and seven bright-eyed faces, I realize that after that epiphany, I still didn't have the educated person question all figured out. Now, as I look around at the thousands of new faces at SMU, I am thankful that this vital question has been brought to my attention once more. I still may not have a "perfect pearl of wisdom" on the subject of education, but I think that's okay. The truth is that no one has ever found this precious pearl. The joy comes from the lifelong hunt.

Works Cited

Higher Learning. Dir. John Singleton. Perf. Omar Epps. Columbia Pictures, 1995. Film.

Jones, Thomas. "The Educated Person." *Criteria 2011–2012*, edited by Mary K. Jackman and Lee Gibson, SMU Department of English, 2011, pp. 11–12.

Warsop, Elizabeth. "Experiencing the Value of an Education." *Criteria 2013–2014*, edited by Mary K. Jackman and Lee Gibson, SMU Department of English, 2013, pp. 34–38.

For Consideration:

1. In your own words, what are the key components of Alexander's multi-faceted definition of what it means to be an educated person?

2. What do you think is the most powerful supporting evidence in the essay? Which aspects of the essays do you feel are most memorable and why?

3. Examine the "Aristotle's Proofs of Rhetoric" piece in the "Tools for Learning Discernment and Discourse" section of this book. Review the definition of ethos. What techniques does Alexander use to establish strong ethos?

Kevin Quinn wrote this essay in response to an assignment asking him to ponder the meaning of community in the world of higher education and to think about his own community experiences at SMU. The essay following this one, also by Kevin Quinn, goes a step further as he shares his thoughtful consideration of the ultimate purpose and benefits of the university experience: to actively claim *one's education.*

A Helping Hand[3]
Kevin Quinn

1   When I began searching for colleges to apply to, I considered many factors. I thought about the location of a school, the food, the athletics, the clubs and organizations, and the academics. However, throughout my college search, I did not really think about the importance of community within the schools I was examining. In fact, I did not even think about the importance of community until my Discernment and Discourse teacher brought up the topic during class. After going over various articles in my Discernment and Discourse class and contemplating my college experience this past semester, I discovered the importance of community in education. Community is an important aspect of education because it influences the intellectual progress of every student involved.

2   One of the articles that helped me discover the importance of community was "The Quest for Community in Higher Education," by Parker J. Palmer. In this article, Palmer suggests that teachers should avoid a "sage on the stage" approach to teaching and try to create a sense of community by following the "guide by the side" approach (51). By a "sage on the stage," he means a teacher who does not do anything to include his students in the lecture, which leads to students not paying attention and not learning. Being a "guide by the side" is a much more effective approach towards teaching because it gives a student the feeling that he or she is involved in the subject matter being taught. By including students in the lecture, teachers are able to create an engaged learning community that encourages students to reach their full potential.

3   Palmer also gives examples of successful learning communities that he himself encountered. Palmer developed a relationship with librarian Dacie Moses and her husband Roy. Many undergraduate students from Carleton College, including himself, would go to the Moses' house to talk about troubles they were experiencing. Palmer learned many things from Dacie and Roy, even though they were

---

3. This essay first appeared in the 2016–2017 edition of *Criteria*.

not teachers at the university. The Moses did not teach Palmer facts he needed to know for the next test, but they created an inclusive community that taught Palmer valuable life lessons he carried with him for the rest of his life.

4   Another example of a successful learning community Palmer encountered was the Princeton Project 55. Instead of donating a bench or major contribution to the school endowment, members of the Princeton Class of 1955 decided to bestow their influence and expertise in building a bridge between the university and the world (Palmer 54). The Princeton alumni created internships and service-learning opportunities for current Princeton students. Instead of choosing the easy option of donating large amounts of money to have their name put on a school building, the Princeton alumni created a community by engaging with current Princeton students and helping the students reach their intellectual goals.

5   In "The Quest for Community in Higher Education," Palmer claims that students develop a sense of community when they feel "seen, known, and respected—when [they are] taken seriously and appreciated" (49). Unfortunately, I have not felt a sense of community at SMU in the way that Palmer describes.

6   I live in Peyton Hall, which is part of the Mary Hay/Peyton/Shuttles residential commons. Students in my hall recognize each other but do not bother to strike up conservations and get to know each other better. I never see students hanging out together in the lobby or their rooms, studying in groups, or going to the events that the residence halls host. I believe that missing such opportunities is detrimental to intellectual progress. I am not saying the people in my residential community are not smart. When I use the term "intellectual progress," I am talking about when students are opened up to new ideas outside of the classroom that force them to think and challenge their beliefs. To make intellectual progress, students should learn things that serve them "in the contexts of life outside the college classroom" and take part in a "lifelong process of learning, study, reflection, experience, and action—not just four years of classes" (Jones 12). However, the students in Peyton Hall fail to step out of their comfort zones and learn new things that could teach them valuable life lessons.

7   Up to this point, I am getting good grades in school, but I have not met peers who have introduced me to new and challenging ideas. If I could change one thing about my residential commons, I would make sure that there is a strong sense of community in which a wide range of ideas is shared among its residents.

8   Similar to my own experience, Thomas Jones was not introduced to new and challenging ideas outside of the classroom. In "The Educated Person," Jones realizes that his learning community failed to further his intellectual progress. He talks about how he just "followed the required path towards graduation" and had "little exposure to interdisciplinary thinking and teaching" (Jones 12). Jones

spends a lot of time after graduation thinking about how much he missed out on during his college career and how he could have applied what he learned to his everyday life. Jones' academic community influenced his intellectual progress for the worse. If Thomas Jones had a caring and supportive community, then he would have been introduced to the educated person question at the beginning of his college studies, not at the end. Jones' community failed to direct him towards the path that he needed to follow.

9   Unlike Jones, the students of Douglass College were introduced to the idea of a strong sense of community at the beginning of their college career. In "Claiming an Education," Adrienne Rich tells the students of Douglass College the importance of actively shaping their academic community. Rich urges the students to form a community where students take responsibility for themselves and push each other to do their best. She also urges the students to form a community where students and teachers take each other seriously (Rich 36). Rich wants students to have a strong sense of community because if students learn in the type of community she describes, then they will be more likely to reach their full potential.

10   Bill Rago from *Renaissance Man* is a great example of a teacher who takes his students seriously just as Rich describes in her speech. In the movie, Rago avoids the "sage on the stage" approach to teaching and acts as a "guide by the side" when teaching his students *Hamlet*. Furthermore, Rago also uses an inclusive teaching style, which creates a strong community between him and the soldiers. Instead of just going through the motions, Rago shows his students that he cares for them; he urges them to get involved and think critically. Ultimately, the community that Rago creates helps his students make intellectual progress. Rago's students do not only pass the final exam, but they also learn valuable life lessons that they will remember for the rest of their lives. Bill Rago was an effective teacher because he showed confidence in his students and wanted to prepare them for a fulfilling life beyond the classroom.

11   After going over various articles and reflecting upon my own experience, I am now more aware of the importance of a strong sense of community in education. Although I have not yet experienced a sense of community during my time here at SMU, I know that I still have three more years to create one. The SMU community consists of people from a great number of interesting backgrounds, and I would be doing myself a disservice if I did not try to learn more about those different backgrounds. When I graduate from SMU, I hope I think about more than just four years of classes. I hope I think about people who helped me broaden my horizons and introduced me to new cultures and ideas. I hope I think about how the SMU community made me a better person at graduation than I was four years before.

Works Cited

Jones, Thomas B. "The Educated Person." *Criteria: A Journal of First-Year Writing 2011–2012*, edited by Lee Gibson and Mary K. Jackman, Southern Methodist University, 2011, pp. 11–12

Palmer, Parker J. "The Quest for Community in Higher Education." *Criteria: A Journal of First-Year Writing 2011–2012*, edited by Lee Gibson and Mary K. Jackman, Southern Methodist University, 2012, pp. 46–55.

Renaissance Man. Dir. Penny Marshall. Perf. Danny Devito. Touchstone Pictures, 1994. Film.

Rich, Adrienne. "Claiming an Education." *Criteria: A Journal of First-Year Writing 2011–2012*, edited by Lee Gibson and Mary K. Jackman, Southern Methodist University, 2011, pp. 33–36.

For Consideration:

1. If Quinn could revise his essay to add more information, where do you think he could add more evidence or supporting details to points already made in the essay?

2. Has your dorm experience been similar to Quinn's or has it been different? Have your friends in other dorms discussed this dynamic in regard to their dorm experience?

3. All of Quinn's source choices work well to help clarify his perspective. If you had to pick one, however, which do think is the most memorable and effectively used? Explain your answer.

Amanda Oh offers a passionate reaction to Adrienne Rich's "Claiming an Education," underscoring what is still valuable about Rich's speech while charging her female peers to pick up the pace in claiming their education and speaking up for empowerment.

The Value of Ownership[4]
Amanda Oh

"I am no bird; and no net ensnares me; I am a free human being with an independent will."

—*Jane Eyre*

1   Adrienne Rich was an English professor at Douglass College, but what she says in "Claiming an Education" teaches a far more important lesson beyond any curriculum. Standing before women at the forefront of their college careers, she challenges the incoming class of female students to view their education as more than just a package to be received and passively enjoyed, but rather as a key to a limitless future they can rightfully claim and defend as their own. She rejects the restrictive paradigm that plagues the female student—one where education is deemed useless for a person destined for the homemaking life, one where sexual objectification distorts the academic relationship between men and women, one where a woman has to prove she is worth listening to before speaking. In "Claiming an Education," Rich argues that a shift away from this paradigm demands that female students actively prove themselves as anomalies in the patriarchal world. In order to accomplish this, she argues, we must first realize that our role in education—and in life—is to reach actively beyond the limits and refuse to stay content with the portion handed to us. In the decades since Rich spoke, we have yet to see the complete breakdown of the sturdy walls of the paradigm; the difficulty is that the walls are not always apparent, not even to women themselves.

2   The existing paradigm of female inferiority is undergirded by the assumption that women are analogous to identical clay pots, molded to hold the content of their schooling. These pots are filled with matter that others decide is appropriate for them to hold. Neither the substance nor the amount can be prescribed by the pot itself. In the same way, Rich describes the paradigm of the woman striving for higher education. Although she may be able to receive *something* to satiate

---
4. This essay first appeared in the 2017–2018 edition of *Criteria*.

her intellect, she is unable to control, and may not even be aware of, the sexism deeply imbued in the information she is given. In fact, so much of history has been defined through the male looking glass that the "total erasure of women's experience and thought from the curriculum" (Rich 35) may not even seem evident to the average woman. Rich points out that students like myself glance over hundreds of "books with titles like *The Descent of Man; Man and His Symbols, and Irrational Man,*" but we never realize that they normalize the idea of "man" as synonymous with "everyone." Since the male perspective is the existing paradigm, women are often unaware that what we learn is actually a function of "how *men* have perceived and organized their experience [and] their history" (36). After all, how is it possible for us to be aware of the inferior position we hold if it is the position we were born into, and the one which has widely been accepted by all for a very long time? The existing paradigm is restrictive and demeaning, but since it has existed for almost all of history, the only way to shift it is for female students to realize the role they have been delegated to and deliberately force an anomaly within the system.

3   Such an anomaly must attract attention. Attention demands boldness and assertiveness. First, it involves the shifting of individual mindsets because thoughts are the roots of actions. This is the micro-shift that occurs on the individual level to support the much broader societal shift that occurs when enough micro-shifts cause an anomaly. Rich pleads with her audience to realize that in order for them to continue their studies as respectable women in their fields, they must make a conscious effort to scorn the passivity of "receiving" an education and instead begin actively "claiming" their education. Proving that we are *owners*—the sole guardians and determinants—of our education and our lives will also mean that our actions will be anomalous. Pots tacitly allow themselves to be filled with traditional disciplines framed in male narratives. Owners purposefully choose women's studies to gain "a new intellectual grasp on their lives, new understanding of their history, and a fresh vision on the human experience" (36). Pots exist for the purpose of servicing the needs of others, whether that means embodying the righteous "self-denying wife and mother" or denying intelligence in accordance with society's feminine expectations. Owners serve the purpose they see best for themselves after careful consideration of their own options, "refusing to let others to do their thinking" (36).

4   Rich encourages her students to live out their lives with the same sense of ownership that they should feel towards their education. However, ownership of

our lives in the context of our relationships with others means more than feeling secure in ourselves; it also means actively demonstrating this to those who may think of us as only pots. Ownership of one's time and body, and peace of mind, means that we should be able to demand that those around us "respect our sense of purpose and integrity" (Rich 37). We must actively be able to prove the second definition of "claiming"—that is, "asserting in the face of possible contradiction" that we are indeed owners of our own future (35). It's not enough to find inward strength in our ownership because in order to gain the true respect of those who have traditionally looked down upon us, we must vocally insist that our education and our life choices be taken seriously. Rich uses the lawsuit of *Alexander v. Yale* as evidence that the contract of mutual respect between students and teachers is something worth actively defending, even if it means becoming confrontational in the legal sense. In order for the macro-paradigm shift to occur—for society as a whole to shift its view of women—we *must* be assertive anomalies.

5   Nearly four decades later, society still grapples with the remnants of the paradigm of gender inequality that Rich condemned. As a student here at Southern Methodist University, I have had first-hand experience with the assumption of male dominance in the world of education. For example, our political science textbook consistently indicates roles such as candidate, official, and incumbent with the male pronoun "he." Why should the default pronoun for a person in political power be male? What kind of underlying message does this convey to female students as they study to become politicians themselves? The contemporary paradigm still defines power as an asset associated with males, an idea too often reinforced by our own classroom texts. Our pots are being filled with information tainted with bias. It is my hope that one day the anomaly of the female politician will be so prevalent that there will be no reason to call her an anomaly anymore.

6   In the time since Adrienne Rich delivered her Douglass College speech, although we have moved forward, progress is occurring at an unacceptably slow pace. Women sit in the same classrooms as men but don't receive the same education. We are taught to receive and not to own—to listen and to accept. There is more "claiming" to be done. Step one is to open our eyes to the small but significant jabs at women—like male pronouns used in a genderless situation—and step two is to work to break the existing paradigm. The goal is to shift the paradigm to one where girls are empowered to reach the upper limits of the education they wish to pursue and the lives they wish to life. In order to do this, we must be the owners of our futures.

Works Cited

Bronte, Charlotte. *Jane Eyre*. n.d., www.planetpdf.com/planetpdf/pdfs/free_ebooks/jane_eyre_nt.pdf.

Rich, Adrienne. "Claiming an Education." *Criteria: A Journal of First-Year Writing 2009–2010,* edited by Mary K. Jackman and Lee Gibson, SMU Department of Rhetoric, 2009, pp. 35–38.

For Consideration:

1. Analyze the author's strategy of placing a quotation from a well-known work of literature before she begins her essay. Having read the entire essay, explain what makes this quotation a pertinent and effective choice. What tone does it set? What links can be drawn between the essay's content and the substance of the quotation? Do you think the quotation works equally well regardless of whether the reader is familiar with the novel? Why or why not?

2. Oh applies her understanding of paradigm theory in this essay, using the terms "paradigm" and "anomaly" throughout. If you weren't already familiar with these terms, does her use of them give you a solid introduction to them? Write out a definition for each of these terms as you understand them.

3. Do your experiences and observations of the gender paradigm in the academic environ here at SMU correlate with the author's? If so, in what ways? If not, why not? Support your position with plenty of concrete evidence.

Tina Hirt makes a compelling and original argument for choosing a liberal arts education. After a lucrative year in the workforce, she decided that "only by learning new ways of thinking could [she] further develop as an individual" and enrolled at SMU to broaden her worldview and skill set.

A Liberal Education: Choices Are the Foundation of Freedom[5]
Tina Hirt

1. Looking back at my college experience, I realize that I have not taken the most direct route. After spending my freshman year at the University of Texas at Austin, I chose to take a gap year because I didn't know what I wanted to pursue for a degree. During my time off, I was fortunate enough to land a job working as the website manager for the Kimbell Art Museum's public relations department. My first months on the job were filled with everyday excitement and innovation due to my exposure to so much new information and so many new people. I found enjoyable the fact that the job did not come with a set of instructions. I spent a large amount of time learning my new website skills by trial and error. I struggled to teach myself the pathways and shortcuts hidden in the website's nooks and crannies. Though my position's tasks were difficult in the beginning, I soon honed and developed a very specialized skill set of which I was proud. Having garnered much pleasure in my new identity within the workplace, I considered never returning to university. However, my initial love of the job began to wane. After a full year, I realized that my role at the museum did not offer much room for growth, and the mental stimulation ebbed. I became a bit like the technical device I managed, passively completing tasks and sometimes turning dark like a computer screen that has gone to sleep.

2. One day, during a conversation with my employer, I had a sudden realization. I not only wanted but *needed* to go back to college and get my degree. I knew at that moment that for myself to grow as an individual, I had to develop skills beyond those I had acquired at the museum. Neither influenced by the wishes of my parents nor the opinions of my peers, I decided for myself that only by learning new ways of thinking could I further develop as an individual. Due to my experience as a specialized employee, I decided that I wanted to attend a liberal

---
5. This essay first appeared in the 2018–2019 edition of *Criteria*.

arts university—Southern Methodist University—where I would be exposed to many different subjects. This would allow me to sample various perspectives and learn myriad skills which would enable me to choose a life path that would enrich my person. I believe that a liberal arts education is the only form that fosters free individuals, enabling people to think dynamically and make informed life choices with confidence.

3   I must first explain what I mean by "free individuals." To my mind, a free individual is someone who pursues his or her curiosities about the world and elects to take ownership of his or her life. A prime example would be Bill Murray's character, Phil Connors, in *Groundhog Day*. During the film, Phil is trapped in a time loop. Initially, he seems to find his repetitious lifestyle pleasing, and he utilizes it to his advantage; however, he soon realizes that he will never find happiness without altering his routine and broaden his perspectives. How does he take control of his situation? Phil chooses to challenge himself, expanding both intellectually and emotionally through liberal arts enrichment, which eventually frees Phil as a person. Using the words of Martha Nussbaum, Phil's ability to break the time loop is fostered after he pursues a "Socratic, active [method of] learning and exploration through the arts" (19). When Phil chooses to educate himself and expand his worldview through literature, music, and art, these areas of study stimulate new, untapped sources of his personality, shaping him into a more informed, empathetic, and invested member of society. His learning causes him to undergo a "metamorphosis of [character]" (Cowan 88). As his thought processes and perspective evolve, Phil is finally able to understand who he truly wants to be. He wants to better himself and his community, and he does so by expanding his mental and social comfort zones, trying new areas of study, and thinking with a newfound complexity about his surrounding world. In short, I believe that by working hard to claim his own education and seeking to educate himself in new and liberal ways, Phil becomes a free individual. I believe that pursuing a liberal education at SMU will result in my maturation into a full and conscious member of the world's larger, interconnected society.

4   I would like to pose the following question: Why should a liberal education be so important and influential to my development or anyone's involvement in our society? In her book *Not for Profit: Why Democracy Needs the Humanities*, Nussbaum states that "leading U.S. educators [can connect] the liberal arts to the preparation of informed, independent, and sympathetic . . . citizens" (17–18). Anyone familiar with what liberal arts education entails would have to agree. If students are only exposed to a single perspective or skill set, how can they ever be able to understand or fully participate in our complex world? Would they even be able to share their skills with others? Though brilliant in their own respective

fields, many specialists struggle to communicate beyond—and sometimes even within—their limited realm of workplace knowledge. I can attest to this first hand. During my tenure at the Kimbell Art Museum, as the sole person managing the website, I tailored my processes of maintaining the site to my own methodologies, and I struggled to explain basic website maintenance processes to my coworkers. In part, I attribute this inability to my lack of a liberal arts background. I began to do my work passively rather than trying to "[challenge my] mind to become active, competent, and thoughtfully critical" (Nussbaum 18) about how I could share my expertise with my peers. Most website managers will tell you that it was my responsibility as a member of the Kimbell's team to educate my department members in case of emergency web maintenance. Unfortunately, I couldn't conceive of how to do so because I didn't actively pursue new methods of approaching my work or interacting with my peers. Without a liberal education, I had isolated myself and limited my intellectual prowess. I came to realize that a liberal education, with its assortment of skills and disciplines, creates people capable of sharing their knowledge and of thinking in a variety of ways while a single-subject education does not.

5   At this point, I would like to address readers who may believe that a technical education or more streamlined education is a better model of learning. They might insist that financial security ensures personal freedom and therefore, our education should solely prepare us for entering a specific workplace position. They might argue that I should have stayed on in my position at the Kimbell Art Museum as "work, getting paid, is really the main point" of life (Crawford 181). There is validity to this point. Crawford asserts that if you have discovered a skill you enjoy and are good at, then work can be your main life focus. I'll admit that I did receive a certain satisfaction whenever I received my salary check from the museum. However, I think that Crawford would understand that as I fell out of love with the day-to-day tasks of my job, I had to "weigh . . . [my] passions more heavily than . . . [my] earnings" (Clapp 16). Akin to Phil Connors in *Groundhog Day*, my intrinsic desires began to outweigh my extrinsic rewards. I know now that in part my slow dissatisfaction with my job was because I hadn't acquired a liberal arts education. I had had yet "to encounter different kinds of people, to discover new interests, and to decide what [I] want to make of [my] life" (Murray 250).

6   It is crucial for every young person to be introduced to new things, and this introduction can best occur within a liberal arts education. By joining the workforce too soon prior to finishing my own liberal arts education, I discovered that working and its acquisition of a paycheck did not fulfill me and bring me true satisfaction. Working prior to discovering my passion did not provide me with the skills necessary to find out who I am as a person. I leave you with this question:

How can people who don't know who they are ever be truly free and complete individuals?

7   I encourage my age group to embrace and savor the acquiring of a liberal arts education. Although four years at college may seem too long of a time, I believe that these years are necessary for myself and my peers to discover how to "be [ourselves, and enjoy life in our] own way" (Emerson). By sampling a wide range of classes, we can find out what makes us true, unique individuals. In Emerson's own words, "school, college, society, [they] make the difference between [individuals]." I concede that many an average college graduate may not view the requirements —the English, Math, Science, and language classes—of a liberal arts education as beneficial to him or her as a person. However, these classes will grant a person a larger body of core knowledge, creating an individual with a greater understanding of the world and the self. Only when you are passionate about your day-to-day existence can you finally embrace life as a complete and liberated person. People should welcome true intellectual growth and leave school well-rounded humans able to make what they do in their personal lives and in society matter.

Works Cited

Clapp, Marissa. "College Majors: The Value of Passion over Profit." *Criteria: Discernment and Discourse Reader and Guide 2016-2017*, edited by Vanessa Hopper and Ona Seaney, Kendall Hunt, 2016, pp. 15–17.

Cowan, Donald. *Unbinding Prometheus: Education for the Coming Age*. Dallas Institute Publications, Dallas Institute of Humanities and Culture, 1988.

Crawford, Matthew B. *Shop Class as Soulcraft: An Inquiry into the Value of Work*. Penguin, 2009.

Emerson, Ralph Waldo. "On Education." *American Transcendentalism Web,* 29 Nov. 2016, www.archive.vcu.edu/english/engweb/transcendentalism/authors/emerson/essays/.

Groundhog Day. Directed by Harold Ramis. Columbia Pictures, 1993.

Murray, Charles. "Are Too Many People Going to College?" *"They Say / I Say": The Moves That Matter in Academic Writing with Readings*, edited by Gerald Graff, Cathy Birkenstein, and Russel Durst, W.W. Norton & Company, 2015, pp. 234–254.

Nussbaum, Martha C. *Not for Profit: Why Democracy Needs the Humanities*. Princeton UP, 2010.

For Consideration:

1. In your own words, explain your understanding of the author's definition of "free individual." When you finish, read over your definition and revisit the author's essay to check it. Did you miss anything? Would you modify your definition any to make it more accurate?

2. In an exercise to reinforce the importance of effectively used sources to build ethos, take the sources from Hirt's essay one at a time and examine her use of each. Answer the following questions in response to each source: What can you learn about the credibility of the source from details in the Works Cited, such as the container and the publisher? In what way(s) does her selection of quotation or example from each source bolster her argument? Be specific.

3. Hirt chose to use a conversational tone in this essay. How does this relaxed tone affect your reading of and reaction to the essay? Would you feel differently about the essay if she hadn't included her first-hand experience and personal reactions to texts and situations? Explain your answer.

In her essay, Megan Meinecke courageously tackles the challenge of overcoming gender bias in her chosen field of engineering while also appealing to students of all backgrounds with suggestions for overcoming adversity and pro-actively pursuing knowledge.

Claiming My Degree[6]

Megan Meinecke

1   While it had been sunny every day since I began my educational career at SMU, making it an exceptionally hot commute back to my dorm from the Fondren Science Building, today's heat reached an all-time high. With the weather app reading 102°F, I could feel sweat droplets beginning to form along my forehead while I crossed Binkley Avenue. Partially due to the heat and partially steaming from my anxiety, tears began to well up in my eyes. Fighting the urge to cry, I looked down at my phone to make sure it was still dialing. Within two seconds of my mother answering my phone call, I began to sob. I tried to explain to her that I had studied fifteen hours only to make a 55 on my first-ever college exam in my Introduction to Physics class. Instead of the disappointed response I expected, to my extreme surprise, she calmly reassured me: "All you can do is try harder the next time. This isn't high school any more. You are going to have to work harder than you ever could have imagined." Realizing that she was right and thanking her for her always-wise advice, I hung up the phone with a new sense of determination. I wouldn't be able to coast through college as I had through high school. Pursuing a degree in mechanical engineering meant I was going to have to claim my education rather than wait for it to be handed to me.

2   As poet and educator Adrienne Rich defines in her speech when addressing a group of women at Douglass College, claiming an education means to "take as the rightful owner" rather than receiving an education by passively "coming into possession of" one (98). Rich emphasizes the importance of a mutual contract that is present between students and teachers that ensures the recovery from the "depersonalizing" and "cheapening" qualities that surround present-day academics (98). This contract requires that the student demand to be taken seriously by faculty as well as engaging in a constant battle to achieve our highest selves by realizing that the "most affirming thing anyone can do for you is demand that you push yourself further" (101). Rich highlights these essential aspects of a healthy

---

6. This essay first appeared in the 2018–2019 edition of *Crtieria*.

student-teacher relationship in order to ensure that our education is maximized to the fullest degree.

3   Going into a field of study that is predominantly male, I relate to Rich's argument. Most females shy away from competing in the field of engineering because there has been little participation by females in the past due to societal beliefs that encourage women to "deny their intelligence to seem more feminine" (Rich 99). By pursuing a degree that is still viewed by some people as an occupation in which only men can succeed, I am "taking responsibility toward [myself]" and demanding that I be respected as an individual as I claim my education (99). Rather than giving up at the first sign of defeat and confirming the false belief that women cannot compete on the same level as men, my phone call with my mother reminded me of my own abilities and encouraged me to push myself harder and learn more despite my first failing test grade.

4   After reading Rich's article in class, SMU student Anna Lee initially experienced feelings of disagreement, believing that Rich's "strong feminist statements" were "too radical to accept" (12). Due to her traditional deep-south upbringing, throughout her childhood Lee had been taught to willingly accept and embrace the societal belief that women should look pretty, cause little disruption, and rarely have opinions of their own. After a second reading, approaching Rich's article with an open mind, Lee decided that there is more to life than achieving the rank of an ideal Southern Belle. Similar to Lee, it took me a while to realize that a legitimate gender prejudice clouds our professional and academic world. While I'm well aware that there is little female participation in the engineering field, I was unaware what that could mean for the few females who do participate. After taking only a month of engineering classes, I have already been exposed to the males' general bias against women and reluctance to take us seriously as academic competitors. My ideas are often silenced or ignored and never considered to be as reliable as those of my male peers. Like Lee, I was raised to accept a limited view of women's intellectual capabilities without even realizing it. In order to claim my education and combat the sexist views that pervade this area of academia, I will continue to contribute my ideas and demand that they be respected.

5   After telling my mother I love her, I hung up the phone and proceeded to get out my daily planner. As I assessed what assignments I needed to complete by that night, I felt an instant wave of panic flood my body. I quickly realized I had an online physics assignment due and a failing class grade, meaning I had no room to falter on this assignment. I would need a perfect homework score in order to compensate for my lacking test grade and was well aware I would not achieve success without help. As former SMU student Emma Richardson states, "No one

is against becoming educated, but many students don't take advantage of all the opportunities [their] campus has to offer" (72). Claiming my education would mean having to go against my stubborn habit of refusing to admit that I need help and taking advantage of the opportunities available on my campus.

6   Suffering a minor blow to my ego and pride, I packed up my backpack and traveled through the sweltering heat once more to reach the ALEC. Upon arriving in the tutoring center, I was intimidated by the organization and professionalism of the atmosphere, making me instantly feel out of place as I nervously walked to the front desk and waited for someone to assist me. A man greeted me and assured me that a tutor was available to assist me with my homework. I hesitantly followed him to a table in the back of the room where I was introduced to an older student who would serve as my tutor. After shyly introducing myself and signing in on his attendance sheet, we proceeded to tackle all twenty of the homework problems I had been assigned. Although the task was not completed without near tears on my part and frustration for both parties, I left the ALEC feeling fully prepared for my next exam in physics. Students don't take advantage of the opportunities their campus has to offer because they are too prideful to do so or they are merely unaware of the options, but the first step towards claiming an education is actively seeking one. I took a step towards claiming my education by abandoning my self-righteous ego and seeking help from others who have knowledge, experience, and wisdom to offer.

7   Practicing what Adrienne Rich, Anna Lee, and Emma Richardson encouraged, Elle Woods from the movie *Legally Blonde* claims her education by pursuing a law degree from prestigious Harvard University despite the doubts of her peers. Although Elle originally seeks a law degree hoping to impress her ex-boyfriend, she ends up developing a passion for law and using her unique knowledge about beauty habits to prove the innocence of one of her clients. Elle, similar to Emma Richardson and me, spent years of her life naively allowing men to dictate the world around her. She goes through her college undergraduate career as a "dumb" sorority girl, allowing her actions to be influenced by what would please her boyfriend. However, Elle changes her ways and actively claims her education by ultimately rejecting the boy who never believed she was good enough and denying a professor who made sexual advances towards her. Rather than making decisions based on what men want, Elle makes decisions for herself and demands respect from her peers, instructors, and competitors, which ultimately allows her to achieve the goals she had set out to accomplish.

8   A few days later, I nervously checked my email, waiting for a notification from Canvas that would alert me if a grade were updated. An email from Canvas

announced that my second test in physics had been graded. Paralyzed with fear, I opened Canvas to find that I had received an A- on my second test. I immediately called my mother to tell her the good news. Like Elle Woods, I claimed my education despite my doubts. I didn't let failure limit my determination. I will continue to claim my education by actively contributing to group discussions, seeking help when needed, and demanding respect from those around me. Once I receive my degree in engineering, I will continue to claim my education by pursuing knowledge in the professional world and leaving an impact everywhere I work.

Works Cited

Lee, Anna. "Claiming My Education." *Criteria: A Journal of First-Year Writing 2005–2006*, edited by Lee Gibson and Kelly Teague Smith, Department of English, Southern Methodist University, 2005, pp. 12–14.

Legally Blonde. Directed by Robert Luketic, Metro-Goldwyn-Mayer, 2001.

Rich, Adrienne. "Claiming an Education." *Criteria: A Journal of First-Year Writing 2005–2006*, edited by Lee Gibson and Kelly Teague Smith, Department of English, Southern Methodist University, 2005, pp. 98–101.

Richardson, Emma. "The Confidence to Claim an Education." *Criteria: A Journal of First-Year Writing 2009–2010*, edited by Mary K. Jackman and Lee Gibson, Department of English, Southern Methodist University, 2009, pp. 71–73.

For Consideration:

1. If you have not read the previous essay, "A Liberal Education" by Tina Hirt, do so. Note that both authors utilize the film *Legally Blonde* and the essay "Claiming an Education" by Adrienne Rich. Articulate the <u>differences</u> in how each author utilizes each text to benefit her argument.

2. Both Hirt and Meinecke open with a personal anecdote intended to engage the audience. Both are successful, but imagine that you must choose one for arguing as the best of the two. Which would you choose? Carefully explain your choice.

3. Megan Meinecke addressed specific prejudice that she will have to battle as she pursues her education goals. Have you ever come up against the barrier of prejudice—sexist, racist, or some other kind—in any aspect of your own education, or do you know someone who has? Explain the situation, and include an assessment of it: Why do you think this prejudice exists? What do you feel are the best ways to battle it?

First-year student Ryan Mendez makes a good case for the value of seeking membership in communities—both social and academic—across campus because "community in education serves as a foundation for knowledge in all aspects of our lives that we continue to build on as we move into the future."

A Community in Education[7]
Ryan Mendez

1   Since the beginning of the academic year, my Discernment and Discourse class has pondered many aspects of education, ranging from what an educated person is to the qualities that a successful teacher must have. Now, in our final writing assignment of the semester, we have been asked to consider the importance of community within education. Former SMU student Maddy Dockery-Fuhrmann says that community is "like a coal burning fire" in the sense that when "all coals are in the fire they stay hot" but if one coal is removed, the "[fire] will cool down quickly" (Fuhrmann 34). What Fuhrmann means is that our education is of greatest benefit when there is a bond or "fire" amongst us all as students. Creating and maintaining relationships with our peers serves as a vital role in the development of all of us into educated people. I believe that having community in education serves as a foundation for knowledge in all aspects of our lives that we continue to build as we move into the future.

2   Before I get to why it is important, what exactly *is* community in education? "Community" signifies the coming together of individuals striving towards a common goal—in this case, to obtain a college education. Where can we find our own specific communities on campus? Author Parker J. Palmer states that students develop a sense of community when they feel "seen, known, and respected" (Palmer 54). Moreover, a community can be found anywhere that we actively seek one out. I discovered this after the fall semester began here at SMU. Before school started, we were told that our residential commons would be constantly bustling with activity and neighbor interaction. The concept of student-life that was advertised excited me because as a high school student, I was heavily involved in my school and community, participating in events from scouts to sports to student council.

3   As a result of graduating from a high school in a small area where I knew everybody and the citizens of the town felt like family, I was disappointed in what

---

7. This essay first appeared in the 2018–2019 edition of *Criteria*.

I initially found in my residential commons. The Mary-Hay Peyton Shuttles commons seemed to be one of the smallest, quietest, and least social dorms on campus. Because of my need to be involved, I decided to take matters into my own hands. I made the decision to get involved with activities in my residential commons such as Commons Council and intramural sports. As a member of Commons Council, I contribute to events on campus like Dr. Bob's Block Party, which was the opening of the new health center, and the boulevards before football games; in addition, I serve in the Dallas community through volunteering and fundraising for good causes. I also participate in intramural sports such as flag football and basketball through our commons. Competitive sports are an easy and effective way to create camaraderie. As a member of these two groups, I feel like an engaged part of my dorm community. Because of my choice to engage in residential life, I can happily say that some of my closest friends have been made through participation in both Commons Council and intramural sports.

4   I have also joined the Methodist college ministry, the Wesley Foundation. Through the Wesley, I have befriended people that I would not have met otherwise. Nayra Salamanca, a former SMU student, claims that as we grow, we need others that "we can rely [on] to fortify our weaknesses with their strengths" (68). The family that I have found within the Wesley Foundation is wonderful. I came to SMU with low self-confidence, only knowing that I wanted to help others. Through the Wesley, I have participated in packaging over 15,000 meals for those in need and served by aiding in the construction of a new home for a family, on top of the weekly activities I engage in on campus. I have made numerous friends while engaging in activities programmed by the foundation. I have not yet decided on what career path I wish to set out on, but I do know that I have invaluable support from the community I found at the Wesley.

5   While community in education clearly has social benefits, it must be stated that is has academic benefits as well. Relationships between students and teachers play a vital role in class performance. Former SMU student Evan Giacomini asserts that a lack of connection between student and teacher "would hinder any learning that occurs and would destroy education's full potential" (13). If we do not establish relationships with our professors, how can we expect to maximize our educational potential? Our professors should be held accountable to instill their knowledge into us as well. Poet and educator Adrienne Rich states that there is an "intellectual contract" between us and our teacher that must remain "intuitive, dynamic, [and] unwritten" and be referred to "again and again" if our education is to be "claimed" (Rich 95). By creating relationships with our teachers, we are actively pursuing our education and forming a key to academic success.

6   Parker J. Palmer describes the qualities of a "guide by the side" teacher versus a "sage on the stage" lecturer (51). A teacher who tends his or her students' needs and builds a community within the classroom is considered a guide by the side. An example of this occurs in the film *Renaissance Man*, where freshly-employed Bill Rago finds himself teaching at an army military base. Rago embodies the traits of a guide by the side as he teaches his students about *Hamlet*. Rago exemplifies these characteristics when he asks his class to role-play *Hamlet*, understanding that this approach suits the students' specific needs. This teaching style fosters the necessary interaction and growth.

7   Another branch of community in education is the future opportunities it creates for us. As a potential student of SMU, I considered the benefits of attending this world-class university in the heart of Dallas versus other schools I was looking at. What could this area provide me that I couldn't find elsewhere? For me, the answer was the vast networking possibilities found here. SMU is an outstanding school, but the opportunities available beyond SMU that may be accessed through it are even better. Palmer describes the reunion of the Princeton Class of 1955. Instead of making a donation to the school in the form of a bench or plaque, the class used their influence and connections to create internships and opportunities for current students (53). The SMU community has the ability to do similar things, we just have to befriend the right people. By networking across the student-body and establishing bonds with the alumni and our faculty, we can find people in all fields of study with many useful contacts. Friendships that are important now will only become more important as we progress in our careers. The communities that we are a part of now will dictate who we can reach out to later on.

8   Due to the choices I have made to get involved with the SMU community in myriad ways, my overall college experience has been much more enjoyable because I feel "seen, known, and respected" around campus (Palmer 54.) Once we find our niche on campus, that same niche will play a vital role not only in the improvement of our classroom performance but in our social lives and career opportunities as well. If we discover and actively participate in the community here at SMU, we will undoubtedly achieve the coveted status of World Changer.

Works Cited

Dockery-Fuhrmann, Maddy. "Community in High Education." *Criteria: A Journal of First-Year Writing 2012–2013*, edited by Mary K. Jackman and Lee Gibson, Kendall-Hunt, 2012, pp. 34–37.

Giacomini, Evan. "CommUNITY in Education." *Criteria: A Journal of First-Year Writing 2014–2015,* edited by Mary K. Jackman and Lee Gibson, Kendall-Hunt, 2014, pp. 12–15.

Palmer, Parker J. "The Quest for Community in Higher Education." *Criteria: A Journal of First-Year Writing 2011–2012,* edited by Mary K. Jackman and Lee Gibson, Department of English, Southern Methodist University, 2011, pp. 46–55.

Renaissance Man. Directed by Penny Marshal, Touchstone Pictures, 1994.

Rich, Adrienne. "Claiming an Education." *Criteria: A Journal of First-Year Writing 2003–2004,* edited by Annie-Laurie Cooper and Lee Gibson, Department of English, Southern Methodist University, 2003, pp. 95–98.

Salamanca, Nayra. "What is the Importance of Community in Education?" *Criteria: A Journal of First-Year Writing 2011–2012,* edited by Mary K. Jackman and Lee Gibson, Department of English, Southern Methodist University, 2011, pp. 67–69.

For Consideration:

1. Do you, like Mendez, feel "seen, known, and respected" around campus? If so, has being a part of any specific communities contributed to that? Explain your answer.

2. SMU is a large community made up of many smaller communities. Each dorm is its own community, and the Shuttles dorm is one community that Mendez chose to maximize the benefits of. When he found that mere assignment to the building itself didn't automatically create a bond among those who live there, he signed up to engage in activities that proved worthwhile. Have you actively sought membership in any communities within the world of SMU since you arrived? If so, which ones and why? If not, do you wish to? Has this essay given you any ideas or inspiration?

3. Mendez cites the networking opportunities available at SMU as one of the main reasons for choosing this univerisity over others he was considering. Were you aware of SMU's networking opportunities and did this have anything to do with your choice to attend this school? Do you agree with Mendez that some schools offer better networking opportunities than others, or do you think that networking can happen with equal effectiveness wherever one goes, and that it is more about how one utilizes one's contacts? Explain your answer.

TIMED WRITING

Students write in class for a grade on all of the Discernment and Discourse levels. It is an important exercise that helps instructors to evaluate students' essential skills because reference books and notes are not usually allowed. Although stressful for students, writing under time constraints—especially on a previously unannounced topic—is a vital learning experience that can help them sharpen their critical response skills, give them insights on organizing ideas, improve their ability to budget their time wisely, and help them test better in other classes. The reality: in most real-life communication situations, people don't have weeks, or even days, to create a response to a challenging question. We want these examples of successful timed student writings to be inspiring; they will allow students to see what can be done under pressure.

(Note: Works Cited information has been added at the end of this section by the editors for purposes of legality/publication; due to the nature of the testing situation, the students were not required to provide such information.)

Undeveloped Humanity
Sophia Paolo

1   Humanity often finds itself caught up in the churning machine of work, all else lost to demands of society. And when humanity neglects to cease work and pay attention to the psyche, they are no longer able to develop normally. Blake writes intuitively about the problems of humanity, focusing deeply on the problems faced by those succumbing to their surroundings. However, Freud's claims most clearly reveal the problems Blake's unfortunate characters face. By applying Freud's ideas about repression and wish fulfillment to Blake's poetry, we can see how society as a whole fails to develop properly when confronted by these problems.

2   Blake's "London" society is the first to improperly develop due to Freudian issues of repression and neglect. The people in London are bound by "manacles" (Blake), but not literal shackles. What holds them back are the "energetic repressions of certain instincts" (Freud 48). These repressions stem from Marx's ideas about the bourgeoisie's suppression of the proletariat. Because Blake's characters have been repressed by the palace, which has "blood" running down its walls (Blake), the people have been taught from a young age to repress their desires. Therefore, they have completely "neglected what was originally animal in [their] nature" (Freud 60) and have neglected all desires, instead only working and enjoying nothing. All that is left for the people of London is unwittingly contracted STDs and a city with no culture or expression of humanity. Reading Blake's poem in this way shows how deprived of meaning society becomes when societal repressions are forced upon it. The people are no longer able to connect with their unconscious wishes and desires and, therefore, exist in a state of constant depravity that inhibits development of normal and enjoyable life and society.

3   Blake's "Little Black Boy" further demonstrates a society that has developed improperly. The little boy sits on the lap of his mother, who serves as what Augustine would call an interpreter. The boy has such a strong Freudian-life wishful impulse that he relies on his mother to interpret the dreamlike state of the sunset. Their conversation does two things: first, it is a psychoanalytic session in which the boy discovers his unconscious desire to be like the white boy. Second, it reveals that society in "Little Black Boy" is also repressing an entire portion of its people: those with dark skin. Reading the poem this way, we can see how problems arise both in a person's mental state and in society as a whole when repression of an entire people occurs. The boy has nothing but his dreams, and they show how damaged society has become.

4   Finally, "Chimney Sweeper" demonstrates a flawed society that occurs when repressions and resistance are present. The young boy is sold at birth and encounters Tom at his horrid job as a chimney sweep. However, the boys are so overworked (think back to proletariat repression) that they assume their situation should be how it is and make no effort to change it. Tom has a dream that distorts reality, and in it is revealed the boys' "phantasy" that makes up for the "insufficiencies of reality" (Freud). The boys hope only that they will be rewarded for their hard work. Their society is just as broken as the last two: children work in terrible conditions and are forced to undertake an assumed reality that they will be rewarded for their work. They have an unconscious desire to be rewarded in some way and can fulfill that wish only in dreams.

5   Blake's poetry is revealed as a commentary on undeveloped societies when laid alongside Freudian ideas. What is common among each of Blake's poems is a society broken by repressions of race and class. Understanding these repressions in a Freudian light, we can see that, if humanity is forced to live in conditions of repression, it will fail to develop a proper society and will instead resort to false dreams and days deprived of any real substance. Like Freud's example of the horse, Blake's societies starved of culture can be expected to die, churned up and forgotten by the machine of work.

Writing in a 50-minute class period, Sarah McCafferty analyzes the different facets of love. Using examples and quotations from various sources, her essay illustrates what students can do when they have prepared their sources and organized their ideas prior to writing in class.

In-Class Timed Writing
Sarah McCafferty

1   The concept of love cannot be defined, yet everyone chases it. Love has the ability to take different forms and can be found in romantic relationships, friendships, and work or hobbies. All these forms of love are seen in Plato's *Symposium*, *Girls Trip*, and *Babette's Feast*. The characters in these works experience love in varying ways with the same result: clarity. Aristophanes, Ryan, and Babette are all able to gain a new vision of the world and appreciation for their lives through love. Love is an element in life that allows people to better understand themselves and appreciate the life that they live.

2   One common form of love people seek is romantic love. Many people search for "a soulmate," or someone who will help make their life feel full. Plato discusses this idea in his *Symposium* through Aristophanes, who states, "[Zeus] cut humans in half . . . immediately after this division, as each desired to possess the other half of himself, these divided people threw their arms around and embraced each other, seeking to grow together" (Plato 28). Aristophanes believes that in order to feel whole, one must heal the wound of separation. Through this idea, people can achieve happiness and peace internally as soon as they complete themselves externally. This idea of love means that people have two visions of the world, one when they are alone and the second once they have found their other half. Once people find this type of romantic love, the pain in life is believed to be over, and feelings of satisfaction and purpose begin. After experiencing the sadness of being without that other half, the world can be seen in a new light, with appreciation for what is gained when a romantic partner is around.

3   Love between friends is a second source of love in one's life, and can provide clarity for a person. Often people's friends know more about that person than they do about themselves. This is the case in *Girls' Trip*, when Ryan's friends guide her through a messy situation with her cheating husband. Towards the end of the film, as Ryan (Regina Hall) is giving her speech, she says, "There are some people, when you see them, you just can't pretend anymore because they know you. The real you" (*Girls' Trip* 1:52:36–1:53:05). Ryan realizes that she deserves better than

her husband, Stewart, and ultimately decides to leave him. Her friends play a large role in this, as they constantly remind her that she is better than that and deserves to lead a better life. They provide the clarity she needs and help her uncover what she knows deep down. This type of love for a friend is a crucial aspect of life. It can create clarity on what to do in life in times of difficult situations or in times of despair. After friends give advice, one often has a more clear vision on where to go from there. This new view often leads one to live a happier life, as one knows what could have been and what is. As previously discussed in romantic love, this friendship love helps people better appreciate the decisions they make and the world they live in.

4   Love can be seen in romance or friendships but also in a job or hobby. Babette (Stéphane Audran) demonstrates this concept of love in the film *Babette's Feast*. In the film, Babette insists that she make a meal for the two sisters and their father's followers. After the meal she tells the sisters that she is not going back to Paris, as she has spent all of her money making that feast and will be forced to live in poverty. This may be confusing for many people, but she did so because of the love she had for cooking and for gourmet French food. To her this sacrifice is worthwhile because she was able to do what she truly loves one last time. Babette appreciates the concept of love in work and finds pure happiness in it. Once people are able to find this love through work, they can better see the world with and without it. Babette knows she will never have the money to cook such a feast again but realizes the importance of the happiness it brought to her and to others. The new vision of the world as seen through love in work becomes the overall appreciation for finding something so enjoyable.

5   Overall, people find love in many different ways, and it is never the same experience for any two people. Some may find love in a romantic partner. Others find it in friends or work. All of these forms of love are found in Plato's *Symposium*, *Girls Trip*, and *Babette's Feast*. People from each of these works find love in some way, and it allows them to be more appreciative for what they have. It is often helpful to have seen the world in two different ways in order to know what really matters. Love does this for a reason; it helps people understand who they are and to live life fully.

The following essay was written in a 50-minute class period without access to books or notes. The phrases from the text were quoted from memory, demonstrating the usefulness of multiple readings and studying one's annotations in preparation for in-class writing. In-text citations have been added to satisfy legal requirements. This essay was first published in the 2018–2019 issue of Criteria.

In-Class Timed Writing
Sunjoli Aggarwal

1   Plato, in "The Allegory of the Cave," depicts those who live a life defined by material gratification as cave dwellers. If those in the chains of the cave escape, however, they may obtain an enlightened perspective. They must then return to the cave and share this enlightenment with those still in the darkness. In Joseph Conrad's *Heart of Darkness*, Marlow and Kurtz share the bond of seeing the truth beyond the cave in which they and their fellow Europeans are trapped. However, certain complexities in Marlow's character prevent him from achieving true freedom from the cave.

2   Marlow exhibits a trait of an enlightened individual in that he values truth, and this is what draws him to praise Kurtz's famous last words, "The horror! The horror!" (Conrad 68). These words exhibit a striking self-awareness in Kurtz at the end of his life, an admission that he knows everything the Belgians have been doing in the Congo is morally wrong. The words allude to the truth that in no context can the blatant subjugation and exploitation of other humans be justified, whether it be for profit or under the guise of spreading what the colonists refer to as "civilization." Kurtz puts into words what we as readers know Marlow has begun to realize: that the Belgians are intruding upon a valid and preexistinging culture, and that they are insignificant compared to the vastness of the jungle. These acknowledgments suggest that Kurtz might be outside Plato's cave and is worthy of Marlow's loyalty. Kurtz played a role in perpetrating the horrors, and Marlow perceives Kurtz's last words as a "moral victory" (70); in exposing the truths of what white men have done in the Congo, Kurtz takes a step towards redeeming himself. What Marlow admires most in Kurtz is his sense of self, his ability to *own* his actions.

3   Often, what we admire most in others is what we lack in ourselves. When Marlow first begins to struggle with the truth of what it means to be savage, he cuts his own introspection short. His job as steamboat pilot is a solitary one, and

he has the leisure to ponder the meaning of what is happening around him. For months, though, every time he begins to reflect on the truth he uses his work duties as an excuse to avoid thinking about his complicity in the ugliness and lies of Belgian imperialism. Kurtz, on the other hand, demonstrates the strength to withstand the trials of solitude. Although he becomes corrupted by power, he sees that corruption for what it is once he has been away from the influence of Belgian society for awhile. Marlow recognizes the challenge of being alone with one's thoughts, and he fails to grapple successfully with his own conflict.

4   To give due credit, Marlow is troubled by the absurdity of the ivory trade business in Africa. He passionately critiques what the imperialists consider progress and sarcastically refers to the "high and just proceedings" (19) of a trade that is destroying a land and its people, indicating a clear lack of faith. Marlow did not, like the other Belgians, go to the Congo to become rich on the ivory, rubber, or the slave trade; he was merely a curious adventurer, and he reacts with disgust to the treatment of the Africans. However, Marlow makes racist generalizations, and he never seems to realize that Kurtz's initial motivation to "civilize" the African "savages" was not noble but misguided (50–51). If Marlow hadn't stopped at merely admiring Kurtz's acknowledgment of the truth but noticeably changed his own behaviors, showed evidence of a shift in perspective, or if he had spread the word of what was truly happening in Africa so the atrocities could be stopped, it would be easier to say with confidence that he is a virtuous man who has escaped Plato's cave. Unfortunately, his choice merely to tell his story many years later to a group of sailors is too little too late. As Plato urges, an enlightened individual must devote his or her life to turning others' eyes towards the light. Marlow fails to do that.

5   Examining Marlow's moral potential and the nature of his bond with Kurtz inspires us to consider not only how our own motivations alter what we value in others, but also how societal expectations affect what we think it means to be human. Futuristic television shows—such as *Black Mirror* and *Westworld*—ponder this very topic and remind us why it is crucial that we still read Conrad's work today. It gives us a historical context for better understanding how individuals react to new cultures, the impact cultures can have on each other, the dangers of materialism, and what it means to take personal responsibility.

Although first published in the 2018–2019 issue of Criteria, *Baily Sprague's essay is still relevant as national security grows into an ongoing concern. In a 50-minute class period, with no books allowed, Sprague uses several different sources to argue that national security and personal liberties do not have to be mutually exclusive.*

In-Class Timed Writing
Bailey Sprague

1. Throughout the history of the United States, there has been a struggle between liberty and security. The two principles work much like a seesaw; when one is being heavily implemented the other is implemented to a lesser degree. This imbalance has caused many people to question whether liberty and security can coexist. Former Secretary of State Condoleezza Rice believed that they could coexist and said of the PATRIOT Act, "only when [President George W. Bush] was satisfied that we could protect both our liberties and our security did he signal that we could go ahead." I agree with Secretary Rice that liberty and security can coexist; however, there must be checks on how both are protected. Liberty and security can coexist as long as the methods for maintaining security and the unacceptable violations of liberty are clearly defined.

2. Security becomes an issue when the parameters for upholding safety force the public to give up their inalienable rights. One of the largest problems with security is that the majority of the American people are unaware that their rights are being infringed upon. In the book, *Homeland Security and Terrorism*, Vermont law professor Stephen Dycus is quoted saying, "I don't think the American public has even begun to grasp the kind of sacrifices we've been called to make in civil liberties in this war on terrorism" (Golden 407). The organizations that defend our national security are very secretive and leave the public in the dark with regards to their own liberty. I see the need for security measures, but I struggle with the mysterious nature of organizations like the NSA and with not knowing what information of mine is being viewed and connected.

3. Glenn Greenwald takes a more radical stance on surveillance: "Regardless of how surveillance is used or abused, the limits it imposed on freedom are intrinsic to its existence" (174). Here he suggests that surveillance of any kind is harmful to overall freedom. I agree with what he is saying, but I still believe there is a place for surveillance in society as long as it doesn't cause people to give up their basic rights. Our current national security system allows our constitutional rights to

be infringed upon and blurs the line between defending our country and spying on its citizens. In the book *Homeland Security and Terrorism*, Nancy Chang writes, "Section 218 allows law enforcement agencies conducting criminal investigations to circumvent the 4th Amendment whenever they are able to claim that the gathering of foreign intelligence constitutes 'a significant purpose'" (374). This section of the PATRIOT Act shows how our basic freedoms are directly being infringed upon. In order to have a balance between liberty and security, laws such as this one must use more clearly defined terms. Later, Golden writes, "As security is increased, freedom is decreased and the nation moves towards dictatorship" (401). This shift towards dictatorship happens in part because the parameters of what is an allowable sacrifice for security are not clearly defined. If that were to change, I believe security and liberty could strike a healthy balance.

4   Similarly, in order to protect public liberty there must be a definitive list of rights people are not willing to give up. Some people might argue that such a list already exists in the form of the Constitution and Bill of Rights; however, if these documents are not seriously defended, then the rights they stipulate are not guarded. Golden writes that, "The objective of the constitution was to establish the overall system of government that would defend the security of the people and provide domestic peace and welfare. However the greater goal as the constitution was the security of liberty. The purpose of the law was so that liberty might be protected" (403). If this is true, then our government is failing to utilize and uphold the Constitution in the proper way by allowing ambiguous surveillance to permeate throughout society. The documentary *Citizenfour* argues that the right to free speech has no point if it is not protected. I agree with this statement. If the government is going to allow surveillance it must still protect our constitutional rights and have a clearly defined system to ensure this. Greenwald sums up my main point perfectly: "Transparency is for those who carry out public duties and exercise public power, privacy is for everyone else" (174). There must be a stronger system created to balance liberty and security if our country is going to continue to remain in peace

5   The ramifications that poorly defined security measures have on society are grave and often cause a huge blow to liberty. The current system is not functioning at an equal balance between the two, but I believe that a balance can be struck. Once liberty and security can both be protected equally, America will be able to say it truly upholds its constitution.

First published in the 2018–2019 edition of Criteria, *the following two essays by Wright and Meehan display the importance of preparation, close reading, and organization for success on a timed writing assignment. Despite the time limits they faced writing during a single class period, both students created well-structured essays with clear transitions and textual support for their character analyses.*

Structural Parallels and Character Formation in "Tiny, Smiling Daddy"
Anna Wright

1   In "Tiny, Smiling Daddy" Mary Gaitskill tells the tumultuous story of Stew and his daughter Kitty through the interspersions of present events with memories. The story begins with Stew, in present time, finding out that Kitty, his grown lesbian daughter, had written and published an article detailing her relationship with Stew in *Self* magazine. As Stew makes his journey to find and read the article, his memories and thoughts about his contentious relationship with Kitty and his difficulties with her life choices are revealed. The overall content of the story shows a deep division between Stew's life as a straight cut, heterosexual, seemingly middle-class male and Kitty's life as a rebellious, artistic lesbian. However, contrary to these divisions, the structural order of Stew's thoughts and memories illustrate connections and similarities between Stew's character and Kitty's.

2   The first similarity can be seen when Stew, after hearing about Kitty's article, thinks, "How could she have done this to him? She knew he dreaded exposure of any kind, she knew the way he guarded himself against strangers, the way he carefully drew all the curtains . . ." (Gaitskill 230). This proclivity to shield oneself from the gaze and opinions of others is something that Gaitskill, with her order of the included thoughts and memories, uses to connect Kitty and Stew. The structure of the story allows for this comparison since immediately following Stew's thoughts about his self-guarding, Stew reveals memories of Kitty where she transformed from a happy girl to a "glum, weird teenager" whose eyes turned "flimsy . . . as if the real Kitty had retreated so far from the surface that her eyes existed to shield rather than reflect her . . ." (230). Through the close structural positions of Stew's thoughts and memories of Kitty, Gaitskill emphasizes that even though Kitty and Stew may seem different in their life paths, they connect and parallel each other in their desire to "guard" or "shield" themselves from others.

3   Another similarity between Kitty and Stew is structurally illustrated when Stew remembers how Kitty, as a teenager, "viciously" called her mom a "stupid bitch" and how Kitty was an "awful kid, looking ugly, and acting mean . . ." by refusing to help her mother with setting the table (230–231). Directly after this memory, Stew, in present time, is shown mistreating his wife by thinking of her as being "idiotic" and aggressively "snatching" the grocery bags and keys from her (231). Through placing this memory and present action in close order, Gaitskill emphasizes the parallels between Kitty and Stew in how they both can be "vicious" and can mistreat others, like Stew's wife.

4   A very poignant parallel between Stew and Kitty is also displayed when Stew contemplates how ". . . it hadn't really been so bad that [Kitty] hadn't set the table. . . . She was a teenager, and that's what teenagers did" (237). Stew's revelation that Kitty was unfairly blamed and verbally lambasted for her normal teenage actions is then connected to the following paragraph in which Stew remembers his own experience with being unfairly lambasted for his childhood actions. Stew remembers staring at his dad with adulatory feelings and creating a heroic image of his father in his mind, which many young male children tend to do, when his father said, "Stop staring at me, you little shit" (237). In this memory Stew, like Kitty, was vilified and verbally torn down by those supposed to support them. Both, through this structural parallel, are shown to connect through the shared trauma of being persecuted for their normal childish ways, thus connecting them as individuals and drawing parallels between their stories.

5   Consistently through her work, Mary Gaitskill uses structural order and the proximity of Stew's memories, thoughts, and present actions to draw parallels between the characters of Kitty and Stew. These parallels seem to undermine the surface reading of "Tiny, Smiling Daddy" that Stew and Kitty are completely divided and separate characters. Instead, through this structural organization analysis, the reader can recognize and contemplate how Stew and Kitty, although different in details and life paths, are very much the same in their personal characteristics and traumatic experiences.

Spotlight on Daddy
Mary Meehan

1. "Everybody makes his own world. You see what you want to see and hear what you want to hear" (Gaitskill 235). People have skewed perceptions of reality because of their egoistic thoughts. The nature of egoism is being centered on or preoccupied with oneself and the gratification of one's own desires: self-centered. Being that one is constantly in the center of one's own world, an evaluation of the rest of the world is inaccurate. Mary Gaitskill, creative writing professor at Syracuse University, uses point of view and the perspective of the character Stew in "Tiny, Smiling Daddy" to portray how egoism alters memory.

2. In the short story "Tiny, Smiling Daddy," the main character Stew finds out that his daughter Kitty has written an article in a national magazine about her relationship with him. He is extremely shocked and immediately worried about what she wrote because his relationship with his daughter as she was growing up was very difficult. According to Stew, his relationship with Kitty was great when she was young, but at some point "his beautiful, happy little girl, turned into a glum, weird teenager that other kids picked on" (Gaitskill 230). The author writes in third-person, limited view to manipulate the readers' understanding and impression of Stew. Gaitskill originally portrays Stew as a nurturing and loving father whose daughter grew to hate him. However, through the story we realize that this perception of Stew only aligns with his own beliefs about himself and not the truth. Stew was a homophobe and did not love his lesbian daughter. He mentally, emotionally, and physically abused her. He spoke to her with disgust; he says, "You mean nothing to me. You walk out that door, it doesn't matter. And if you come back in, I'm going to spit in your face. I don't care if I'm on my deathbed, I'll still have the energy to spit in your face" (237). Stew does not see anything wrong with his actions and believes that everyone else in his life is in the wrong.

3. Stew not only idealizes his own actions, he also portrays himself as the victim in the whole situation. From his perspective, he did his best to raise a good daughter, and it was misfortune that she chose to become who she became. The story should create empathy for a daughter who was unloved by her father, but Stew twists the memories of what happens to victimize himself. When his wife asks if he is okay, he replies with, "No, nothing is all right. I'm a tired old man in a shitty world I don't want to be in. I go out there, it's like walking on knives. Everything is an attack—the ugliness, the cheapness, the rudeness, everything" (236). Instead of facing the consequences of his wrongful actions, Stew complains about everything that is wrong with the world, as if he is a perfect person always

the martyr to others' mistakes. Stew has the mindsight of "why me." When Kitty's heartbreaking story is released to the world, he doesn't feel bad or guilty; instead, he thinks about how his childhood was bad, but no one wrote any articles about it. It was always about him. Stew is delusional, and his thoughts and memories are so concentrated around himself, it is not possible for the reader to imagine what happened accurately until reading through the whole story.

4   Through Stew's third-person, limited view and his perception of the events of his life, the reader is tricked by his altered memory to feel empathy for him. However, throughout the story, the truth is made present, and Stew's egoistic mindset is exploited. Upon reading the story through, the reader can take into account Stew's altered memories and understand what truly led Kitty to write such an article.

Works Cited

Audran, Stéphane, performer. *Babette's Feast*. Directed by Gabriel Axel, Nordisk Film, 1987.

Blake, William. "Chimney Sweeper." *Poems of William Blake*. Project Gutenberg, 30 Jul. 2008, www.gutenberg.org/cache/epub/574/pg574-images.html.

-----. "Little Black Boy." *Poems of William Blake*. Project Gutenberg, 30 Jul. 2008, www.gutenberg.org/cache/epub/574/pg574-images.html.

-----. "London." *Poems of William Blake*. Project Gutenberg, 30 Jul. 2008, www.gutenberg.org/cache/epub/574/pg574-images.html.

Chang, Nancy. "The USA PATRIOT Act: What's So Patriotic about Trampling on the Bill of Rights?" *Homeland Security and Terrorism*, edited by James J. F. Forest, Joanne Moore, and Russell Howard, McGraw Hill, 2005, pp. 369–384.

Citizenfour. Directed by Laura Poitras. HBO Films, 2014.

Conrad, Joseph. "Heart of Darkness." *Heart of Darkness: A Norton Critical Edition*, 3rd edition, edited by Robert Kimbrough, W.W. Norton, 1988, pp. 7–76.

Freud, Sigmund. *Five Lectures on Psycho-Analysis*. Norton, 1990.

Gaitskill, Mary. "Tiny, Smiling Daddy." *Scribner Anthology of Contemporary Fiction*, edited by Lex Williford and Michael Martone, Touchstone Books, 2007, pp. 228–238.

Golden, Roger Dean. "What Price Security? The USA PATRIOT Act and America's Balance between Freedom and Security." *Homeland Security and Terrorism*, edited by James J. F. Forest, Joanne Moore, and Russell Howard, McGraw Hill, 2005, pp. 400–413.

Greenwald, Glenn. *No Place to Hide*. Picador, 2015.

Hall, Regina, performer. *Girls Trip*. Directed by Malcolm D. Lee, Universal Pictures, 2017.

Plato. *The Symposium of Plato: The Shelley Translation*, edited by David K. O'Connor, translated by Percy Bysshe Shelley, St. Augustine's Press, 2002.

Rice, Condoleezza. *A Nation under Attack*. George W. Bush Library and Museum. Dallas.

ENGLISH AS A SECOND LANGUAGE (ESL)

In the Fall of 2018, over 2,000 international students came to SMU representing over 80 countries. Without having first visited SMU's campus and, in some cases, with no previous experience of the United States or its culture, these students have the courage and determination to travel over 10,000 miles from their hometowns to pursue their goals and dreams at SMU.

The essays in this section represent the work done in the English as a Second Language (ESL) sections of Discernment and Discourse, bringing new worldviews to Criteria. *Although these essays have been edited for grammatical correctness, the editors have striven to preserve the authenticity of the authors' voices.*

A native of Shanghai, China, first-year student Yinzhe Qian writes a process analysis paper to help Western players learn the ancient Chinese board game GO. Comparing the game to life, Qian shows that the game can help not just individuals progress in their own lives, but humanity progress in general.

How to Make Progress in GO
Yinzhe (Mark) Qian

1   GO, originating from ancient China, is an extremely complex strategy board game which simulates the battlefield. The basic unit of GO is called a "stone," which is divided into two colors, black and white. Each player takes charge of a color and then takes turns putting the stones on a board. Different from chess, in which the final aim is to kill the rival's King, GO is run by those accumulative stones, which are intended to surround more territory than the opponent. However, not every stone is safe on the board. If stones without two separate empty spaces, called "eyes" in GO, are unfortunately surrounded by rival's stones completely, those stones will be regarded as "dead." The rival player can "eat" the dead stones, and then they will be removed from the board and counted in the eater's territory. Typically, the player who takes the black stones needs to surround a little more territory to win the game than the player who takes white due to his/her advantage in an offensive move. For instance, in a formal game, the black side needs to surround 185 units to win, but the white only needs 176 on a board with 361 units.

2   Although GO is mainly popular in East Asia, more and more people in Western countries are beginning to learn it because of the great potential value it has in helping human beings research the brain and understand Artificial Intelligence. However, making progress in GO is not an easy task. In my opinion, it is the efficient and scientific learning strategies that count most. Generally, amateurs are supposed to follow these three steps to become an expert: learning the protocol of GO, strengthening the ability to fight in a part of the board, and competing with different rivals and making reviews on a regular basis.

3   GO is not only a game but also a culture. Thus, the very first thing beginners need to know is how to respect others. Once the game between two players starts, just like chess, any noises made during the game will be regarded as rude and are forbidden. Although one game may last for several hours, players are still required to pay full attention to any change on the board no matter who takes the turn. In

addition, winning and losing are deeply rooted in GO, which is not only revealed in the last result but also every period of a game. For instance, if one player is ahead of the other at the beginning a lot but then plays carelessly, he may pay for it in the middle of the game and finally lose the game. Nobody can win all the time, even if he is Napoleon. In the same way, nobody loses all the time. Therefore, players should strive for the victory at every minute of the game. Giving up is not encouraged in GO, especially during the very beginning. Of course, learning to accept the loss matters as well. On one side, it helps us recognize our current status. On the other side, it makes us even stronger by motivating us to improve ourselves continuously in the future.

4 Since the whole war of GO is composed of every small battle, the partial fight plays an important role in deciding the result of the game. Whether players are good at partial fights depends much on their abilities to foresee the future situation by calculating a rival's movements. One great way to make progress in calculation is to practice as much as possible. Those practices are designed by professional players, typically some problems involving the life and death, which means that the player can solve the puzzle only by a unique movement. Even though those problems will probably not appear in the game directly, the ability people develop during the process of figuring out the solutions to the puzzles will enable them to solve the actual situation in a game. Step by step, amateurs will find themselves more powerful and dominant in the fight because they can foresee the rival's movements and then respond reasonably and calmly. Practicing may sometimes be boring and tedious, and doing more does not necessarily mean a higher level, but it will determine a player's lower limit. For example, no matter how magnificent a building is, it is the base that supports it to stand on the ground. Hence, mastering the great ability to calculate by practice is the foundation to become a good player in GO.

5 When amateurs finish the construction of the base, they can feel free to go up without limits. As a two-player game, the competition between different people is where the core of GO lies. However, although some amateurs compete a lot with others, they do not gain much progress. In fact, what matters most is not the number of the games people have played but the quality of the game. A smart person would rather enjoy one good game than ten low-key games. In whatever fields, the time when a player makes progress is the moment he/she finds his/her weak points. This rule applies to GO as well. Thus, a game without a review is not a useful game. The review, typically, is held after the game immediately, in which both sides recall their movements in order and then discuss whether there exists a better movement in each step. Through the review, players can have access to the

mistakes they made and where they can improve. By repeated practice, amateurs take countless lessons from every game and will make progress spontaneously.

6   The three steps above may help people gradually become expert in GO, but the process to learn GO is unlimited. Many masters in the history of humankind spent their whole life in study of GO because they knew it's a game about life. The final goal to learn GO is never just for fun but to understand our life in a deeper way. For example, amateurs always try to kill all rivals' stones when they are more powerful. But experienced players won't do that. Conversely, they will take advantage of the situation to surround more territories by pretending to attack rival's stones. Such perception of GO will help people understand why killing never solves problems in our real life. Therefore, when our skills are improving, we players are growing at the same time.

7   Two thousand years ago, our ancestors collected their intelligence from the war into this small board. It never occurred to them that today this small board would continue to thrive, even connecting the past and the future of humankind. Recently, Google created a machine called AlphaGO, which was designed to challenge the best human GO player, Lee Sedol, by combining the most advanced algorithm and Artificial Intelligence. No one thought AlphaGO could beat Lee before the match because GO is such a complex game that its all potential movements exceed the computer's capacity. But AlphaGO made it. The victory of AlphaGO not only represents the formal arrival of the age of AI but also signals a big step for humankind to the future. Scientists claim that they will continue to improve Artificial Intelligence by taking a further research into GO. It is this small board where our future lies!

For Consideration:

1. Do you have a better understanding of the game GO from Qian's essay? Why or why not? On your own or with a partner, explain which sections of Qian's explanation give you a clear understanding of the game's strategy and which sections do not.

2. In 1997, IBM's computer Deep Blue beat then reigning chess grandmaster Garry Kasparov, the first computer ever to do so. In 2016, as Qian states in his essay, Google's AlphaGO beat GO world champion Lee Sedol. Is using ability in a strategy game like chess or GO a valid measure of the progress of artificial intelligence (AI)? Why or why not? Remember to give explanations and examples that support your claim.

3. Qian states that ancient Chinese GO masters studied the game their whole lives because "they knew it's a game about life." Reflecting on your own experiences and after speaking to older family members and friends, explain why you think the games humanity have played for centuries are usually a reflection of the way we live our lives.

For ESL Consideration:

1. Go through Qian's essay and mark where he uses analogies. In at least one paragraph for each analogy, explain why it is effective or not in helping to explain Qian's points.

2. Is there a game native to your country that those outside your culture would not understand? Explain what the game is, its goal, and why a game player from outside your culture might find it interesting to learn.

3. Although this is a process analysis paper, notice that Qian introduces other aspects of the game of GO besides how to improve one's game. Do these extra pieces of information help the paper's focus or detract from it? Why?

Steven Zhang and Yuxuan Zhou, both first-year students from China, wrote comparison/ contrast essays previously published in the 2018–2019 issue of Criteria. *Comparing two paintings from the Meadows Museum collection, the students produced clear, well-structured essays despite having had no previous experience with Western art and the vocabulary of the art world.*

Natural Beauty
Steven Zhang

1   The real definition of beauty has been a big argument as individuals pursue their own opinions of beauty. Naturally, it becomes the subject of countless artistic masterpieces that represent the thoughts of their crafters. Both *Lady at the Paris Exposition* (Jiménez Aranda, 1889) and *Portrait of the Duchess of Medinaceli* (Casado del Alisal, after 1864) are portraits of very beautiful and well-dressed women. The painters obviously wanted to demonstrate the definition of beauty in their points of view since the main subjects of their paintings are the two pretty ladies. However, although the two paintings share a similar style, they present two different kinds of prettiness: natural and decorated. The natural grace is arguably more beautiful than factitious elegance because it truly shows beauty without excessive decoration.

2   Simply having a glance at the two paintings, the audience can already differentiate two types of beauties from their initial impressions. The overall mood of *Lady at the Paris Exposition* is relatively more relaxing than that of *Portrait of the Duchess of Medinaceli* since the color used in the first painting is fairly light, which is totally opposite to the bright color used in the second painting. On the one hand, in *Lady at the Paris Exposition*, the dress of the lady, most of the buildings behind her, and the sky mostly turn out to be light colors including blue and white, which form a cozy atmosphere. On the other hand, in *Portrait of the Duchess of Medinaceli*, the florid dress of the lady, the big curtain next to her, and even the sky mainly consist of bright colors like red, which develops a sense of boldness.

3   As a result, the second painting definitely expresses its theme more strongly by decorating the whole picture with bright color. However, the nature and gracefulness presented by the light color used in the first painting is more attractive because it comes in a natural manner rather than an affected purpose. In other words, the first painting makes the audience detect its beauty from its overall style rather than showing beauty for the sake of expressing it while the second one just reaches out to grab the attention of the audience and impresses them with the beauty it directly reveals. Thus, it is the pattern and color of the two paintings that

highlight their different styles of beauty. The natural beauty without much decoration indicated by the overall relaxing pattern with light color of the first painting is more charming than the emphasized beauty with bright color presented by the general strong expression of the second painting because it does not depend on embellishment to fulfill its beauty.

4   Zooming into the paintings are the direct representations of beauty in the two paintings—the ladies themselves, who play the most significant roles to illustrate that natural beauty is better than factitious beauty. The lady in *Lady at the Paris Exposition* has a natural posture, comfortably leaning on the block behind her, and she looks to her right just like a random person on the street; the lady in *Portrait of the Duchess of Medinaceli* remains formal with one arm akimbo, her body facing left, and faces straight at the painter's perspective. Moreover, the lady in the first painting wears a semi-formal everyday dress with gloves, umbrella, and a hat. However, the lady in the second one wears a colorful, formal dress with necklaces and ornate hair and makeup. It is very clear, then, that the first lady behaves in an unaffected way that shows her natural gracefulness while the second lady fully expresses herself to present her dignity.

5   Admittedly, the two ladies perfectly present their own type of beauty, but the lady in the first painting that shows her elegance in an inartificial way is no doubt prettier than the other lady that prepares herself for the impression. This is not because of one looking or dressing better but because of the way each lady expresses her beauty. The artless elegance displayed by the lady in the first painting surely defines beauty better than the overly garnished dignity exhibited by the other lady since a natural state overweighs a deliberate one where affectation determines a big part.

6   The argument that prettiness without excessive decoration is more beautiful is again proven by the different settings that the ladies blend into. The lady in *Lady at the Paris Exposition* is surrounded by objects that people see every day in life: chairs and a table that has a newspaper and a drink on it. In addition, behind her are buildings and the Eiffel Tower, which create an ordinary view. The lady in *Portrait of the Duchess of Medinaceli*, though, possibly is located at a very big house with a huge curtain next to her and, very significantly, a servant behind her. Therefore, the background of the first painting reveals a sense of daily, natural life that is able to show its beauty anytime, yet the second painting shows a combination of beauty and nobility brought by her status and wealth. Both the setting of her big house and the appearance of a servant indicate that she is rich, therefore suggesting that money provides physical beauty. Obviously, that is a corrupted way to view beauty, which can be displayed by anyone no matter their social class and wealth. That being said, the second painting does not intend to present the

idea that money makes people beautiful; it can definitely lure people to think about that opinion. In conclusion, the background also supports the statement that natural beauty looks better than artificial beauty by contrasting the ordinary landscape to the luxurious environment behind the figures.

7   Overall, both portraits perfectly illustrate the definition of beauty in the painters' points of view but each one, by contrasting colors, figures, and settings with one another, represents a unique style of beauty. Thus, the first painting strengthens the natural beauty that is exhibited by ordinary actions anytime while the second one reinforces the decorated beauty that requires both character and materials. Out of the two, the natural beauty undoubtedly attracts people more than the affected one does since it shows the true loveliness within oneself. The fact is, people, especially viewers of the paintings, tend to accept what they are able to experience and are less likely to understand what they can only imagine.

Works Cited

Casado del Alisal, José. *Portrait of the Duchess of Medinaceli*. After 1864, Meadows Museum, Dallas.

Jiménez Aranda, Luis. *Lady at the Paris Exposition*. 1889, Meadows Museum, Dallas.

For Consideration:

1. Zhang's overall thesis is that natural beauty is more attractive than affected beauty. Do you agree with this thesis? Why or why not?
2. Notice that Zhang gives specific details regarding the figures' position, dress, and look. In what ways do these details support his arguments?
3. What other points of comparison would you have liked to read about regarding the paintings? Why?

For ESL Consideration:

1. Pay particular attention to the way Zhang structures each argument. What does he do for each comparison? What does he do after he gives his point of comparison? How does this structure support his thesis?
2. Read through Zhang's essay again and mark the transitions he uses between each paragraph. Why are these transitions useful in creating a sense of coherence and readability for his essay?

Mother Mary and Virgin Mary
Yuxuan Zhou

1   Religious paintings, as spiritual art, significantly influenced the culture and belief in Europe, especially in traditionally Catholic countries like Spain. The artists present their own imagination and demonstrate individual understanding of Christianity while giving audiences images of God, saints, and angels. Even though religious artworks predominately share the same characters and reflect equivalent topics, they still differ on spiritual meanings. For instance, Luis de Morales' *Pietà* and Juan de Juanes' *Christ in the Arms of Two Angels* are religious paintings illustrating diverse identities of the Virgin Mary through Jesus' crucifixion.

2   *Pietà* and *Christ in the Arms of Two Angels* share historical backgrounds, painting techniques, basic settings, and themes. They are both religious paintings created by two Spanish artists in the 16th century. Four hundred years ago, Catholicism was the national religion of Spain; Jesus and the Virgin Mary were two of the most popular religious subjects in spiritual paintings. Morales and Juanes both use oil on panel as material and technique. In both paintings, Jesus was painted deadly pale, and the Virgin Mary was wearing a blue and white robe. The use of cool colors gives feelings of death, seriousness, and sadness. The cross, Jesus, and the Virgin Mary are all elements that reflect the context of Jesus' crucifixion; all of these subjects are found in both paintings, and the presentation of them provides insight into each artist's interpretation.

3   Initially, *Pietà* and *Christ in the Arms of Two Angels* are immediately distinguished by the varying sizes of the paintings and the positioning of the subjects. *Pietà* paints the subjects vertically near one another only showing upper torsos of both Jesus and Mary. This puts them in the center of the canvas implying an intimacy between the two subjects. Therefore, the relationship between Mary and Jesus is apparently strong, perhaps mother and son. Contrary to *Pietà,* the other painting focuses primarily on angels shown in the foreground and gives lesser emphasis on Mary. The subjects, shown full-body, are two angels taking Jesus after crucifixion; Mary is praying in the right corner. The audience pays less attention to Mary because she is comparably far away from Jesus. As a result, the audience may assume Mary is just a lady or an apostle rather than Jesus' mother. In doing this, the painter places more importance on the two angels, shown as human-looking spiritual beings with wings and a halo. Since angels are commonly recognized as a symbol of Christianity, this puts a more religious tone on the theme.

4 The artists not only differ in their choice of sizes and positions for subject illustration, but also in their color hues to evoke deep visual feelings and emotion. Morales uses bright colors to make the surface of *Pietà* glossy. More specifically, the glossy surface creates a realistic feeling drawing the audience in to what appears like a live video; it is as if the audience is not looking at a painting but witnessing a lady crying sorrowfully with her son dying in her arms. Conversely, *Christ in the Arms of Two Angels* has a dull surface with dark colors, which creates a somber, but less emotional, mood by showing only the result that Jesus is dead and taken by angels after the crucifixion. These two artists both show the same story but differ in the story that is told. One is of the religious importance of this event; the other is the emotional relationship of mother and child. The artist purposely made *Christ in the Arms of Two Angels* less realistic and more religious.

5 Another difference in the two painting is the artists' use of diverse art elements to illustrate dead Jesus. In *Pietà*, Morales puts the color cyan on Jesus' cheek, nose, and lips, and he paints Jesus' skin in an off-white color. However, instead of using color, Juanes adds abundant details for subject illustration. He draws whip scars, wounds, and blood all over Jesus' body. Viewing both paintings stirs Christians to grieve deeply for Jesus' sacrifice and that He was tortured and killed; believers rethink their sins and appreciate God's mercy. The variation on the method of illustrating Jesus' death basically differentiates the two paintings in an artistic way.

6 By presenting different body postures and facial expressions of Mary, the artists Morales and Juanes create two distinct identities of the Virgin Mary with individual opinions. *Pietà* depicts the Virgin Mary embracing her dead son, and *Christ in the Arms of Two Angels* illustrates Mary praying with hands clasped. Morales puts Mary's gaze at her son's face and uses nearly invisible brushwork to present her crystalline tears. Mary is fully shaped into a sorrowful, loving mother who cries for her lost son. The tears are falling from Mary's cheek onto Jesus' pale face. Even an audience who does not understand the religious meaning will have sympathy for Mary from the bottoms of their hearts. Conversely, Juanes portrays Mary facing upward and seeking God's mercy. *Christ in the Arms of Two Angels* enjoys a deeper religious meaning by illustrating a faithful Mary who is praying to God and begging the Holy Father to take her son to Heaven. At this point, the artist is not presenting Mary's motherhood but her holiness, which affects the audience spiritually rather than emotionally. Thus, the audience, especially Christians, will see a Virgin Mary. Due to different purposes, the two artists use the subject's body posture and facial expression to express various emotions and illustrate diverse identities of Mary.

7   The religious paintings, *Pietà* and *Christ in the Arms of Two Angels,* share the theme of Jesus' death and present Mother Mary and the Virgin Mary to the audience. Many assume religious paintings are incomprehensible due to the deep meanings. Even da Vinci's *The Last Supper*, one of the best-known art works, is difficult for a non-Christian to understand without knowing the religious significance. Without academic knowledge, even a believer may struggle with understanding a religious painting. Nevertheless, audiences can still form impressions by feeling emotions, analyzing artistic elements, and observing subjects' facial expressions and body positioning. Enjoying an art piece does not require specialized knowledge, and audiences do not have to share the same opinions and understanding. Just like the different religious beliefs, art creates diverse thinking patterns. And just like religion, art inspires different interpretations without absolute judgement.

Works Cited

Juanes, Juan de. *Christ in the Arms of Two Angels*. n.d., Dallas Museum of Art, Dallas.
Morales, Luis de. *Pietà*. 1550–70, Meadows Museum, Dallas.

For Consideration:

1. Zhou's essay contains a paragraph focusing on the paintings' similarities. Zhang's essay contains no such paragraph. How does this difference affect the efficacy of the two essays?

2. Zhou states in the essay's conclusion that "enjoying an art piece does not require specialized knowledge." Do you agree? Why or why not?

For ESL Consideration:

1. Read through Zhou's essay again, and highlight, underline, or otherwise mark the details used to support the essay's thesis. Then, write a paragraph explaining why these details are key in persuading you of Zhou's point of view.

2. Compare Zhou's transitions with Zhang's transitions. Which ones do you feel create better coherence? Why? Give a detailed explanation for your answer.

Phuoc Dinh Le writes a causal analysis that explains why his fellow Vietnamese males will put everything else aside to watch a soccer match at a stadium. The result is a paean to the sport and those who support it.

Why People Love Watching Soccer at Stadiums
Phuoc Dinh Le

1 Three middle-aged women gather in a coffee shop; they seem unhappy. The first one complains: "My husband is so funny. He bought an expensive 4K TV and then still goes to soccer stadiums. What a waste of money!" Then the second woman continues angrily: "It is still fine. My dumb husband is always going out from afternoon till late at night for soccer matches. It spoils our weekend nights. Why does he not stay home and enjoy the match with me?" "Well, I tried following my husband to a soccer stadium once. It was such a terrible memory! The weather was hot, and I felt very tired. Watching games on a couch is always better," the third one sighs. If going to stadiums for soccer matches is that terrible, why do people still neglect lots of things like time or money for it? Those husbands definitely have various explanations, and the three most typical are extra activities during the match, the atmosphere of support, and immersion in a real match.

2 First, a lot of people, including both soccer fans and those who are not interested in it much, go to soccer stadiums since it is fun and looks like a festival. Soccer has become more and more popular, and business is now an essential part, which also means soccer fans now have more and more available services when going to soccer stadiums. At big stadiums, there are always various extra activities before, during, and after the matches. Kids, for example, may not have enough knowledge to enjoy a complete soccer match; however, they are always the most excited to go to stadiums. With kids, stadiums are ideal places to gather because stadiums usually provide them a big playground outside, where they are able to play with others. Therefore, they can always find plenty of friends there with the same hobby. In addition, the hosts often run various mini games for kids like shooting to a small goal or throwing a basketball to a small basket. Those games really attract kids because they are very fun and, sometimes, they can receive tiny and cute prizes.

3 Adults, on the other hand, care more about the match. However, they still look for necessary stuff like food and drinks. Fortunately, these are indispensable around soccer stadiums; there are always a lot of stalls outside stadiums serving

almost everything, from fast food like burgers and pizzas to cold drinks like water, beer, or soft drinks. This gives adults a lot of conveniences; they do not have to prepare anything to bring to the stadiums, only go to the stadium and enjoy. And it is such a relaxing time for them to drink with friends or their family while enjoying their favorite sport at the same time and in a great atmosphere. Sometimes, spectators can have chances to listen to live music by pop stars or attend mini games between the halves, such as playing soccer with mascots or a lottery.

4   Second, there is nowhere better for fans than a stadium to cheer for their favorite teams. It is where fans can express all their love to the team without concerning anyone around. In fact, one of the inconveniences people have to face when watching soccer at home or in a small area like coffee shops is, most times, they have to lower their excitement since it may disturb others. For instance, a husband cannot shout loudly to support his team while his child is sleeping or his wife is reading. However, he is able to act like that comfortably at stadiums, where everyone around also shouts loudly almost the entire match.

5   Also there, people sing traditional songs the whole match, create "human waves" together, or express their support through traditional ways like scarfing. Indeed, a stadium is the only place they are able to do those activities because, usually, nowhere else has sufficient conditions, such as the number of people, available space, or the lively atmosphere. Even with someone who is not energetic or open-minded, they would find a great place to unleash and express their inside passion since everyone else becomes crazier than usual. In short, there is no barrier between people and people in stadiums, only a common love for soccer.

6   Moreover, people going to soccer stadiums may meet many bigger fans, who can flame the enthusiasm and love inside them. They may be sexy cheerleaders, who are able to bring fans joy and hopes even when their team is losing. They may be a band who creates an exciting space with optimistic drumbeats and melodies. They may also be a fan club who cheers and shouts tirelessly the entire match. Or they may just be normal fans, with creative and emotional ways of expressing love. For example, one may bring a big national flag to their national match, and then the flag is moved hand to hand around the stadium stands. It spreads pride not only to fans but also to players on the field. Everyone loves being a part of such a great community.

7   And, of course, everyone loves wins and celebrations. Definitely, the greatest moments in a match is when it comes to a goal. The stadium explodes; fans go crazy; noises overwhelm everything else at that moment. There will be nothing inside stadiums that can stop fans' high feeling; they could express it in any way: jumping around, crying, or even hugging strangers; they could unleash their deep

emotions without any worry in mind. Although these actions may attract weird looks from other people if they happen in another space, they become strangely normal at a stadium. People may imagine them vaguely when watching soccer on TV but experiencing them directly in stadium stands always brings fans great and hard-to-describe feelings. Furthermore, it is a lot better if we have many others around to share our happiness and do not feel alone when we are the most excited. In those moments, even strangers may look like the closest friends ever. It would be a little bit disappointing and shameful if one celebrates crazily in a coffee shop and then realizes everyone else is sitting calmly and staring at him.

8   Third, people go to stadiums to enjoy and immerse in a real soccer atmosphere, from real players, real fields, and real views. TV, although they have plenty of considerable developments recently, never is able to bring spectators the most genuine views like watching from the stadium stand. And it is not only watching; fans may feel like they are participating in the real match. "Shoot," "Pass," "Go back!" are some instructions that make us think about the coach; however, in a stadium, those mostly come from the stands, where fans become coaches in their imagination. In controversial situations like handballs or penalties, they even argue more drastically than players and coaches on the field. All the time, they share the feeling and moments with players. Imagine a player standing in front of a penalty shot: everyone would stop breathing and silently watch every one of his steps. They feel the same pressure as the player at that time. It is something that watching soccer on TV cannot bring completely to fans, a real feeling of attending a real match.

9   Some fans are simpler; they come for their favorite teams or idols. Love for idols is a special affection. Like people going to music concerts for their favorite singers, going to a soccer stadium is the best way for soccer fans to express their love and send their energies to players. For these fans, witnessing their players play with the ball and perform their playstyle is a great honor and happiness. It is even greater if they can share big moments, like a big goal or an important win with their idols. And with long-time fans, going to stadiums has become their habit and an important part of their weekends. It is like one who loves watching *American Ninja Warrior*, so he or she will schedule other activities around the show hours weekly. And it would be quite disappointing and strange if the show is not broadcast one week. Soccer fans feel the exact same way if they cannot go to the stadium on game day.

10   Soccer, naturally, is still a normal hobby, and everyone has the right to choose their best way to enjoy it. The fact that non-soccer lovers find going to stadium weird is very similar to the situation that men cannot understand why their wives

waste a lot of time in shopping centers. As engaging as other hobbies, watching soccer at stadiums brings people joys, beautiful moments, and special feelings. Although fans now may have more and more convenient choices to watch a soccer match, there is still nowhere more appropriate to watch it than in a soccer stadium.

For Consideration:

1. Le uses parallelism and repetition in this essay to good effect. In two or three paragraphs, analyze several examples of these methods, explaining why they strengthen the essay and draw the reader's attention.

2. As mentioned in this essay's headnote, Le is an international student from Viet Nam. On your own or with a partner, explain how much of what he describes is particular to the Vietnamese experience of soccer and how much can be seen in the behavior of various sports' fans around the United States.

3. The tone of Le's essay is more informal than is usually acceptable for academic essays. Explain how the tone for this essay either benefits or detracts from its purpose. Make sure you give specific examples to support your claims.

For ESL Consideration:

1. Le's introduction is not a typical introduction for an academic paper, yet it fulfills all the requirements of an introduction (see "Introductory Paragraph Evaluation Exercise" in the Learning Tools section of this text). In one or two paragraphs, explain how Le's introduction accomplishes the goals of an introduction.

2. Although Le's introduction grabs the reader's attention, the conclusion contains elements that are stereotypical, and some might say sexist. On your own or with a partner, re-read Le's essay and then fashion a new conclusion to avoid these drawbacks.

The United States has been the number one education destination for international Chinese students for several years. Once they arrive, however, how do these students fair in a new environment and new culture? Linda Chen, herself a native of Nanjing, China, explains how the Chinese students' previous education sometimes does not benefit them once they start studying at SMU.

The Effects of Chinese Education on International Chinese Students in the US
Linda Chen

1   Education is a fundamental building block in one's life. From pre-school education all the way to graduate school education, all knowledge will affect people's behaviors, thinking, and perspectives. Moreover, this is a chain reaction because the education one receives a step before impacts largely on the one right after. Therefore, if one receives two educations in two different countries, the first education's impact cannot be eliminated. During the past twenty years, more Chinese international students have decided to come to the US for college education. However, most of them struggle during the first few years because they had received a total different style with Chinese pre-college education. These Chinese students find it hard and stressful to transition smoothly into the new American style college education, and these difficulties affect their well-being and performance on a large scale. Three of the largest and most common effects of a Chinese pre-college education on Chinese international students in the US are lack of creativity, the idea that one exam determines all, and not seeing all classes equally.

2   One of the first effects that the Chinese education has on the international Chinese students is that those students lack creativity. In China, education is more like a "monopoly." The only correct person in the classroom is the teacher, and he or she has the one and only legitimate answer to all the questions. In a traditional Chinese classroom setting, it is only the teacher that delivers the lecture to the students for all 40 minutes. There is seldom or literally no discussion time during the class period, and students are forced to listen carefully and be quiet at all times. Every time a question is thrown out to the class, the teacher is looking for only one right answer. If the students' answer does not include that specific word or phrase, they are wrong even if they convey a similar idea. Moreover, if students did give the specific word or phrase in the correct answer, extended answers are not allowed. Students can answer only what is asked in the question, and any

other extended ideas related to the question asked can make the whole answer wrong.

3   Therefore, most Chinese students studying abroad lack creativity and cannot figure out knowledge on their own, and these defects from their previous education strongly affect their educational well-being in America. Memorization is the way that Chinese students learnt to study back home. They can memorize math formulas and definitions fairly well. However, this way of studying knowledge affects those students negatively in the US when American education prefers different approaches to a concept or question rather than a single memorization. International Chinese students cannot receive and process their knowledge well in the US classroom settings if professors here only give general ideas. They are used to being given answers rather than figuring out by themselves using creative and extended thinking. This is why Chinese students cannot do group discussion or activities easily. Lastly, most international Chinese students find it hard at first to write English essays because in an American college, essays require all kinds of creative thinking toward a topic. Usually, an essay topic will have at least three arguments and many concrete details to support. However, this does not match the Chinese students' way of thinking that one topic can have only one argument. Compared to the American students that approach questions from all perspectives, Chinese students studying abroad become more single-minded and inflexible. Thus, they still need to practice on how to build several creative answers into a strong persuasive essay.

4   The second effect that the Chinese education has on the international Chinese students is the idea of one determines all. In the Chinese educational system, a student's final grade in a class is determined by a single exam at the end of the school year that covers all materials. Even though teachers still assign pop quizzes and homework throughout the year, those grades do not count at all in students' final reports. Therefore, the final exam is the one and only chance to see how a Chinese student performs during the year. If they ace the exam, then students get an A; if not, then students fail the class. This makes Chinese students cram only for the last exam and try less or not at all during regular class time. However, in all American colleges, students' grade reports consist of so much more than just the final exam. Professors grade students on their attendance, quiz and homework grades, chapter tests, and then the final exam. Also, final exams in American colleges are not big percentages of the grade, and they are mostly 50 to 60 percent. This kind of system makes American college students try throughout the year and do every class assignment carefully.

5   Therefore, American colleges expect Chinese students that come here to study to do the same. Unfortunately, many international Chinese students still bring this idea of one determines all with them to their US colleges, and this causes them to perform less ideally in academics in regard their abilities. Most Chinese students in the US try less on pop quizzes and homework, and this causes their grades to drop unnecessarily. Also, since Chinese students care less about regular quizzes and homework, they cannot get enough practice on the knowledge taught in class. In the US, college professors only teach the ideas of the knowledge, getting hands on and familiar with the knowledge is the students' own responsibilities. Thus, a lot of Chinese students studying abroad are not responsible for their own knowledge and grades.

6   Lastly, most Chinese students still end up receiving a non-ideal grade even if they cram hard before the final exam. These students usually stay up all night to cram, and it is a less effective way to learn knowledge because the process is tiring. Moreover, a regular US college course requires seven to eight hours outside classroom time to review. Thus, the Chinese students' cramming time cannot compare to the time supposed to be spent on homework and quizzes. The cramming process can be said to be useless and cannot contribute to those students' grades.

7   The last effect that the Chinese education has on the international Chinese students studying in America is that it makes those students not see all classes equally. The Chinese educational system divides classes into "big" class and "small" class. Classes are considered "big" if they are literature and science based. For example, math, physics, and biology are included in the big classes. On the other hand, "small" classes are art and social based classes like drawing, music, and social studies. In China, big classes are the more important classes, and they compose a great percentage of students' GPAs. On the other hand, small classes compose less than 10% or even none of the GPA. Therefore, most Chinese students care about and try less on small classes. Not only do students care less, big class teachers sometimes do not even respect the small classes. When it is the midterm season, big class teachers will "borrow" the small classes and teach a big class or give out practice exams during that time. Thus, Chinese students do not even get full time in the art and social based classes.

8   The above, therefore, contributes to the Chinese students not viewing all classes equally when they come to study in the US. In an American college, all classes are viewed equally. They compose the same percent of GPA, and they get the same time for lecturing and reviewing. Yet because of Chinese students' old ideas, the students care less about the classes they categorized as small. Most Chinese

students do not even attend small classes because they think they are worthless. This makes international Chinese students' GPAs drop and gives them a hard time that could be avoided easily. Moreover, not attending these small classes will have a negative impact on Chinese students' overall development and even opportunities to find a job. American companies value well-rounded job seekers. Those kinds of people are good in every field of study, really flexible with their knowledge, and are well developed overall. Losing the chance to get knowledge and information in those small classes will make Chinese students inflexible and think simply and have fewer opportunities to find a job in America.

9   The differences between a Chinese pre-college education and American education are huge, and these differences affect international Chinese students largely when they first come to the United States. However, being aware and noticing these differences can help students better transition into the new American college life. Chinese students should be willing to try to adapt to the new education style in order to receive full benefits of what a US college has to offer. This will help the international Chinese students achieve good grades and success later in the workforce.

For Consideration:

1. Although a causal analysis focusing on the effects of their previous education on Chinese students' experiences at SMU, Chen also incorporates elements of comparison into her essay. Re-read each of her arguments and explain how the comparison between Chinese teaching methods and American teaching methods helps to clarify the effects her essay focuses on.

2. Chen mentions that Chinese students see their classes as either "big" (important to their overall GPAs) or "small" (of little importance or irrelevant to their GPAs). In two or three well-written paragraphs, explain how students in the United States reflect this attitude or one similar regarding liberal arts classes. Remember to give specific examples and details to support your points.

3. Chen states that Chinese students must answer their teachers' questions exactly and "extended answers are not allowed." Reflect on your own high school experience. Were you an AP student? Were you taught how to write AP exams? What were guidelines? In a comparison/contrast of your own, explain the similarities and differences between what Chen describes and what American students are "taught" to score well on placement tests.

For ESL Consideration:

1. Did you have an educational experience similar to the one Chen describes? What was similar? What was different? How do Chen's examples and details match your own reflections and memories?

2. If you had educational experiences similar to the ones Chen describes in her essay, do you agree with her conclusion? Are these teaching methods detrimental to students once they arrive in the United States for study? Why? Just as Chen gives details and examples to support her main arguments, supply your own.

3. After reading Chen's essay, reflect on your own experiences here at SMU. If you have been having difficulties, what will you now do to address those? If you have not been facing difficulties, what will you do to continue your success?

LEARNING TOOLS

In this section, you will find a trove of everything from specific aspects of the writing process to constructing an oral presentation. Our faculty have shared these proven-successful tools to help you create your best work.

From VANESSA HOPPER

Writing at the University: Insight and Advice from a Professor Who Cares

On Reading (Don't skip this section! The more effectively you read, the more effectively you will write!):

Have you ever been told that you need to "go deeper" when analyzing a text? If so, you probably need to work on your critical reading skills. Look beyond the mere plot/surface details; read for what is *implied*. Critical reading is about *excavating*. Consider not only a word's denotations but its connotations. Read "between the lines" to dig out the author's agenda. Be a detective. Consider figures of speech as clues to what the author wants you to get out of the reading. Note not only what is present and what is stated, but what is missing and what is left unsaid. What is not there is often just as relevant as what is there. If you are analyzing a work of fiction, consider the possible significance of nuances like names, colors, locations, dates, and times. Begin your critical reading with the title. Titles can cleverly foreshadow what's coming. The gender of the author and the era in which the piece was written may also be important to determining meaning and function. If a text has a prologue or a headnote, don't skip it: it was placed ahead of the text for a reason and may have clues or background information to help you understand the reading.

. . . and BY ALL MEANS: Take notes in class if there is a discussion on a text! When your professor directs a discussion, he or she will ask specific questions and lead you deliberately in directions that will help you grasp the deeper meaning therein. Writing down what goes on during discussions will create a record of insights and observations to study and/or use as a starting point of preparation for writing about that text later on.

On Creating an Essay:

When you receive a writing assignment, read it actively. Make sure you understand its challenges: What, exactly, is the professor requiring of you? At the university, you don't have free rein to write whatever you feel like writing about—not for a class, anyway (That's what journals are for). Professors design writing assignments to challenge you in particular ways. Practice discipline, making sure that you keep the ultimate goal of a writing assignment in mind at all times. Trust me—this does not mean you must sacrifice your own voice. You can still be original and interesting while working within the bounds of your assignments.

Were you forbidden to use first person in your high school writing classes? There are writing situations when doing so can be beneficial. In my Discernment and Discourse classes, students' opinions and life experiences are always relevant; <u>your "I" is of critical importance</u>, and you may certainly use first person in your writing if it will strengthen your ethos (this is defined in a separate article) and contribute to an argument or interpretation. I **want** you to think about your reactions—to consider your relationship with the material you encounter and what that relationship says about you as a person.

That said, this approach will not be relevant to or acceptable for every single college writing situation. Use your judgment. If you are ever unsure if a professor might have a problem with your use of first person for an assignment, simply ask him or her, explain why/how using first person might contribute to your project, then accept his or her decision on the matter.

When you are writing an essay, you always have a responsibility to communicate clearly and articulately what you think and know, and you also have a responsibility to engage the reader. <u>If you stifle your "voice," your writing may be unoriginal and uninteresting</u>. Be prepared to tailor your "self" to accommodate various types of assignments and levels of expectation.

When writing an essay, <u>maintain appropriate tone and content</u> for your audience. In this course, your audience is made up of me and your academic peers who are familiar with the work you will be writing about. This means that no summary will be necessary when you begin an analysis of a text. You should use medium to formal language (avoid clichés, slang, colloquialisms, and conversational speech which may include features that are unacceptable in academic writing, such as run-ons and sentence fragments). In some scholarly writing, professors will require a strictly formal tone, and you might be asked to write for a general audience who is wholly unfamiliar with your subject matter. If you aren't sure of a professor's stance on tone or audience, just ask.

<u>Writing is a process</u>. Prepare to write more than one draft and revise methodically, actively scrutinizing your essay to improve it. Realize that you will have to rewrite passages, move bits and chunks of writing around, add, and delete during the revision process. Revision is part of good writing for every writer.

An essay should be **unified and coherent**. Your writer's handbook will elaborate on these terms. If you aren't sure how to properly select, cite, or integrate quotations, your handbook will enlighten you. It includes myriad legal methods for modifying quotations to do anything from cut out unneeded information to help a quotation fit grammatically with your own language.

<u>Make sure that your **introduction** and **conclusion** serve the appropriate functions for a sophisticated essay</u>. In addition to featuring a strong thesis, your introduction should include a hook: an engaging lead-in designed to provoke your audience's interest and give your essay individuality. Your conclusion should never merely summarize what you've said in the essay. Where a brief summary of points covered in the body might be useful at the end of a long and complicated essay, summary is unnecessary at the end of a short essay and should <u>never</u> be the only component of a conclusion: a conclusion should actually *draw conclusions* and offer closure. If you are at a loss as to how to conclude an essay, brainstorm through the following questions and mine through your responses for gems that may be compelling:

- What did I learn from this project?
- What might others learn from contemplating this text or these issues?
- How and why is this material relevant today?
- Does this material have bearing on any of *my* communities (school, neighborhood, state, nation, etc.)?
- What are the far-reaching implications of this material or these issues?
- Do I have any relevant personal relationships with the material that others might benefit from understanding (gender, race, class, firsthand experience/observation, etc.)?

(Hint: The list of questions above can also be useful for brainstorming lead-in material for your introduction.)

<u>Utilize resources</u>. Conference with your professors if they make such opportunities available. Visit tutors for help when needed if they are available. Utilize reference books like your style manual. Engage in ethical peer evaluations in class if required and, if possible, on your own time. Form study groups and talk about the material you are encountering in your classes: this can be more helpful than you might imagine.

On Essay Grades:

Writing is a skill and an art. Some are born with a natural talent for writing, but even they must work hard to create an excellent final product. Those who were not born with a talent for the art of writing can still produce excellent work: but it isn't going to happen overnight, and it will take dedication.

Producing an essay is nothing at all like studying for a multiple-choice test. Writing isn't about memorizing and proving mastery of facts or formulas. Students regularly ask me what they can do in order to guarantee an A on an essay, specifically in my class. The truth is that there isn't a magic formula, precisely *because* writing is a skill and an art.

There are, however, certain steps you can take to increase the likelihood of writing a successful essay. For every assignment, consider the directions and the language of the prompt with great care, making sure that you do exactly what the professor is asking of you. If you have the opportunity to visit a professor for a conference, don't miss that opportunity. If your professor makes clear that evidence from the text, quotations from the text, original critical thinking, or some other specified component must be present in the essay for it to qualify as excellent work, naturally you should strive for that. Of course, you should always edit carefully for technical correctness, select your diction painstakingly, and heed all formatting requirements. Your many years of education thus far should've given you a strong sense of your writing weaknesses on a technical level: *Do you have only the vaguest sense of when to use a comma vs. a semi-colon? Are misplaced or dangling modifiers a problem for you? Do your pronouns and antecedents fail to agree? Are you guilty of sentence fragments or run-ons and have no idea why?* Your professor required you to purchase a writer's handbook for many reasons: waste no time getting started reviewing rules of grammar and punctuation that you should've mastered long ago but didn't. Your handbook will also have guidelines for not only MLA formatting (which your Discernment and Discourse professor will require) but for many other documentation methods you may be asked to utilize in other courses.

Here is the bottom line: Earning a particular grade on an essay (be it an A, B, C, D, or F) is never a guarantee that you will duplicate that grade on a subsequent essay. Why? Because each assignment provides a new and different challenge, and each time you're hit with an assignment you have other responsibilities and distractions in your own life. So many factors—the nature of the assignment, your health, your work load in other classes, etc.—affect the outcome of any project. The many variables make it impossible to guarantee the same level of performance every time. When you take on any essay assignment, here is what's important: (a) Stretch your brain, put in the necessary time and work, and do your 100% best—if that's the case, you should never be ashamed of any grade, whatever it may be. (b) Learn from your mistakes.

From JOAN ARBERY

Some Chronic Essay Issues

THESIS STATEMENTS: A thesis should be argumentative—not descriptive, not factual, not ambivalent, but rhetorical.

- A thesis should:
  —be both interpretive and persuasive
  —make a claim that matters/picks a fight.

- Normally, thesis statements are[*]:
  —cause/effect
  —proposal
  —definition
  —evaluative

[*]See "What Is a Thesis" section for greater depth regarding these kinds of arguments

TOPIC SENTENCES/CLINCHERS:

- Topic sentences should not just relate to topical points or to specific details but should show what the argument of the body paragraph is both at the beginning and end: How is the argument developing here? Why? Where are you headed? Why?

- As you conclude the body paragraph, reiterate what you were hoping to prove. In short, avoid ending a body paragraph on a transition to the next body paragraph. Instead, wrap up the main theme of the body paragraph proper. That's called a clincher because it sews up, ties back together, and clinches the top and bottom of the paragraph together.

EVIDENCE: To defend your argument, you need evidence.

- Evidence-based arguing means directly citing, be it from an essay, chapter, book, film, or any other source material. You can't analyze evidence well if you only paraphrase and summarize. Especially when you are dealing with literary analysis, you want quotations to prove your points. Many textbooks might recommend summarizing and paraphrasing evidence specifically as regards research documents, but a strong research paper still incorporates and interprets direct evidence. Here's more on how to do that.

- In citing, don't call attention to quotations or lines (e.g., *This quote says . . .* or *This line from Shakespeare's sonnet means . . .*).
- Instead, if you've just quoted, write something that refers to the action being described, the idea being relayed, or the thought being conveyed within the passage:

    —Here, Orwell articulates the problem of power . . .
    —In making this comment, Winston proves that . . .
    —When Wiesler says, "You are a great artist," he helps Christa Maria see that she does not need to rely on . . .

- When you include a quotation, you must contextualize and embed it. Do not leave it dangling (i.e., with nothing to introduce it or nothing to conclude it). To frame a quotation, you can use signal phrases, or you can embed the phrase within your own sentence:

    —Orwell writes, ". . . . ." (#).
    —When situating Winston's predicament as a watched man, Orwell carefully creates the illusion of security only to dismantle it, as when Winston thinks that ". . . . ." (#).
    —In speaking to Julia, Winston remarks that ". . . . ." (#).
    —". . . . .," says Winston to Julia (#).
    —Yet even as Winston remarks that ". . . . ." (#), he still indicates that power is . . .

- After you have included your quotation, interpret and then analyze it.

    —Tell me how you interpret the passage rather than restating what the quotation means. You can do so by saying things like:

    - What I take X to mean here is . . .
    - X's point here seems to be . . .
    - To my mind, X's ideas suggest the following . . .
    - Essentially, X's claim here is . . .

    —Tell me how you analyze the passage by relating the quotation both to the body paragraph's topic and to the larger argument that topic sentence entails. This action differs from interpretation in that you are showing how your interpreted source information now applies to your own argument. See the section "Using Your Voice" to get a better sense of how to show how you are analyzing something.

TRANSITIONAL PHRASES:

- Transitions are necessary from one sentence to the next. Failure to transition from one sentence's content to the next one forces me to pick up the missing logical pieces. Use words like *yet, nevertheless, despite, instead of, at the same time as, by the same token, furthermore, additionally, moreover, on that note, that said, however, in contrast to, as opposed to, for example, for instance, to elaborate, to clarify, to illustrate, further to my point, first, second, third*, etc. These little words act as the segues from one idea to the next.

- Transitions are also very necessary between paragraphs. However, transitions are not just words/phrases. Between paragraphs, every transition should act both thematically and argumentatively. That is, transitions should not lose your argument's focus. You want to move logically from one theme or topic to the next. Thus, if you're raising a counterargument as you transition, include that fact: *Contrary to what I've just argued, I now want to raise the question of…*

- As a rule of thumb, keep topical transitions to the beginning of a new body paragraph, not at the end of the last one. That way, you don't confuse your reader about what the body paragraph's main point has been.

RUN-ONS/FRAGMENTS/COMMA SPLICES:

- If two independent clauses come together with no terminal punctuation separating them whatsoever, that's a run-on.

- If a sentence is incomplete, that's a fragment.

- If a comma is trying to do the work of a period or semicolon, that's a comma splice.

- See the "Basics: Some Conventions of Correct Writing" in the Appendix for examples.

VAGUE *THIS*: Show what the antecedent before *this* is.

- To correct the earlier sentence: "The pronoun *this* can often be confusing: it can point to any number of words within earlier sentences, let alone the one in which it actually figures."

- For such reasons, if *this* or *it* frequently appears within a paper, that pronoun prevents you from carrying your major points over, which prevents you from transitioning logically from one idea to the next.

- Thus, always clarify what *this* refers to by adding the noun, concept, or idea it points back to.

STYLISTIC HELP:

- Avoid expletive construction and *to be* verbs.
    - **EXAMPLE:** There is a dog running down the road who is panting. He is thirsty.
    - **REVISED:** The panting dog running down the road is thirsty.
    - **OR:** Thirsty and panting, the dog runs down the road.
- Avoid passive voice.
    - **EXAMPLE:** The cake was made by the baker, and the frosting was put on by the designer.
    - **REVISED**: The baker made the cake, and the designer frosted it.
- Use compound (use *for, and, nor, but, or, yet, so*), complex (use subordinating conjunctions), or compound complex sentences (use both coordinating and subordinating conjunctions).
    - **EXAMPLE:** This sentence is simple. (One independent clause comprised of subject, verb, and object.)
    - **EXAMPLE:** This sentence is no longer simple, for it uses two clauses. (Two independent clauses separated by a coordinating conjunction.)
    - **EXAMPLE:** This sentence, because it uses *because*, is now complex. (An independent clause that uses a subordinating conjunction to signal a dependent clause.)
    - **EXAMPLE:** This sentence takes on both a compound and a complex nature because it uses *because*, and it becomes compound and complex with the use of *and* between the two clauses. (Two independent clauses linked by a coordinating conjunction as well as a subordinating conjunction signaling a dependent clause.)
- Use appositives: these add another noun or group of words to help combine sentences.
    - **EXAMPLE:** The man was sad; he was lonely; and he was tired, but he was still full of hope.
    - **REVISED:** Sad, lonely, and tired, the man was still hopeful.
    - **EXAMPLE:** The woman was a professor at SMU; she taught in the physics department; she specialized in astronomy.
    - **REVISED:** A professor of astrophysics, the woman taught at SMU.

- Use participial phrases: these phrases provide action to your sentence and cut down on wordiness.
    - **—Example:** The monster was eating the stinky cheese, and it became smelly as well as scary.
    - **—Revised:** Eating stinky cheese, the monster became both smelly and scary.

WORKS CITED

- In 2016, MLA style changed. *Easy Writer* tells you exactly what to do for citations.

- You are responsible for figuring out how to cite according to MLA. In general, Works Cited pages should not take more than ten to fifteen minutes. Doing them correctly is an easy way to get a 90–100 on that section of your paper.

- Often, a student's in-text citations and works cited page give a general indication of the quality of the whole essay.

- On that note, using MLA format—headers with a page number, heading, and titles—all indicate a similar rigor and attention to detail. Do those things well so surface technicalities do not distract from the essay's content.

From JOAN ARBERY

What Is a Thesis?

It is not a statement of fact: Mary Shelley wrote *Frankenstein*.

It is not a list of various subtopics: In *Blade Runner*, the replicants show they are human by their feelings, their fight, and their speeches.

It is not a weak assertion: Because candy tastes good, young children get too many cavities.

It is not a half-hearted attempt at picking a fight: Greek life is the only life—anyone else can shove it.

What is it? It's what keeps you on course, guided in a single direction, not without peril and possible attack, but always ready at the helm to steer your reader along. All of the parts of your paper are responsible to that thesis. To use a different analogy, it's like the electric socket: all the parts of your paper plug into it. Your introduction guides with a hooking metaphor, followed by your claim, your topic sentences, your evidence, your analysis, your clinchers, your conclusion. At any given point, your reader should be able to plug that information back into the socket without facing electrocution.

Let's go back to those four bad thesis statements and expand on them (don't think thesis statements need to be one sentence. They can be an extended argument).

1. Published in 1818, Mary Shelley's *Frankenstein* might be the most important work ever written on artificial intelligence. If so, then we should ask ourselves why the Enlightenment, the late industrial revolution, and the romantic period spawned a monster that has yet to lay in peace. If we answer that question, we will have found the solution to our worst fears regarding the AI explosion.
2. Because their feelings, fight, and force show them to be far more concerned about what human life means than any of the film's actual humans, *Blade Runner*'s replicants prove that they are indeed "more human than human." In short, the replicants deserve more respect than Scott's humans do.
3. The peddling of Willy Wonka-like sweets in every grocery store, with the checkout lane a cornucopia of various chewy, sweet and sour, succulent candies, speaks to the American Dental Association's vast concern with childhood cavities. Far from being something that just falls out by the time they're seven, children's teeth set up a lifetime of good or bad dental hygiene. Since the candy corporations have an

incentive in marketing their products to kids at a young age, I would argue they're the main culprit in kids' cavities. They should front the bill when kids get cavities.
4. Recently, Harvard decided to prevent students belonging to supper clubs or certain Greek life institutions from nomination to leadership positions. This non-admittance is like the old fear that Freemasons were members of a "secret" order. Don't get me wrong; I'm not saying Greek life doesn't have its downsides, of which I'll speak later. But I am arguing that a university shouldn't impugn a whole part of its social fabric—or, if it does so, it first has to explain why Greek membership excludes one from leadership. For, far from what Harvard conveys, I would claim that to be Greek is to be most like a leader.

Those might be somewhat longwinded arguments, but they all fall under the four most common kinds of arguments you're bound to make:

> A proposal argument: we should, we must, we ought to, I propose, the solution is . . .
>
> An evaluation argument: better than, worse than, is more, is less, the best, the worst (compare/contrast)
>
> Cause/effect: because, is the result of, effected by
>
> Definition argument: is, comprises

The four I've outlined above fall within these four categories.

Back to what is a thesis? It's not just what the paper's about or what it's trying to aim at occasionally. It's what the whole paper's purpose rests upon. Every time you're thinking to yourself, "Man, I'm getting a little lost here. What am I writing about again?," you go back to that thesis and you plug yourself back into it.

That should matter to you because you don't want to get lost, and it matters to your reader, who is more often than not your grader, because you don't want him/her to get lost in the thicket.

Weak theses tend to start to develop warts and outcrops pretty quickly. Strong thesis statements, ones where you've really developed your standpoint and know at every turn what you want to say, help you see the overview of your argument quickly. Back to Thesis 4, for example. With it as your argument, you can quickly see the shape of your paper, where you'll:

- Maybe have three body paragraphs really trying to prove that Greek life is much better than Harvard claims;

- Then play the naysayer and really try to see the other side's perspective about why they think Greeks can't be leaders;
- Then turn around and concede a small point, but then spend two more paragraphs and knock that argument out of the park with evidence as to why Greek life makes leaders again.

In short, a strong thesis makes it hard to sink your ship.

From LEEANN DERDEYN

A Good *BET*: Forming the Thesis

A friend of mine recounts his early days at UC-Berkeley. When writing papers, he was frustrated with how much time he had to spend coming up with a genuinely arguable thesis. He wanted to come up with a quick-and-dirty formula to make his life easier. Since he was a philosophy major, and a prodigy, he discovered he could use the basic format of a Hegelian argument (thesis, antithesis, synthesis) to create a formula usable across many disciplines. He called his discovery "B-'s Emergency Thesis."[*] I've christened it *BET* because it is the best BET for finding the necessary components of a successful thesis. It goes something like this: "It might seem like *X*, yet *a*, *b*, *c*. Therefore, *Y*."

Since I am neither a philosophy major nor a prodigy, I'm happy to use and teach my friend's discovery to students who are usually not philosophy majors or prodigies either. Everyone knows that a thesis should be arguable, debatable, controversial, intriguing, surprising, and risk-taking, right? But how do you find that? Often you don't, and you're writing about something obvious in the plot. You end up with a literary review or a plot synopsis, something descriptive, but neither expository nor analytical, with very little of your own thinking shown in the process.

I'll give you an example of *BET*, but let me first take you through the process. *BET* starts with a broad, generally accepted *X* claim: *it might seem like* . . . If the *X* claim is not broadly acceptable, it won't work. If the *X* claim is an argument you think you want to write about and is obviously just thrown out there, it won't work. That's a logical fallacy called the *strawman* argument—a *faux* opponent is set up so it can easily be knocked down with no risk.

After a broadly acceptable premise is achieved, the *a-b-c* counter-arguments come next. There are three of them because several thousand years ago, Aristotle illustrated that three points make a sufficiently convincing argument (my friend knows his philosophy). These *a-b-c* counter-arguments should have an obvious connection to the *X* claim, but they should not be examples of *X*. These counter-examples should also not entirely negate or refute the broadly acceptable *X*. If it's that easy to find three things that completely refute *X*, then *X* can't be that broadly acceptable to begin with. The *a-b-c* should expose hesitations or modify, amend, nuance, or refine *X*. They should raise questions. They should make you, the writer, think differently about *X* and make your reader ponder it. Then comes the real thing. The "Therefore, *Y*" synthesis brings

---

[*] My friend modestly wishes to remain anonymous.

the broad *X* claim and the *a-b-c* amendments into conversation in a not-quite-so-obvious blended claim—or even a not-at-all-obvious blended claim—that now will take you the length of the essay.

However, what often happens in initial efforts (especially before a student masters the logic of the form) is that *Y* turns out to be the broadly acceptable claim because what's fairly easy to see is what students often think they want to argue. This won't work, but it is what most theses look like, and a major cause of shallow, surface-level expository papers that masquerade as literary analysis (or historical analysis, or philosophical analysis, or social sciences, or advertising, communications, law, and even the sciences, but that's another topic). If *Y* is broadly acceptable (i.e., if any intelligent reader of the literary work would already know and see this), then start over. In fact, start there. Make *Y* your new *X* claim and repeat the process, seeing what can be discovered, uncovered, and unmasked. *BET* format often needs tweaking to help with syntax and grammar. If, for instance, the *a-b-c* ideas are not single nouns or short phrases but sentence-length, then they need to be separated. The idea of *a* can be in its own complete sentence, followed by sentences for *b* and *c*—or combined into compound sentences. Remember, though, *Y* is almost always its own sentence.

Still, I promised you an example. I'm going to make it pretty random and simplistic, so the efficacy of *BET* is full pomp and circumstance.

Every good essay starts with an intriguing title that does some work for the essay: the title of my essay is "Pokémon GO-ldilocks." Good essays also begin with hooks or broad introductory sentences and then introduce the authors and works (or concepts, or issues, or products) the essay will address before transitioning into the thesis, but I'm not covering these topics, so pretend I've already done these, and now I'm ready for *BET*.

Here's my *X* claim: "It may seem like *Pokémon GO* and *Goldilocks and the Three Bears* have nothing in common." Hopefully, readers concur that my *X* is broadly acceptable: the summer 2016 mega-hit augmented reality game and the Mother Goose children's fairytale don't in any immediately perceptible way easily link up.

Here are my *a-b-c* claims: Yet, like the key player of the children's tale, Goldilocks, players of *Pokémon* occasionally trespass if they think there's something they want within the boundaries of someone else's property, and both intentionally appropriate other people's property. Additionally, like Goldilocks, *Pokémon* players have tunnel vision about the world around them, blindly putting themselves in harm's way (while I presume my various *Pokémon* points are obvious to those who know the game, I might argue here about Goldilocks that if she stopped and looked around, she would likely have seen signs that she had blithely fallen asleep in a *bears' house*).

My *Y* could be several things, but I've chosen the following: Therefore, while both *Pokémon* players and Goldilocks seem to get what they're looking for in the short term—Porygon, Lapras, and Snorlax or porridge, rocking chair, and feather bed—they both risk their health and welfare following whims.

Both *Pokémon Go* and *Goldilocks and the Three Bears* have sufficient critical coverage out in the real world, so I know I'll be able to find good outside sources to provide grounds for my claims. I've mapped out my arguments, and it's easy to see how I could get a decent four- or five-page paper out of this. I might, in fact, discover a lot of new information about my two primary sources in the process—maybe even more than I wish to know—making new connections in the process. Cultural capital is a good thing (even sometimes pop cultural capital). Although you're likely to be writing about more highbrow topics, I hope you see in this quick gesture how having a plan such as *BET* is a good thing.

From VANESSA HOPPER

Ten Steps to Building the Brightest Essay

STEP 1: UNDERSTANDING your assignment.

If you have any questions—about formatting, source use, style, length, content expectations, or anything else—ask before you get started.

STEP 2: DISCOVERING your focus.

Once you know what is expected, you can get your head in the assignment and start thinking within the necessary parameters.

STEP 3: BRAINSTORMING . . .

which means figuring out what you want to write by doing any of these: unfettered freewriting, creating lists or idea trees, clustering or webbing.

STEP 4: CREATING *YOUR* THESIS: what you will explain, defend, or prove in your essay.

Don't create an outline or begin writing body paragraphs until you have articulated your main idea/goal. (This would be like building a house without measuring your lot, collecting the proper materials, considering logistics, and having carefully thought out the floor plans!)

STEP 5: ORGANIZING your ideas by creating an essay plan or an outline.

Don't just haphazardly dump ideas into paragraphs or your essay will likely have coherence and unity problems; at worst, it will become a stream-of-consciousness mess. (If you had an event to get to in Boston, you wouldn't just set out on the drive from Dallas with only the vaguest sense of which direction to go in! Yes, you might get there eventually, but you'd likely waste a lot of time and gas, and you'd almost certainly miss your event.)

STEP 6: DRAFTING:

- **First—an introduction**.

  It should *engage* the audience with a lead-in/hook, *set the stage*, and *present your thesis*.

See "Introductory Paragraphs Evaluation Exercise" in *Criteria* to be sure your intro has all the components that it should. (Hint: Sometimes the lead-in/hook is easiest to write once you've completed the essay; however, you should never start working on body paragraphs until you have the thesis statement and you've adequately set the stage for what is to come.)

- **Second—body paragraphs**.

  Each should be coherent and controlled by a single main idea, supported with reasons or evidence.

- **Finally—your conclusion**.

  Don't regurgitate your thesis or summarize your main ideas (yawn!): offer satisfying closing remarks that justify your project. If you have problems concluding in interesting and relevant ways, tips are in various places in *Criteria*.

  [Note: Even drafts should be typed and formatted according to your professor's required style guidelines, which are usually determined by discipline.]

STEP 7:   REVISING:

- After a cooling-off period, examine the content (the ideas, organization, and overall delivery) of your own work critically to make sure it flows and is unified.

- Engage, if you can, in an ethical peer evaluation session with another student who is struggling with the same challenges. See *Criteria* for guidelines and follow them carefully.

- If possible, get critical input from a professional: your professor and/or an SMU-employed tutor. Be open to constructive criticism! If your professor offers to conference with you, take him or her up on it and make the most of the opportunity by preparing with "Office Conferences with Your Professor: What to Expect and How to Prepare" in *Criteria*.

- Be prepared to cut material, move material around, and add new material: all of this is part of revision, and revision is a crucial and regularly practiced stage of the writing process for all good writers.

STEP 8: EDITING:

Check carefully, line by line, to make sure you correct all grammatical and mechanical mistakes. Refine your diction so that your word choice is as effective and accurate as possible. Keep in mind that the *Criteria* "Basics" review in the Appendix is there to help you avoid common grammar mistakes. *Easy Writer* has sections for referencing specific rules of grammar and mechanics and style tips.

STEP 9: PROOFREADING:

Assure that your format is correct. Are your margins as they should be? Is your heading constructed as required? Do you need a header or footer? Have you used the proper font and font size, and did you eliminate all typos?

STEP 10: FINALIZING the project:

Do not forget to put a good title on your essay. It should (a) be specific and foreshadow what the essay is about, and (b) be interesting enough to spark your reader's curiosity. Lazy titles like "Essay 1" won't do your credibility any favors. Avoid giving your essay the title of the text you are analyzing because, after all, that title has already been taken: by the author who wrote the original piece! When one thinks about the writing one sees in the world, one can't help but notice that titles are important and serve a vital function. Why would your own essays be an exception to that rule if you are here to hone your real-world communications skills?

Staple your essay. College professors move from classroom to classroom and do not carry office supplies for students to use. Be certain you follow all directions for submission. Not doing so can cost you points. Do not wait until the last minute to have your essay ready for class. Finish it the day (or night) before it is due, and be sure it is in your backpack before you go to bed.

If your professor uses Canvas, give yourself plenty of time to upload your paper before the due date. Again, do not wait until the last minute to upload as you may suffer computer glitches, connectivity problems, or other issues that can make you miss the deadline.

From PAULINE T. NEWTON

Newton's Four Laws on Writing

Show little fear. You're afraid to express your opinion for fear this will affect your grade. Shake this notion off. No, you don't want to offend your reader. Yes, you want to consider, carefully, contrasting or supporting opinions. What you have to say (and not just what they say)[1] merits attention.

Forget the five-paragraph essay. Yes, this method enables you to organize your ideas when you're learning to write, and, yes, paying attention to the order and organization of paragraphs and ideas is important. However, think about the magazines and books you read. Do those writers write in five paragraphs? Of course they don't, and neither should you.[2]

Don't tweet sources. You did a research paper in high school, where you learned to find and summarize twenty or more sources. Doing the research is easy. Applying and engaging that research, thoughtfully and scrupulously, is the challenge. Show that you've considered an article carefully; explain your response to the article (which should be relevant to your thesis as a whole). Inserting brief and unsubstantiated quotations won't push your paper toward a convincing effect.

Use your magnifying glass. Look at your chosen text, painting, or play in depth. Rather than studying the work as a whole, choose a small slice. My students write an entire paper on one panel of a graphic novel or a sculpture from the Meadows Museum, using no outside sources.

---

[1] See Gerald T. Graff, Cathy Birkenstein and Russel Durst. *"They Say/I Say": The Moves that Matter in Academic Writing: With Readings.* W.W. Norton, 2009.

[2] For further information on breaking away from the five-paragraph mold: www.thefreelibrary.com/Escape+from+the+5-paragraph+essay:+tired+of+reading+dry,+formulaic...-a0192853542

From VANESSA HOPPER

Aristotle's Proofs of Rhetoric

<u>Always strive for strong logos and ethos in your writing</u>: These are the critical properties of successful argument and of persuasive communication in general. Study the definitions below and use them as guidelines (or create a checklist of your own) for use when you construct an essay or oral presentation.

LOGOS (from the Greek, meaning "word," referring to reason or the rational—as in "logic"): The substance of the argument/essay/speech itself. Your piece has strong logos if

- your thesis is reasonable.
- your piece shows logical thinking and common sense.
- your points are supported reasonably and sufficiently.
- your piece is coherent and unified, articulate, well-organized, and free of mechanical/grammatical errors.

ETHOS (from the Greek, *ethikos*, meaning moral—as in "ethical"): Ethos is about how you communicate your own character and credibility through your writing or oral presentation. Your piece has strong ethos if

- you use a tone that shows you as fair, ethical, and polite.
- you show your opposition respect in spite of your differences.
- you take care not to offend members of your audience.
- you demonstrate authority and credibility with regard to your subject via responsible documentation, the sharing of viable firsthand experience, and/or the use of respectable and reliable outside (re)sources.

PATHOS (from the Greek, alluding to feeling—as in "em*pathy*" or "sym*pathy*") is a deliberate appeal on the part of the writer/presenter to a specific emotion (such as sympathy, anxiety, patriotism, or sentimentality) in the audience. Pathos is usually exercised in the form of examples, narratives, and scenarios deliberately constructed or chosen for their emotional resonance, or the general use of evocative language. Unlike strong logos and ethos, pathos is not a necessary element for the success of every argument/presentation; however, if put to good use in an appropriate situation, it can be quite effective.

From LORI ANN STEPHENS

Note-Taking Techniques

Note-taking is probably the most well-known but least appreciated skill in university classes. Most students don't like to take notes. I know this because I can hear them groaning as they hunch down to retrieve their notebooks. A few years ago, I stumbled across Bruce Ballenger's *The Curious Researcher,* which offers the best (and relatively pain-free) note-taking approaches I've seen in action. When I asked my students to select a note-taking technique and to use it all semester for every reading assignment, the results were remarkable. I noticed a significant improvement in my students' research papers, and my students reported a significant reduction of anxiety in the writing and research process. For both teachers and students, taking good notes is a win-win practice.

So what are "good" notes? Good notes are *thoughtful responses to a text*. Underlining or highlighting a sentence is not note-taking. Jotting a note in the margins is a step better because you're interacting with the sentence in a thoughtful way. Still, when you sit down to write a paper, it's inefficient at best (and maddening at worst) to wade through hundreds of pages, hunting for a brilliant marginal note you scribbled at some point. At least you think it was brilliant. It's all too vague to remember.

Good notes *keep your ideas organized, but allow lateral thinking*. Sometimes you read a sentence that stands out because the content is shocking, because it reinforces your assumptions, or because it points out some nugget of truth or logic you hadn't considered. Good notes allow you to record your initial responses along with the quotation in a format that is easily accessible.

Good notes *significantly reduce the time it takes to craft the first draft* of your paper. Your notes become the fledgling commentary to the sources you quote in your paper. All your parenthetical citations and MLA entries are included in your notes, which reduces the time and stress it takes to create that daunting Works Cited Page.

Finally, good notes help writers *create annotations*, those summaries of sources that not only help contextualize and support your own thesis, but also help prevent plagiarism and "quote-mining" (quoting someone out of context, distorting the original message).

Here are two note-taking techniques, based on Bruce Ballenger's model, that helped my own students research and write their own papers. I've included a few of their notes, the annotations that were written after the notes, and, finally, an excerpt from their final drafts.

First Note-Taking Approach: Considering Sources

Chasitie Brown researched the effects of standardized testing on mental health. Her notes considered each source in three ways: immediate impressions, notable quotations, and thoughtful **ten-minute** reconsideration.

Madus, George, et al. *The Paradoxes of High Stakes Testing: How They Affect Students, Their Parents, Teachers, Principals, Schools, and Society*, Information Age Publishing, Inc., 2009.

Initial Reaction:

What strikes me the most is the close relationship that this former student has with his test grades. I thought it was interesting to witness the way other students viewed their peers who did not test as well.

Quotations to Consider:

"I did well in school and seemed to be peculiarly able to learn what the teacher said—I never mastered a subject, though—and there was the idiotic testimony of those peculiar witnesses, IQ tests: those scores invented me" (Madus 63).

"Those scores were a decisive piece of destiny in that they affected the way people treated you and regarded you; they determined your authority; and if you spoke oddly, they argued in favor of your sanity. But it was as easy to say and there was much evidence that I was stupid, in every way or . . . as my mother said in exasperation, 'in the ways that count'" (Madus 63).

Reconsidering the Source:

The student stating that "test scores invented me" is a strong indicator of the powerful effect that test scores have on students' mental image of themselves. Although he performed well in his classes it was of no measure to his true "intelligence." His inability to achieve high scores on his IQ made him feel less than intelligent. Test scores not only affect the way that students view their own intelligence but also how they are regarded by their peers. The student in this passage said that his test scores influenced how much power or authority his peers gave him. He was regarded as stupid solely because of his test scores. This demonstrates the crucial role that test grades play in shaping the way students view their (and their peers') intelligence. Students who receive low grades on these tests believe they are not intelligent.

Kohn, Alfie. *What Does it Mean to be Well Educated.* Beacon Press, 2004.

Initial Reaction:

I thought it was interesting to note how students are actually being deceived in how intelligent they are based on test scores. Grades do not accurately depict a student's intelligence. I was also interested in the competitive nature of school in the article.

Quotations to Consider:

"SAT scores turned out to be significantly correlated with both the surface and achieving approaches, but not at all with deep approaches" (Kohn 67).

"Grades and tests, at best, will predict future grades and tests. There is good evidence that grades don't predict later-life success, in occupational or intellectual terms" (Kohn 70).

"One series of studies, for example, found that students given numerical grades were significantly less creative than those who received qualitative feedback but no grades" (Kohn 77).

"The same effect is witnessed school wide when kids are not just rated but ranked, sending the message that the point isn't to learn, or even to perform well but to defeat others" (Kohn 79).

Reconsidering the Source:

SAT testing, in particular the verbal section, is just a measure of how well a student can memorize. It does not measure how deeply or intellectually a student can think about a given subject. The students that score lower often believe that they are not intelligent when, in fact, the SAT does not even measure intelligence. While the general consensus in the academic field holds that grades are a determinant factor of success, it is indeed not the case.

The article suggests that students who are numerically graded are less creative than students who are not numerically graded. This supports my claim that students are not driven for the sake of learning but are driven for the sake of performing high grades. It is tragic in my opinion that students who receive lower grades believe that they are less capable of thinking intelligently when, in fact, they are probably more creatively intelligent than the former.

Students are learning how to beat each other in terms of grades rather than actually learning. As a result of this competitive environment, they are now assessing each other on the basis of grades and test scores. Therefore, students who receive low grades and scores will invariably be shunned by their peers as opposed to those students who score high on their grades and scores.

Janz, Julia. *High Stakes Testing: Students in Grade Four through Eight Report Effects of Standardized Testing.* Dissertation. Capella University, 2011, Umi Dissertation Publishing, search.proquest.com/docview/884326317.

Initial Reaction:
What strikes me the most is how mild pressure can increase a student's motivation. I thought it was useful that this quotation was backed up by scientific data, which I need. I was shocked to see the number of young children suffering from anxiety.

Quotations to Consider:
"Studies have shown that although mild pressure can be a useful form of motivation, intense or prolonged pressure was counterproductive to learning and unhealthy for the student" (Janz 6).

"The research showed that the emotional state of students was directly related to their ability to learn" (Janz 7).

"In one study on test anxiety with 200 elementary students, Beidel et al. (1994) found over 40% of the students reported significant anxiety" (Janz 19).

Reconsidering the Source:
This article brings up an issue that opponents of my argument would bring up and refutes it well. Mild pressure is good for students—it motivates them more to pursue higher academic goals. However, it is the intense pressure sprung upon students today that leads to high anxiety and handicaps students' mental health. PET scans show that students' emotions are contingent upon their ability to learn. The correlation here is easy to see: higher scores equate more positive emotional states while lower scores equate to more negative emotional states. Students' emotions being so intertwined with their academic life is a problem. With high-stake testing rampant in the United States, we are bound to breed a generation of students with anxiety issues because they cannot measure up to these standards.

Test anxiety is beginning at an earlier age now. Elementary students are now subjected to the evils of test anxiety. Not only is test anxiety rampant in these young students but over 40% of them are diagnosed with significant anxiety as well. This is a huge problem! We cannot have such small children suffering so immensely for an arbitrary number.

Second Note-Taking Approach: Double-Entry Notes

Kaycee Smith was researching the correlation between violent video games and gun violence. Her notes took the form of Double-Entry:

Vossekuil, B., et al. *The Final Report and Findings of the Safe School Initiative: Implications for the Prevention of School Attacks in the United States*. U.S. Department of Education, U.S. Secret Service, National Threat Assessment Center, 2002, www.secretservice.gov/data/protection/ntac/ssi_final_report.pdf.

Notes from Source	My Response
"However, most attackers showed some history of suicidal attempts or thoughts, or a history of feeling extreme depression or desperation" (30).	This quote demonstrates the prevalence of suicide and depression among a subject pool of 41 attackers. Although they did not share many characteristics, this is one thing in common that many of them did share.
"Although most attackers had not received a formal mental health evaluation or diagnosis, most attackers exhibited a history of suicide attempts or suicidal thoughts at some point prior to their attack (78 percent, n = 32). More than half of the attackers had a documented history of feeling extremely depressed or desperate (61 percent, n = 25)" (31).	These statistics support the quotation above. 78% and 61% are two very large numbers. Also, it's important to remember that these are just the documented thoughts of suicide or feelings of depression. I'm sure that many other attackers were feeling suicidal and depressed as well, but this was not documented. It will be important for my paper to know how prevalent mental illness was among the school shooters.
"Over half of the attackers demonstrated some interest in violence, through movies, video games, books, and other media (59 percent, n = 24)" (31).	Of course not all of the shooters were impacted by media violence, but over half of them were. This will contribute to my paper by demonstrating the depth of exposure that these attackers may have had to media violence, including video games.

Kinkel, Kip. Diary Entry. "Kip's Writing and Statements." *Frontline*, www.pbs.org/wgbh/pages/frontline/shows/kinkel/kip/writings.html.

Notes from Source	**My Response**
"Every single person I know means nothing to me. I hate every person on this earth . . ."	This quote demonstrates the severely depressed and angry state of Kip Kinkel. His violent actions were obviously very planned and predetermined. He had been thinking about this killing for a long time, and even telling friends and teachers about it. Yet, they did nothing.
"I feel I could snap at any moment. I think about it every day. Blowing the school up or just taking the easy way out, and walk into a pep assembly with guns. In either case, people . . . will stop breathing. That is how I will repay all you . . ."	Kinkel is clearly very angry and depressed in all of his comments. His thoughts are really disturbing and troubling to read. I cannot imagine giving someone in this state access to guns or access to video games that allows them to premeditate on their killings and practice their actions repeatedly.
"Oh God, I am so close to killing people. So close."	In the progression of these quotations, Kinkel seems to be getting more and more serious with his threats. I feel like video games would only increase these emotions and the desire to kill people.
(Two images from the article captured by student but not included in this example of note-taking techniques.)	These are two images that Kinkel drew. The bottom one was even on a worksheet that he turned in, and his teacher saw it. These images reflect the mental instability of Kinkel very well. These are not drawings that would come from a sane person. He seems very obsessed with death and violence in all of his statements and drawings. Video games would just give him another source to explore and deepen his fascination with death.

Feldmann, Theodore. "Bipolar Disorder and Violence." *Psychiatric Quarterly Journal,* vol. 72, no. 2, June 2001, pp. 119–129. *Academic Search Complete,* accession number: 11303877.

Notes from Source	My Response
". . . serotonin exhibits inhibitory control over both affective and predatory aggression" (125).	According to this author, serotonin can inhibit the occurrence of aggression, which then as a result inhibits violence. However, I also know that a person with low serotonin levels is likely to be depressed. Therefore, if serotonin levels are low, a person is more likely to be depressed and aggressive. All of the shooters in the school shootings were depressed.
"In general, the greater the number of psychiatric illnesses a given individual has, the greater his or her risk for violence" (126).	All of the shooters in the school shootings had a number of psychiatric illnesses, which increases the likelihood of their violent acts according to this quotation. This statement makes sense because it seems logical that persons with many disorders, such as depression, bipolar disorder, social anxiety, etc., would be less likely to be able to control their emotions and impulses.
"The characteristics of predatory aggression include minimal or absent autonomic arousal. There is no conscious experience of emotion. When violence occurs, it is planned or purposeful violence. Aggressive behaviors take place in the absence of a perceived threat. The behavioral goals of the individual are multi-determined and variable, but generally do not include threat reduction" (123).	This article states that there are two types of aggression: affective aggression and predatory aggression. In relation to my paper, I will be looking at predatory aggression. The violent acts that occur due to predatory aggression are planned; there is no immediate threat or arousal. In the case of the shootings, they were all planned and the shooter was in no immediate danger. Their violence was instead predetermined and purposeful.

Kaycee immediately moved from her notes to her Annotations, which helped her separate her own thoughts and aims from the original thesis or message of the source. Here is her translation of the previous notes into annotations:

(Working) Annotated Works Cited

Feldmann, Theodore. "Bipolar Disorder and Violence." *Psychiatric Quarterly Journal,* vol. 72, no. 2, June 2001, pp. 119–129. *Academic Search Complete,* accession number: 11303877.

> Feldmann argues that there is a strong positive correlation between psychiatric conditions, such as bipolar disorder, and aggression. The distinction between affective aggression and predatory aggression is one of Feldmann's first points. Affective aggression occurs immediately, and it is a reaction to reduce threat (122). Conversely, predatory aggression is planned and there is no immediate threat to the aggressor (123). Either of these two types of aggression can then lead to violent behavior. Feldmann states that "In general, the greater the number of psychiatric illnesses a given individual has, the greater his or her risk for violence" (126). It is important to understand the relationship between any psychiatric condition and violence to help predict the dangerousness of those with a specific psychiatric condition. Many hormones can be linked to violence, but specifically the hormone ". . . serotonin exhibits inhibitory control over both affective and predatory aggression" (125). This source helps me determine that the school shootings were a result of predatory aggression. Additionally, I know that these patients were depressed, which is usually caused by low serotonin levels. This is key because serotonin helps prevent violence.

Kinkel, Kip. Diary Entry. "Kip's Writing and Statements." *Frontline.* www.pbs.org/wgbh/pages/frontline/shows/kinkel/kip/writings.html.

> Kinkel expresses his violent thoughts and severely depressed emotional state through the use of journal entries and drawings. His thoughts initially read, "Every single person I know means nothing to me. I hate every person on this earth. I wish they could all go away. You all make me sick. I wish I was dead" (Kinkel). They then progress to a more violent condition, and he begins making death threats. For example, he writes, "It is clear that no one will help me. Oh God, I am so close to killing people. So close" (Kinkel). I plan to use Kinkel's drawings and quotations in my paper to demonstrate the kind of emotional state that some shooters are in prior to their attack. Then, I will consider the impact that playing video games would have on one in this kind of emotional distress.

Vossekuil, B., et al. *The Final Report and Findings of the Safe School Initiative: Implications for the Prevention of School Attacks in the United States.* U.S. Department of Education, U.S. Secret Service, National Threat Assessment Center, 2002. www.secretservice.gov/data/protection/ntac/ssi_final_report.pdf.

> The U.S. Secret Service and U.S. Department of Education conducted research to determine the average profile for school shooters, and they determined that while there is no "average" profile, many of the shooters did share certain characteristics. Thirty-seven school shootings and 41 shooters were examined for this study. The subjects ranged from age eleven to twenty-one (28). They came from a variety of different ethnicities, family backgrounds, education, and social groups (29–31). Even though there did not seem to be many patterns among these characteristics, the researchers did discover that most attackers had a history of some kind of mental illness. Seventy-eight percent of the shooters showed signs of suicidal thoughts prior to the attack (30). Sixty-one percent of the attackers had ". . . a documented history of feeling extremely depressed or desperate" (30). Additionally, "Over half of the attackers demonstrated some interest in violence, through movies, video games, books, and other media (59 percent, n = 24)" (31). These statistics will contribute to my research because they help give me a clearer picture on the prevalence of mental illnesses and video game exposure among a large group of attackers that were involved in school shootings.

Chasitie's notes and annotations directly benefitted her drafting process. Here, you can see how her notes worked their way into one paragraph of her research paper on testing and mental health:

> Even more disheartening about this issue is that standardized tests do not even accurately depict a student's intelligence. Society convinces our children that high scores on standardized tests equate to intelligence and vice versa. In fact, high scores are needed to gain admission into prestigious universities. Alfie Kohn's *What Does it Mean to be Well Educated?* shows that standardized tests are "significantly correlated with both the surface and achieving approaches, but not at all with deep approaches" (67). The surface and achieving approaches mentioned here refer to shallow thinking. Students employing a surface approach during test-taking look at fragments of articles and fail to make bigger connections. Students with achieving approaches only seek to learn in order to achieve high grades. Therefore, standardized testing only succeeds at measuring a student's ability to recall facts and how effectively a student can employ test-based strategies. What is more startling is how the use of numeric grading serves a

student's creativity. Another study by Kohn demonstrated that "numerical grades were significantly less creative than those who received qualitative feedback but no grades" (77). The arbitrary weight that a grade carries can control the way that students think, thus robbing them of their creativity. The discord between society's beliefs of standardizing testing and grades versus what they actually measure further strains a student's identity. Unfortunately, it is those students who receive the lowest scores and grades who view themselves as unintelligent when perhaps they may remain some of the brightest and most creative students in class.

Kaycee's paper on gun violence also benefitted from her careful note-taking process. Consider the way she introduces Feldmann's original thesis, then synthesized two more sources to provide backing for her own main argument:

> The effects of violent video games are amplified on those with mental illnesses. Dr. Feldmann, from the Department of Psychiatry and Behavioral Sciences at the Louisville School of Medicine, argues that people with mental illnesses, such as antisocial behavior disorder or depression, are predisposed to violence (126). Antisocial behavior disorder, along with the effects mentioned earlier, decreases one's awareness of human rights, depresses their "ability to feel empathy" (Larkin 149),[1] and causes a "lack of remorse for wrong doings" (Larkin 149). Eric displayed many of these characteristics during the shooting, especially considering he laughed and smiled the whole time. He showed no remorse or empathy toward the students and teachers he was firing upon. On the other hand, people with depression, such as Dylan, have low levels of serotonin. This neurotransmitter contributes to the overall well-being and happiness in humans (Myers, "Biology of Mind" 54).[2] Doctors also know that ". . . serotonin exhibits inhibitory control over both affective and predatory aggression" (Feldmann 125). Therefore, those with low serotonin levels are more likely to be depressed and aggressive. Dylan exhibited both of these side effects during the shooting. The impact of playing violent video games on those who are predisposed to violence by their mental illnesses proved to be deadly.

Taking good notes is the short but scenic path from critical thinking to critical writing. It takes a little discipline to make a habit of this note-taking practice, but the long-term benefits are immense and rewarding. Try it on your next paper. You won't be disappointed.

---

1. Larkin, Ralph W. *Comprehending Columbine.* Temple UP, 2007.
2. Myers, David G. "The Biology of Mind." *Psychology.* 10th ed. Worth, 2013, pp. 46–81.

From JOAN ARBERY

Writing with Your Own Voice

Throughout grade school all the way up to graduate school, there's a strong impetus against writing with the first-person pronoun, *I*. Some of the arguments go like this:

- Write objectively. You can't help but be subjective if you're using *I*.
- This is not a memoir. Don't share your touchy-feely stories of personal discovery.
- Your job is to convince with argument—logos—not to emote. What you believe, think, or feel doesn't matter.
- We're not interested in your personal beliefs about God, politics, or the weather.
- Everyone writes in the third person point of view.

I used to ascribe to all of the above, and quite mindlessly, let me add. But then I read Russel Durst, Gerald Graff, and Cathy Birkenstein's invaluable book *They Say, I Say*. One of the first things they disabused me of was the idea that I shouldn't use *I*. In their view, the first person can be a very persuasive, lively way of writing. Indeed, with their helpful set of templates dealing with voicemarkers, naysayers, and metacommentary, I soon learned that using your voice, your *I*, doesn't mean creating a saccharine, puerile paper—it can actually distinguish your paper from the dross and drudgery of many essays. After taking their points to heart, I started seeing and hearing the templates they talked about everywhere. As a result, I've actively encouraged my students, however begrudging and fearful they are about it, to use various forms of *I*, *me*, and *my* in their writing.

Why? Because one of the things that Durst, Graff, and Birkenstein note is that many good writers tend to use *I* both in their written and oral work. I've found that giving a lecture without once referencing myself, my own point of view, and why I think the way I do is like a chef trying to give orders to his sous-chefs and line cooks without explaining why these ingredients are the best ones, what's made him so confident in his recipe, and what he thinks the customer will get out of the eating experience.

Likewise, you want to direct your audience to your point of view. Of course, you want to use evidence but do that with a few little turn signals that show your reader where you want them to go. Borrowing from Durst, Graff, and Birkenstein's own perspective, I would say that using *I* in academic writing is a skill all students need to learn. It does, of course, make writing more personal in the end, but it's not about personalizing so much as persuading.

Let me give a few ways to do it, using Durst, Graff, and Birkenstein as a model:

> What I mean to say here:
>
> Don't get me wrong; I'm not trying to say . . . but I am trying to say . . .
>
> What I understand from X's work is that . . .
>
> In my opinion, much as X is correct, he fails to see why . . . .
>
> To my mind, there's nothing worse than a boiled egg. Here's why my experience proves it:
>
> While the skeptic in me would argue, the idealist in me would say . . .
>
> Even though some would claim that you should call a spade a spade, I would say . . .
>
> Now you might be wondering, how could any reasonable person argue that someone should use *I*? Well, to that I would say, many intelligent people do . . .
>
> Some teachers have argued that using *I* is a weak way of proposing an argument. Lest I offend those teachers, I would respond that failure to engage with your own viewpoint can make writing deadly boring.

All this to say that *I* isn't about how you feel or propounding your belief systems. Rather, it's about showing where you stand and why; using reasoned arguments and evidence to arrive at your conclusions; and actually engaging with your own convictions and claims as you go.

I assure you that it'll make writing far less tedious and much more intentional and engaging for you. That said, always ask your teacher what s/he prefers because you don't want to face the firing squad.

From LORI ANN STEPHENS

The Art of Embedding Quotations

As you begin writing academic papers at the college level, you may hear your professors tell you to embed your quotations, to incorporate outside sources, to introduce all quotations, or to sandwich quotations with commentary. These are all ways to deal with meshing someone else's quotation into your own writing, but what do we mean exactly when we tell you to do this task? This short article will give you a brief introduction to the art of embedding quotations. The following examples will demonstrate ways to incorporate quotations smoothly and logically into your analysis. This essay will not explain how to create a unified, cohesive paragraph, nor will it tell you how to craft substantive analysis; you have a semester of classes to learn and practice those skills. The purpose of this article is to give you the basics of embedding quotations, from simple to more skillful methods.

INEFFECTIVE QUOTING METHODS

Most commonly, instructors see these hazardous kinds of quotations:

Example A: A dropped, or unincorporated, quotation

"He learns to lie, to plot, to conceal his opinions, to pretend, to resort to bluff and braggadocio, in order to carry off the prize of social recognition" (Baldwin 93).

Example B: A comma splice

James Baldwin explains the lengths people go to become popular, "He learns to lie, to plot, to conceal his opinions, to pretend, to resort to bluff and braggadocio, in order to carry off the prize of social recognition" (Baldwin 93).

Example C: A run on

James Baldwin explains the lengths people go to become popular "He learns to lie, to plot, to conceal his opinions, to pretend, to resort to bluff and braggadocio, in order to carry off the prize of social recognition" (Baldwin 93).

In Example A, the readers get lost quickly. They don't know who wrote this information until they get to the end of the sentence, they don't know who the mysterious "he" is, and they don't know why the quotation is significant. As authors, we need to be kind to our easily-distracted readers and always be clear about who says what and why it's significant. Examples B and C have fatal punctuation errors. (Professors die a little when we stumble across these.) Example B uses a comma to separate two independent clauses. If we correct the error by replacing the comma with a period, the quotation turns into a dropped quotation, so the problem of embedding isn't resolved. Example C has no punctuation between the two independent clauses, and adding punctuation does not solve the problem of embedding the quotation. Turn to the "Basics: Some Conventions of Correct Writing" article in the Appendix to learn how to avoid comma splices and run-ons.

THREE STEPS TO EMBEDDING QUOTATIONS SUCCESSFULLY

You've read the text and understand the essay assignment. Your thesis and topic sentences are looking pretty good, and you've even begun drafting parts of your essay. Now you need some textual evidence to support your claims. Rather than selecting the first sentence that sounds vaguely similar to your argument, treat your textual evidence as a process.

Step One: Select an excerpt from the source that is informative, surprising, or particularly salient.

Too often, the quotation is self-evident; your readers wonder why you would quote something that everyone already understands. If the quoted material is something that you could easily paraphrase in your own words, then do so and include a citation. Save the quotations for lines that are so articulate, artful, or surprising that you could not possibly paraphrase them without losing their spark.

Step Two: Decide how much of the excerpt you actually need to quote. One sentence? One phrase? One word, a term coined by the author?

You'll almost never block a quotation in DISC courses; the essays simply aren't long enough to merit a block quotation.[1] Occasionally you'll quote an entire sentence. Quote only the key words or powerful phrases to underscore or highlight their effectiveness. Whatever you decide to quote—a short phrase or an entire sentence—commit to discussing the significance of those words in the next sentence or two.

---

1. A block quotation is a passage of more than four typed lines of continuous quotation. The passage is indented one inch from the normal margin and cited slightly differently than a shorter quotation.

Step Three: Embed the quotation into your own sentence. The simplest, grammatically correct embedded quote includes a signal phrase and the quote.

Example A

Larraine claims, "I can't leave money in my bank" (Desmond 217).[2]

Example B

Emerson states that "every heart vibrates to that iron string."

Further Discussion: "Larraine claims" and "Emerson states" are signal phrases: they signal who is speaking in the quotation. Use a comma to separate the signal phrase from the quotation (Example A); don't use a comma when you use words *that*, *whether*, and *if* in the signal phrase (Example B). Sometimes, simple will suffice. However, in academic papers, you'll more often want to incorporate some context into the same sentence. More sophisticated writing weaves analysis alongside embedded quotations:

Example C

Desmond also reveals a pattern of unequal opportunities by stating that the government "legitimizes and defends" landlords' rights to accumulate as much income as possible in the affordable housing market (Desmond 308).[3]

Further Discussion: Notice that Olivia selected Desmond's phrase "legitimizes and defends" because it was startling to her that a democratic government would support a pattern of unequal opportunities. She didn't need to quote the entire, unwieldy sentence from the book.

Here are a few more examples of weaving phrases and sentences into the beginning, middle, and ends of sentences:

Example D

Lola says, "I was waiting to begin" at the end of the short story, which succinctly summarizes the journey for Lale, too (Díaz 17).[4]

Example E

The African American Troop feels jealous because the girls in Troop 909 have "long, shampoo-commercial hair, straight as spaghetti from the box. This alone was reason for envy and hatred" (Packer 5).[5]

---

2. From student Olivia Shawkey.
3. From student Olivia Shawkey.
4. From student Caroline Kester.
5. From student Michael DeFrank.

Example F

Furthermore, Twain urges the audience to be wary of "dump[ing] [one's] life-long principles into the street, and [one's] conscience along with them" in order to stand well with society (Twain 253).[6]

Every once in a while, you might choose to use a colon to introduce a quotation. First, write your analysis as an independent clause, followed by a colon. Then insert your quotation. When you use this method, your quotation should be delivered like a stroke of divine clarity, so make it count by crafting a thoughtful independent clause. This is illustrated in the next example.

Example G

Perhaps Desmond's most convincing evidence that the government actively discourages poor people from saving money is Larraine's irrefutable response: "I can't leave money in my bank" (Desmond 217).

Further Discussion: Don't introduce all of your quotations with a colon. As with good music and good food, variety keeps people engaged.

PLACING YOUR EMBEDDED QUOTATION WITHIN THE PARAGRAPH

Now it's time to pay attention to the sentences surrounding your embedded quotation. You'll learn more about this skill in your Discernment and Discourse workshops. For now, consider this three-step process to positioning a quotation within a paragraph:

> Introduce the source (title and author) if you haven't already done so in the paper.
> Embed the quotation to correlate with your own argument.
> Address the significance of the quotation.

The best way to explain the process is to provide a few more examples from students. These excerpts are lifted from the middle of the students' paragraphs, and each excerpt supports the paragraph's main claim (the topic sentence).

Example A

Each character's reaction to the insults seems to confirm the validity of their own stereotypes. Baldwin would argue that it is in the nature of these characters "to lie, to plot, to conceal his opinions, to pretend . . . in order to carry off the prize of social

---

6. From student Taylor Grace. Sometimes we need to change words or letters in the original quotation to fit the context of the analysis; do this by placing brackets around the altered words or letters. We use brackets mostly with pronouns or vague references that need clarity.

recognition"; they are overcompensating for their own insecurities in order to defend their social status (Baldwin 93).[7]

Example B

Baldwin also explains that men "learn to lie, to plot, to conceal [their] opinions, to pretend, to resort to bluff and braggadocio, . . . to carry off the prize of social recognition," which is similar to the way McCarthy gains his following in *Good Night, and Good Luck* (Baldwin 93). In fact, none of McCarthy's opinions is ever verified.[8]

Example C

They give up their rights for their own security, which Emerson, a fierce individualist, does not tolerate. In his "Self-Reliance," Emerson points out that "society is a joint-stock company, in which the members agree, for the better securing of bread to each shareholder, to surrender the liberty and culture of the eater." In other words, society is comprised of people who buy into one ideal at the expense of civil liberties, which is exactly what happened during McCarthyism.[9]

Further Discussion: Each one of these examples follows the three-step process of signaling the text or author, embedding the quotation in correlation with the paragraph's argument, and addressing the quotation's significance.

As you craft your embedded quotations, follow the process to create syntactically sound sentences that reveal thoughtful analysis.

Works Cited

Baldwin, James Mark. "Social Competition and Individualism." *The Individual and Society or Psychology and Sociology*, Richard G. Badger, 1911, pp. 77–117.

Díaz, Junot. "Wildwood." *The New Yorker*, 11 June 2007. www.newyorker.com/magazine/2007/06/11/wildwood.

Emerson, Ralph Waldo. "Self-Reliance." *Emerson Essays: Self-Reliance*, archive.vcu.edu/english/engweb/transcendentalism/authors/emerson/essays/selfreliance.html.

Good Night, and Good Luck. Performance by George Clooney, David Strathairn, Patricia Clarkson, Jeff Daniels, and Robert Downey, TVA Films, 2006.

Hansberry, Lorraine. *A Raisin in the Sun*, Vintage, 1994.

Packer, ZZ. "Brownies." *Drinking Coffee Elsewhere*, Riverhead Books, 2003, pp. 1–31.

---

7. From student Olivia Shawkey.
8. From student Hunter Tatham.
9. From student Taylor Grace.

From VANESSA HOPPER

Introductory Paragraph Evaluation Exercise

A strong introduction is critical to a successful essay. This exercise should help you become more successful in the creation of your own introductions by way of offering thoughtful, constructive criticism of others' introductions.

Reminder: You should have your essay assignment sheet out for quick reference every time you work on essay evaluations in class and every time you work on your essay outside of class.

An effective introduction . . .
   . . . **has a lead-in.**

A lead-in (or hook) is something that engages the reader's attention, makes the introduction interesting and original, and gives it personality. Avoid generalized, hackneyed statements (such as "War has plagued mankind from the beginning of time"). Do not look up a quotation about your subject on a quote-generator website, either; doing so says that you are too lazy to think about the issue yourself and come up with a way to open that is all your own.

   . . . **promises an essay that will deliver on what the assignment requires.**

Hint: Incorporating key words from the prompt can be useful.

   . . . **has a strong thesis statement.**

The thesis should indicate with specificity and clarity the direction(s) the essay will take.

   . . . **sets the stage by providing relevant context for what is to come.**

If you are writing for an audience unfamiliar with the material, some background information and/or defining of terms or concepts may be necessary at the start.

For Today's Activity:

Step 1 Reread the topic on the essay assignment sheet. (Really! Students often just skim the assignment, not considering the connotations of certain words and overlooking details of the requirements. Always read the topic multiple times, on separate occasions, with a critical eye.)

Step 2 Consider the properties of an effective introduction listed above.

Step 3 Read your peer's introduction carefully several times, "listening" to it in your head.

Step 4 Write <u>a well-developed paragraph</u> of evaluation in response to his/her introduction. Think carefully before you begin your response. Use the properties above as a springboard but go beyond the properties if you wish and articulate other perceived strengths and weaknesses. Be as specific as you can. Be sure to offer constructive criticism. Perfect paragraphs are rare, and they are naturally quite rare in the early stages of writing. Every writer should want to know what he or she can do to create an improved piece of writing.

Remember: **This is an evaluation exercise, *not* an editing exercise. It is not your job to edit your peer's introduction. Do not correct, revise, or rewrite any words or phrases.**

From MARTA KROGH

Says/Does Exercise

This assignment asks you to organize your thoughts after you finish your essay. The assignment serves as a means for you to determine if your reasoning is sound. Second, it serves as an assurance that all of your sentences are lucid and functional. The "says" portion of the exercise demands that you clarify and simplify the idea of each sentence; the "does" portion demands that you evaluate the purpose of the sentence.

You will choose one paragraph of a major paper and provide a "says/does" description of every sentence of that paragraph.

Says

The "says" part of this assignment is reasonably self-evident, if not always easy to do: using different words, restate the point of your sentence. Your paraphrase should try to capture the heart of the sentence, as well as strive for clarity, simplicity, and brevity.

Does

For most, the "does" statements are more challenging than the "says" statements. Becoming aware that sentences do things, not just say things, is half the battle.

The "does" of critical writing is foundational to its meaning. How you reason—what you do to prove your argument—is as important as what you have to say.

Here are some of the things a critical writing sentence may do:

1. State your essay's thesis—the thesis sentence
2. Establish the argument you will make in a body paragraph—a topic sentence
3. Be a reason in support of your argument
4. Support or develop your argument
5. Provide evidence for your argument—including quotations from the text
6. Transition between sentences, arguments, or paragraphs—a transition sentence

Does and Doesn't

As you examine your paragraph, you will notice that some sentences aren't doing anything. When this happens, note this in your "does" sentence. For example, you may find sentences that repeat information already presented or you may find that a sentence introduces a new idea not related to the argument in the paragraph. If you make such a discovery, then the exercise is working—it allows you to critically analyze your own writing so that in your next assignment, you won't have sentences that don't "do" anything.

From VANESSA HOPPER

Loving Lit:
A Conversational Response to the Question,
"Why do I have to read this book?"

It should be obvious why every SMU student must take at least one level of Discernment and Discourse. "Discernment" is thinking critically: not just taking ideas at face value, but considering them deeply, questioning them, and thoughtfully developing your own responses to concepts and problems relevant to daily life. "Discourse" is the art of verbal communication: how to best articulate beliefs, opinions, thoughts, and ideas in writing and in speech. Discernment and discourse are skills every person needs to be highly effective in any career and in personal relationships, too, right? Right!

Something that you may be called on to do in your Discernment and Discourse class, though—and possibly other classes as well—is to read novels or short stories. In my years of university teaching, I have had many students ask me (typically in a tone of annoyance), "Why do I have to read literature? What does *that* novel have to do with anything?" This question doesn't bother me. It's a good question, and I'm always happy to answer it. What *does* bother me is that so many students get all the way to the college level, no doubt having been required to read a heap of literature, yet they really have no idea why reading literature is required of all students pretty much everywhere.

So why *is* literature a vital aspect of the tradition of education? Let me tell you: Because there are things we can learn about the human experience as represented within the artistic medium of fiction that we cannot learn any other way. It's that simple. As Virginia Woolf asserts in *A Room of One's Own,* "fiction... may contain more truth than facts" (4). Your education is as much a search for truth as it is an exercise in skill building and collecting information.

Think of it this way: History presents us with an organized compendium of facts. Psychology offers us a scientific way to understand our motivations and behaviors. Political science courses help us understand our systems of government. Literature can present us with concepts from all of these disciplines (and more) across hypothetical scenarios that help us understand the unique challenges of being human. People aren't machines—we have emotions, and we have unique perspectives and personalities. Literature explores these rich complexities and provides readers with scenarios that help us understand ourselves and our place in this world. When we do, we are better equipped to meet the challenges that come with interacting with our inventions, nature, and the people around us.

Here is a practical, personal example. My father is a veteran of the Vietnam War. I was born within a year of his return from the front, and he was broken in ways I once felt I could never understand. The journey to understanding my father began with my own explorations, as early as junior high, into American history. *What were we doing in Vietnam? What was the war all about?* Although I gained a factual perspective in my independent history studies that was valuable, it didn't help me understand how my father saw the world or why he behaved the way he did. The psychology articles I read on Post Traumatic Stress Disorder and post-war trauma gave me technical language and a new dimension of scientific understanding, but this still didn't connect me in a meaningful or realistic way to the man I grew up with. It wasn't until I read the novels of Tim O'Brien—an American novelist whose fiction is based in his own experiences in the war that so indelibly shaped my father—that I began to understand what my father possibly *felt* . . . how the war had impacted his emotions, and his perceptions of himself as a man, a soldier, and a citizen. I asked my father to read these novels, and they gave us a common ground upon which my father could share his war memories and discuss his trauma. Our relationship is better because of it, and these stories offered him an avenue to healing that no therapy ever had.

Know that the novels and stories your professors will assign have important perspectives for you to consider, perspectives that may help prepare you for life in ways that no other text or medium could. Also remember: books and stories are written to entertain! All writers want their work to make an impact, but they also know that for this to happen, the reader must *want* to read on.

As you read a novel or story, to get the most out of it, try this:

1. <u>Approach the text with an open mind</u>. If you haven't read it before and you have preconceived notions, get rid of them. If you've read it before, expect a new experience: after all, you've had experiences and changes of perspective as you've grown. If you aren't the same person today that you were your sophomore year in high school, why would your experience with a book or story be exactly the same?

2. <u>Whether you're reading a novel or story for the first or second time, think of it as building a friendship</u> because friendships teach us about ourselves. In order to really "get" a novel or story, you have to read it carefully, and let it into your heart and head. Question the actions of the characters! React! Ask yourself if you would behave the same way a character does if you were in her situation. Then ponder your reaction: Why do you feel that way? What does your reaction say about *your* values? Think about a character's motivations: Does someone act the way he does because of society's expectations? Or have his past experiences influenced his behavior? Do you admire him? Do a character's actions frustrate you? Why?

3. <u>Realize that novels and stories can be an exciting way to get educated</u>. Many writers extensively research the periods in which they set their stories, so they can realistically represent the culture of that period. When reading John Fowles' humorous, surprising, suspenseful novel *The French Lieutenant's Woman*, readers don't initially realize how much they are learning about the Victorian Age because the novel is so much fun to read. Countless students have told me after reading Toni Morrison's *Beloved* that they didn't have the slightest conception of the emotional toll of slavery's legacy before reading the book—that it taught them about aspects of slavery they never even touched on in history classes—and that they loved the symbolism and ghost story aspect, which made a difficult topic into a mystery that was rewarding to solve.

4. <u>If it's a requirement anyway, don't fight it—embrace it</u>. Trust that your educators have good reasons for assigning the books that they do and enjoy breaking the code: dig into the book or story to figure out what's important about it, why the author created the characters a certain way, why the plot twists in just the way that it does. Think about the characters' names, the use of color and figures of speech, and clues to when the story was written because every detail may be relevant to solving the puzzle of "the big picture"—and who doesn't love the feeling of satisfaction that comes when that last piece slides in and suddenly everything makes sense! And remember that if a book or story is really tough to decode, your professor is there to coach you through it.

I'd like to say that if you follow the steps above, you'll end up loving every novel and story you're required to read. That's not realistic, though, and it wouldn't be nearly as much fun anyway. Try instead to love (or at least appreciate) the experience of reading it for what it can show you about your own humanity and about our past, present, and possibly even future world. If you don't like a story or a book, or some aspect of it bothers you, use that as a springboard for discussion in class or with your peers. Think about why and talk about it. Even books and stories you end up not liking very much can and should be an enlightening experience; remember that your reactions are valid, and your professors want you to feel you've gained something from what you've read, even if it doesn't land on your list of favorites.

Happy Reading!

Works Cited

Woolf, Virginia. *A Room of One's Own*. Harvest Books, 1989.

From VANESSA HOPPER

Universal Peer Draft Evaluation Guidelines

Everyone needs and should desire constructive criticism! It should take you a substantial amount of time to complete one evaluation. Write in complete sentences, write legibly, and be thorough. Remember that your peer may not refer back to your written comments for a few days; it must make sense to him/her when he/she is alone and working on the essay. You may also use these guidelines on your own as a revision checklist.

Always remember when engaging in a peer evaluation in or out of class:

- **Be tactful and diplomatic.** Thoughtfully and constructively explain your reactions to your peer's writing.

- **Follow-through is key.** It is important that you <u>be as specific and thorough</u> when you react to the writing of another as when you are writing your own essays.

- **Learn from how others write**. We all have different strengths and weaknesses. Never "steal" ideas from a peer's paper to put in your own! Do, however, consider how his/her approach to the assignment differs from yours.

- Feel free to <u>ask each other questions and debate</u> the texts as you work.

IMPORTANT:

- **Resist the temptation to make "corrections"** to your peer's essay. This is an evaluation, not an editing exercise. This is neither the appropriate time in the writing process nor is it your responsibility to "fix" what you see as spelling, punctuation, diction, or sentence construction errors. If you suspect a student might be using commas incorrectly or that a certain word doesn't work in a particular sentence, you may indicate that you think the problem exists, but you may not edit it.

- **What you take away from these exercises is up to you.** I hope that each of you will seriously consider your peer's comments.

Ready to Begin?

Before you read your peer's essay, reread the topic, and always have the assignment sheet handy for quick reference. Read the essay in its entirety before beginning your comments.

I. **Introduction**
   a. A good introduction has a lead-in or hook, something to engage the reader, an element that gives the intro personality and originality. Does the essay have that? Is the lead-in successful? Is it relevant? Any suggestions for improvement?
   b. A good introduction has a strong thesis statement. Reread the essay topic and consider what is required of a good thesis statement for this essay. Can you find the thesis statement? Does it serve the function it should? Explain any weaknesses.
   c. Does the introduction as a whole successfully promise to deliver on what the assignment requires? Is it of reasonable length for this assignment?

II. **Body Paragraphs**
   a. Each body paragraph should have a single, controlling main idea: that's *unity*. Look at body paragraph one. Is it unified? Is there any irrelevant material? Is there any repetition? (Look for multiple sentences that say exactly the same thing only in slightly different words.)
   b. Is body paragraph one *coherent*? That means the order of sentences is working effectively. This is what makes a paragraph "flow" smoothly. Does the paragraph feel disjointed? Are transitions needed anywhere? Point out any rough spots.
   c. Does body paragraph one need any more supporting evidence? Are the ideas developed fully? Is there follow-through? Explain any areas where more development or explanation would benefit.
   d. There is a difference between reinforcement and repetition. To reinforce an idea is to offer further justification or evidence, thereby strengthening it; to repeat an idea is simply to say the same thing again in different words. Repetition is to be avoided. Is there any repetition in the paragraph?

   Now look at each subsequent body paragraph and evaluate it based on the criteria above.

   e. After evaluating each body paragraph individually, consider the organization of the body paragraphs. Do you think the essay is organized effectively? Are there any parts that you would shift around? Would you re-order the paragraphs? Explain your answer(s).

III. Quotations and MLA Format
Examine each quotation in the essay individually.
- Are there any disembodied quotations (quotations that are not meshed with the writer's own text)? If so, point them out and indicate that the writer needs to work on meshing them properly.
- Does each quotation have a correctly formatted MLA citation? Point out any and all problems you suspect exist.
- Is each one meshed to preserve grammatical correctness?
- Is each quotation necessary and relevant to the area of the paper it is meant to enhance?

IV. Accuracy

(The questions below are designed to inspire healthy and constructive debate about the material.)
  a. Consider the content of your peer's address of the author's ideas. Do you feel that s/he has made any errors?
  b. Does s/he clearly understand the key concepts of the text that is the subject of analysis?
  c. Do you think s/he misread or misunderstood any aspects of the text? If so, ask him/her questions and engage in some constructive discussion/debate about the content. Call on me if you need a mediator.

V. Conclusion
  a. Is the conclusion provocative and relevant?
  b. Does it truly "conclude" the essay?
  c. Does it make you think? It mustn't be a regurgitation of the introduction or a summary of points already made.

VI. Diction/Clarity
Are there any phrases, sentences, or passages that don't make sense due to possible problematic word choice(s)? If so, indicate where they are and perhaps discuss the problem with the writer.

VII. What Works
  a. What do you like best about this essay?
  b. Are there any phrases or ideas that you find particularly strong or interesting?
  c. What, in your opinion, are its greatest strengths? Explain your reaction(s).

From PAULINE T. NEWTON

Tips for Writing a Timed Essay

Read the prompt carefully. Are you writing a short answer or paragraph-length response? An essay? If you are writing short responses, then don't write an essay. Do what the assignment requires of you; doing more may not earn you extra credit because your instructor may think you cannot decipher/follow instructions.

Do a "brain dump" immediately after you read the prompt. Your mind will flood with ideas when you first see the question, so jot those down to have in front of you.

As you learned in high school, spend a few minutes at most, particularly for a 50-minute or 80-minute class, outlining what you will write. These notes can be simple lists or just keywords. You don't need to compose a fancy outline, especially given your time constraints.

Get to the point. If you are writing an essay, start with your thesis statement as your first sentence (unless otherwise instructed). As an instructor, I often get essays that include a very long opening; only one body paragraph follows because the student ran out of time.

If your instructor tells you to answer Question A or B or to select two questions out of three, don't do additional work unless your instructor encourages you to do so. Again, your instructor may think you cannot follow instructions. Moreover, your response(s) may seem underdeveloped because you didn't fully devote the allotted time to a specific question.

Engage the text in question when applicable. You want to demonstrate, as you write, that you've read the assigned materials carefully and know them well.

For a 110-minute class, my timed essays generally run about 1–3 pages (typed). Your instructor may have guidelines on this, but do what you are able to do, given your time constraints.

If you have a documented learning difference, make arrangements with DASS well ahead of time—two weeks if possible. Do not ask your instructor for accommodations while you are taking the test. She or he should not disclose or discuss your learning differences in front of others.

Use the language of the prompt in your response. Highlight and use keywords.

Don't drop the thesis after the opening statement; remind the reader of the purpose/answer and/or the keywords, when applicable.

Use clear, concise, and direct language.

Save a minute or two at the end to review your brain dump scribbles. Re-read your ideas/response. Proofread for grammar and spelling errors.

From VANESSA HOPPER

Planning Rubric: How to Create an Excellent Oral Presentation

Preparing a successful speech requires many of the same skills as producing an effective essay. As for an essay, there are specific techniques for opening and closing, and you must think carefully about unity and coherence as you build the bulk of your presentation. Like an essay, an excellent speech cannot be produced at the last minute. An oral presentation must be crafted, practiced, honed, revised ... and practiced some more! Before beginning, have all the details of the assignment: objective, audience, and venue. Knowing who will be hearing your presentation and what your goals are will determine not just your main points, but also your vocabulary and attire.

Remember: Giving a good oral presentation does not entail simply reading some notes aloud in front of a class. Using the guidelines below will help you to build the best presentation possible. Be sure to understand what your professor wants before you begin; if you have any questions, do not wait until the last minute to ask. Understand the expectations early on so you will have plenty of time to devote to building the best presentation.

Overall Content:

- *Introduction*: Always introduce yourself. Warmly welcome your audience. Do not abruptly launch into your material: state your purpose before you begin.

- In the body of the presentation, make sure that you adhere precisely to the assignment. Create content that properly satisfies all of the requirements.

- Demonstrate college-level thinking and convey depth.

- If you are offering an analysis or making an argument, support with plenty of strong and specific examples, and make sure your reasoning is solid.

- *Conclusion*: Do not end abruptly. Offer substantive and meaningful closing remarks, and thank your audience for their attention before you step down or away from the group.

Tone and Presence:

- Use language appropriate for your setting and audience. (For example: If you are presenting to a group of student peers sitting on the grass in front of Dallas Hall—a casual setting with a friendly, known group—you would use different vocabulary/tone than you would if you were presenting behind the podium in a classroom to a group of professors from the business school—obviously a more formal situation in which you would be addressing authority figures who probably do not know you.)

- Convey your ideas with energy and enthusiasm. If you seem bored with the material, your audience will be bored, too. Even the driest material can be made engaging by a lively speaker.

- Practice coming across as confident and focused. If you do, your audience will not only pay attention, they will be more likely to believe and trust what you have to say.

Organization:

- Make sure your points flow logically and are easy to follow. This is helped by crafting smooth transitions from point-to-point.

- Avoid repetition (one exception: deliberately doing a re-cap of main points at the end of a long presentation).

- Always stay on track, avoiding distracting tangents and drifting off-topic.

Use of Time:

Manage your time wisely! Know your time limits and practice your presentation as many times as necessary to achieve your goals effectively in the time allotted. Nothing says that you planned a speech at the last minute like not having enough to say or being cut off before you are ready to conclude.

Physical Aspect:

- Make eye contact with as many members of the audience as possible. This helps everyone to feel respected and included, it encourages the audience to pay attention, and it shows confidence and focus on your part. The less you have to look at your cue cards, the more of an expert you will seem.

- Maintain good posture. Don't slump over the podium and don't fidget.

- If you need cue cards, use the smallest index cards and don't fill them with fine print; truly use them just to "cue" each section of your presentation. You should know your speech well enough in advance that you don't need to read it word-for-word (which prevents you from making eye contact and keeping your audience engaged).
- Watch your voice projection and articulation. Don't speak too quickly; you need your audience to be able to follow your thoughts. Enunciate carefully and speak loudly enough for the back row of the audience to hear.
- Dress appropriately for the situation and audience. If particular attire isn't specified, dress business casual, even for an informal presentation. Never wear baseball caps, flip-flops, logo t-shirts, or anything that looks rumpled or sloppy.

Pre-Presentation Prep:

Get good sleep before a presentation day and have something healthy to eat before it's time for you to be "on stage." If you haven't procrastinated, you won't have to stay up all night working on your speech. If you aren't well rested or you are low on fuel, you are more likely to forget your lines, have shaky hands or voice, be overly nervous, or be less confident in the material than you should be. Most speakers get a little bit of stage fright; it's pretty common and somewhat natural. If you've prepared well, just breathe deeply and go out there with a smile, ready to do your best job. If you trip up or experience an awkward pause, just give your brain a second to catch up, and you'll be fine. An audience you've greeted with respect and clearly made an effort to engage is going to be forgiving and grateful for the knowledge you have to share with them.

I won't wish you good luck because if you've followed these steps, you won't need it!

Advice for New Discernment and Discourse Students

At the end of the semester, DISC students were asked, "What little bit of advice would you give to new DISC students?"

Here's what they offered:

Do not procrastinate on essays! Writing an essay is a process that takes time and many drafts. It is extremely difficult to receive a desirable grade when the essay is rushed, so don't wait until the last minute to start.
—Katie Lei

In this course, it is very important to put effort into the draft for conferences. The individual conferences are extremely helpful, but only if you complete a full draft beforehand.
—Andrew Plax

Turn in everything on time. Whether it's complete or not, anything is better than nothing. Also, don't be afraid to ask for help when you need it.
—Ryne Osborne

I would just reiterate not to do essays the night before. Spending time on your essay and preparing for them properly (1) makes the essay turn out much better, (2) reduces stress, and (3) actually helps you grow into a better writer rather than wasting your time here by winging assignments.
—Thomas Alcorn

Do the work and show up. This class will help you survive more than any other class here. Oh, and I know it's tempting, but don't B.S. your paper at 3 a.m. It's not worth it.
—Jeffrey Kelley

I would also say to make sure to participate in class because you will get more out of the class, and it will be more enjoyable. Finally, make sure to try to improve your writing based on feedback from conferences and essay grades.
—Christiana Brandt

Do the assignments and readings given to you. While many times I felt the work I was completing was not helpful, upon completion I could always look back to recognize the purpose of the assignment.

—David Haimbaugh

Go to every class to stay caught up on assignments; it moves faster than you realize. Most importantly, take reading homework seriously. You'll be glad you did when writing your essay.

—Patrick Hurley

Revising on your own is key because papers are much more about [revising] than the initial writing. Really focus on making the paper great.

—Grant Phelps

APPENDIX

Discernment and Discourse: Course Descriptions

DISC is an abbreviation for Discernment and Discourse, words that have relevance throughout the undergraduate curriculum, suggesting not only necessary skills but also habits of mind. *Discernment* suggests critical thinking and evidence-based analysis, while *discourse* refers to purposeful verbal communication. The Discernment and Discourse sequence introduces students to the fundamental principles of academic thought and communication, invites them to become members of our community of inquiry, and equips them with the skills necessary to present their work effectively in writing.

DISC 1311: Foundations of Written and Oral Discourse
This course gives students practice in the reading, writing, and analytical skills necessary for the successful completion of DISC 1312 and 1313. Students will approach writing as a process of drafting, revising, and editing. They will work on sentence-level and paragraph-level writing skills as they build toward essay-length writing projects. Students must earn a C– or better to proceed in the sequence of DISC courses. *This course cannot be dropped.*

DISC 1312: The Individual and Community
Students will read texts that explore themes of identity and community and will write essays that practice summary, analysis, interpretation, and evaluation. This course introduces students to a variety of discipline-based modes of inquiry and expression. The texts students read and create will employ and exemplify the principles of academic discernment and discourse. Students must earn a C– or better to proceed in the sequence of DISC courses. *This course cannot be dropped.* **Prerequisite**: DISC 1311 or 550 on the SAT Critical Reasoning or 24 on the ACT English section.

DISC 1313: Inquiry Seminar
This course is a topic-based seminar in which students continue to develop their critical reading and writing skills, employing analysis, evaluation, synthesis, and/or integration, while learning to employ research protocols for the discipline or various disciplines represented in the course. Students must earn a C– or better to complete their DISC requirement. *This course cannot be dropped.* **Prerequisite: DISC 1312.**

ESL Discernment and Discourse Writing Sequence
(DISC 1311, 1312, 1313) These courses focus on the special needs of non-native speakers of English, offering additional practice in reading comprehension, vocabulary

development, grammatical accuracy, and compositional "fluency." The ultimate goal of these sections is to provide ESL students with the tools they need to produce written and spoken work that conforms to the standards applied to their native English-speaking peers. As in regular sections of DISC 1312 and 1313, a final grade of C– or above is required for successful completion of the ESL sections. *These courses cannot be dropped.*

DISC 2305: Honors Humanities Seminar I
The seminar considers insights from literature, linguistics, philosophy, psychology, and science that became major modes of interpreting the world in the 20th Century and define what constitutes knowledge in the 21st century. *Restricted to students in the University Honors Program.*

DISC 2306: Honors Humanities Seminar II
The seminar studies ethical questions derived from history, literature, psychology, and philosophy that focus on what constitutes a meaningful life. The course also explores historical challenges to the bases of ethics. *Restricted to students in the University Honors Program.* **Prerequisite: DISC 2305.**

PLEASE NOTE:
Courses in the Discernment and Discourse Program cannot be dropped. All students enrolled in DISC will remain in DISC until the end of the semester and receive a grade for the course. This is both a program policy and a General Education policy.

Awards

The Laura Kesselman Devlin Award

The Devlin Award commemorates Laura Devlin, a first-year writing teacher distinguished for academic rigor, intellectual adventure, and human concern. This award for continuing excellence is presented annually to a full-time faculty member whose major teaching responsibility is in DISC.

The Laura Kesselman Devlin Instructor for 2018–2019 was Marta Krogh.

Class Attendance

Discernment and Discourse classes are workshop classes; therefore, attendance, preparation, and participation are expected and required. **Be aware that courses in the Discourse and Discernment Program cannot be dropped. Each student enrolled in DISC will remain in DISC until the end of the semester and receive the grade he or she has earned. This is both a program policy and a General Education policy. You cannot drop DISC, and your professor cannot drop you from DISC.**

The following attendance policy applies to every section of DISC: If you have more than three absences of any kind (except for those sanctioned by the university and excused via official SMU paperwork from the proper office) in an MWF section or more than two absences in a TTH section, your grade will suffer a penalty of a full letter grade: for example, a final average of 85 would become 75. If you have more than six absences in a MWF section or four absences in a TTH section (except for those sanctioned by the university and excused via official SMU paperwork from the proper office), you should expect to fail the course. If you have more than one absence during a summer session, expect your grade to suffer; if you have more than three absences, you will fail the course.

Knowing that you are allowed only two (for TTH) or three (for MWF) absences before you will suffer a major penalty, use your absences wisely. Save them for sick days. Notes from doctors or the campus health center are not included in official SMU paperwork that will excuse an absence.

Office Conferences with Your Professor: What to Expect and How to Prepare

In any Discernment and Discourse section, expect to meet with your professor in his or her office at least once. Conferences are highly beneficial at any stage of the writing process. These meetings are an opportunity for your professor to give you individualized help in a setting where you can both focus intently on your writing. Because your professor's goal is to improve your critical thinking and writing skills while encouraging your accountability, he or she will not edit your paper for you, tell you what to write, or predict your final grade. None of that would help you grow. What he or she will do: draw your attention to specific aspects of your essay that still need work, point out skill areas in need of improvement, answer your questions, and coach you in the right direction via useful suggestions.

There is no guarantee that your final product will be an A simply because you attend your conference; only so much can be covered in a session, and much must be accomplished between meeting with your professor and the ultimate due date. What is guaranteed: if you are prepared for your conference and you make the most of it, your final product will be stronger than it would have been otherwise. It is important to realize that conference sessions do not just function with the immediate goal of improving the current writing project, but with the long-term goal of helping you evolve into a more effective inter-disciplinary thinker and writer overall.

Preparation:

Do not procrastinate.

Professors usually cancel some class periods to make time to meet with every student. Make the most of that time out of class by making headway on your essay. Do not wait until the last minute before your conference to prepare the materials your professor has asked you to bring. You should spend some time on your writing assignment every day until your appointment day comes, so you can present your best possible effort.

Know that "writer's block" is an invalid excuse.

In college, the work simply must get done, and you must do whatever it takes to get moving on an assignment. If you're at a writing stand-still, have coffee or even a short chat in the dorm with a peer—someone who is not in your class—and talk to her about your writing project. Explain your assignment and verbalize your ideas and struggles. Articulating your writing situation to an objective party and answering questions about it can be a great way to get out of a creative rut. It gets ideas brewing. Also, remember that the Writing Center can help you in the early stages of writing your essay. If you hit a stumbling block before your conference, you can meet with a writing tutor for help getting over it. Tutors can help you at any stage of the writing process, including brainstorming, planning, and shaping a thesis statement. If you take advantage of the Writing Center or any other authorized SMU tutor, make sure you bring along a printed copy of your assignment, so the tutor clearly understands the goals and requirements of the paper or project. "Writer's block" is not an excuse for being unprepared. Don't be surprised if a professor counts your conference period as an absence or deducts point from your grade if you show up to a conference without anything to work with.

Follow all instructions.

Did your professor specify that you have a certain number of paragraphs or pages completed? Did he specify that you need to bring a Works Cited page or have quotations incorporated into your essay? Did your professor ask you to upload your draft to Canvas in advance of your conference? Did she ask you to make two hard copies to bring to your session? Showing up unprepared makes you look as if you aren't invested in the class, and it will prevent the professor from giving you the maximum help she could. If you are required to take a three-page draft to conference and you take an introduction only, your professor will be limited in what he can evaluate. If you show up with only an outline, there is very little he can help you with if the plan was to evaluate your essay-writing skills.

Know what you want to know.

Before you visit your professor's office, it's a good idea to come up with three questions about your draft—and, in fact, some professors require it. Why? Because identifying your uncertainties requires thinking more critically about your own work, and preparing and writing down those three questions can save time in conference by providing the session with more focus.

Getting the Most Out of Your Conference:

- Be a little early. When the student before you finishes up, you will be ready to go right in and get started.

- Never go to conference empty-handed. In addition to anything the professor has specifically asked you to bring, have pen and paper for note-taking. If you have a question about something specific in a course text, have the text with the page marked and ready for reference. If you have questions about specific spots in your essay, have them highlighted. Have all questions written down for quick and easy reference.

- Be alert during your conference. Focus on your professor's words. Write down all that you can. Since this will be your only conference, you want to make the most of it!

- **DO NOT MISS YOUR CONFERENCE.** As soon as your conference date/time are set, record that appointment in numerous places: on your course calendar, in your personal planner, and on your assignment sheet. Most professors will count a missed conference as an absence, and some deduct points from the essay grade. It is likely that your professor will not be able to reschedule you if you don't show up; after all, she must make time to meet individually with fifty to seventy students in a single week. The time investment this requires of the professor is intensely demanding. It is generally not possible for professors to see each student more than once, and the tight schedule makes rescheduling extremely difficult. Do not expect your professor to allow you to make up a missed conference in some alternative format (i.e., via e-mail). Bottom line: If your professor reserves this time to meet with you one-on-one, don't procrastinate on preparation, and don't miss out on this highly valuable opportunity. The penalties may be manifold.

The Writing Center

. . . is a resource for all SMU undergraduates who need help with a writing or reading project of any kind. The Writing Center is staffed by Discernment and Discourse faculty members.

30-Minute Consultations by Appointment

Whether you need help understanding a writing or reading assignment, getting started in the writing process, revising a draft in progress, or applying your teacher's comments to subsequent assignments, the Writing Center offers one-on-one tutorials that will send you in the right direction. Writing Center faculty can provide strategies that will help you learn how to understand reading and writing assignments, generate your own ideas, revise and edit more efficiently and effectively, and benefit as fully as possible from your teacher's suggestions.

Even if you're not working on a specific assignment, if you think that you have a particular area of weakness, such as organization of paragraphs or use of the possessive, the Writing Center faculty members can teach you how to eliminate such problems, thus making you a more confident writer.

If you are working on an essay for a course, it is a good idea to schedule your tutorial well in advance of the due date, thus allowing yourself ample time for revision, a conference with your teacher, and perhaps even a follow-up appointment.

You may schedule an appointment with the Writing Center through Canvas.

Drop-In Consultations

Uncertain about citation form? Need to look over topic sentences? For questions that don't require a 30-minute session, you can work with a Writing Center faculty member during drop-in hours.

Drop-In Writing Lab

In Writing Lab, you can work independently on your writing project with a Writing Center Faculty member available to answer questions or offer suggestions as you work.

Writing Center for ESL Writers

Most first-year ESL students take a section of Discernment and Discourse (DISC) taught by an ESL specialist. These professors are students' most important writing resource, and students should take full advantage of their instructors' office hours and opportunities for individual conferences. When students need additional help, Writing Center resources are available.

ESL writers who have completed the DISC sequence or those who took their writing courses at other universities and now have writing projects for other classes can also get help understanding a writing or reading assignment, revising a draft in progress, or applying teacher's comments to assignments.

The Writing Center can offer support during Writing Lab and drop-in hours, and ESL writers may also **drop in to work with the** Writing Center faculty member who specializes in helping ESL writers.

The Writing Center is located in the Altschuler Learning Enhancement Center, Suite 202, in the Loyd All Sports Center. For more information, including the current Writing Center schedule, go to www.smu.edu/Writing Center.

The Altshuler Learning Enhancement Center

The Altshuler Learning Enhancement Center (A-LEC) provides a variety of services to support the academic success of SMU's undergraduates. Most students who arrive at SMU find that the learning strategies that worked for them in high school need upgrades. We're here to help. Students at all levels have found that working with the LEC can make a huge difference. All LEC services are offered without charge to SMU undergraduates.

Our programs include:

- **Reading and Learning Strategies/HDEV 1110:** A one-credit elective course, HDEV 1110 helps students improve reading comprehension and rate while developing a personalized system of strategic learning techniques. HDEV 1110 can help make a successful transition to college, whether students excelled in high school without ever studying, have multiple courses with heavy reading loads, or aim for a 4.0 in three majors while running for Student Senate.

- **Success Strategies/HDEV 1211:** A two-credit elective course, Success Strategies introduces academically struggling students to specific approaches to help them achieve greater success in their academic, professional, and personal life. In this course, students will engage in ongoing self-assessment and journal writing to explore strategies and to identify academic challenges, as well as strengths they possess to overcome these obstacles. Students will also be introduced to learning strategies and study skills and explore campus resources they can use to succeed at SMU.

- **Learning strategies workshops:** Students who can't take the Reading and Learning Strategies course can develop college-level learning strategies by attending one-hour drop-in workshops on a wide variety of topics including time management, note taking, study-reading, concentration, and test preparation, test taking, and test anxiety. Check the LEC Web page for a complete schedule of this semester's workshops, and then drop in for one or all. Workshops are also listed on the back of each Semester-At-A-Glance sheet.

- **Individual academic counseling:** For one-to-one help with learning strategies, call the LEC to make an appointment for individual academic counseling. We can help assess reading and learning skills, develop new strategies, and apply them to the demands of the student's specific courses.

- **Drop-in tutoring:** The A-LEC offers one-to-one or small group sessions, Sundays through Fridays, for most key first- and second-year courses and many higher-level ones. Use A-LEC tutoring to raise a B to an A or to repair a disaster. Tutoring works best when you start soon and come frequently, least well when you wait until the night before a test. Writing tutors, trained by the Writing Center director (an English faculty member), are also available during all shifts. No appointments are necessary for tutoring—we operate on a drop-in basis. Check out our website for tutor availability by class at http://www.smu.edu/Provost/ALEC/Tutoring/TutorSchedule.

- **Disability Accommodations & Success Strategies (DASS):** DASS is the primary contact for all SMU students with disabilities. This office, within the A-LEC, assists students with disabilities to effectively utilize resources and helps them work with professors and staff in obtaining appropriate and reasonable accommodations. DASS will evaluate and accommodate those students who are significantly impacted by a condition that is disabling, even if only temporary. This includes learning disabilities, physical disabilities, psychiatric disorders, and others. It is up to the student to request DASS services. Academic coaching for undergraduates with learning and attention disorders is also available. For more information, check out https://www.smu.edu/Provost/ALEC/DASS.

We invite you to check out our website at **www.smu.edu/alec** to learn more about our programs, or to stop by in person at 202 Loyd Center. We look forward to working with you to help you meet your academic goals.

Sue Bierman, Ph.D.
Director
Altshuler Learning Enhancement Center

How the Library Can Help You with DISC

SMU Libraries have assembled a team of librarians, led by Jonathan McMichael (jmcmichael@smu.edu), specifically dedicated to helping DISC classes. Our primary focus is helping students get the most out of their DISC experience. We've found that the best learning outcomes occur when the library is part of your everyday academic experience. You will see us in your classrooms sometime this semester and we are always available and willing to help with the unique research challenges offered by DISC.

Below you will find a summary of a few of the things the library does that might be of use to a DISC student. However, if you can imagine a way that we might be able to help, contact Jonathan. We are specifically dedicated to the needs and experience of the DISC student. Do not hesitate to reach out.

Fondren Library

Fondren Library is the main library on campus for undergraduate students. Fondren is one of the best places on campus to study with flexible study spaces, reservable study rooms, and Starbucks for your caffeine needs.

Need to print? The library has both color and black-and-white printers. Log-in to http://printing.smu.edu with your SMU ID and password to add funds and send print jobs.

Web site

http://smu.edu/cul should be one of your go-to places for research while you are at SMU. From here you can:

- Start your research using our "Everything" search, which connects you to SMU's print and online resources
- Get more in depth with our Research Guides
- Reserve a Study Room (http://smu.edu/fondrenrooms)
- Make a research consultation with one of our librarians

The best part, all of this is available whether you're on or off campus. All you need is your SMU ID and password, and you can access all our online resources from anywhere as if you were in the library.

DISC Research Help
You can always feel free to stop by the Main Desk or chat with us using our Ask service (http://guides.smu.edu/ask). We also offer online bookable consultations specifically for DISC students.

These one-on-one appointments are a way to meet with a librarian familiar with your class, assignment, and instructor expectations. It is the best way to get customized research help from a knowledgeable research professional.

Visit http://www.smu.edu/cul/services/disc to view librarian availability and make an appointment.

Check Stuff Out/Course Reserves
You can check out books, movies, and technology with your SMU ID card at the Main Desk. Course Reserves are at the Main Desk, too. Honestly, if you are looking for something just ask the Main Desk, and they will get you what you want or at least point you in the right direction.

Workshops
The libraries offer many types of workshops to help students, faculty, and staff learn research skills and how to use library resources. They are interactive sessions specifically designed to help you develop meaningful skills. Check out what is up this semester on our Web site.

We are here for you!
We are a team that is solely focused on DISC because success in the class will set you up for the rest of your time at SMU.

Jonathan McMichael
User Experience Librarian

jmcmichael@smu.edu
http://www.smu.edu/cul/services/disc

Photo by Rob Walker, © 2014 Norwick Center for Digital Services, SMU

Researching Like a College Student

In high school, you may have written at least one research paper. To write the paper, you probably reported evidence by authors who agreed with you. Your teacher had you turn in the assignment incrementally and helped you plan for each step. In college, writing papers will be a different experience.

Research is a quest and a conversation.
A researcher questions the information that came before and responds to it. Research papers involve an inquiry on a specific issue then communicating the intellectual conversation you had with other scholars. You will not simply tell what others have said; instead, you will give your standpoint with regard to the interpretation of text, data, or events. You will seek useful disagreements on a subject and show how your position is supported by experts, as well as where others interpreted the material differently. You may need to use primary sources (and find out the difference between primary and secondary sources). You will actively seek opposing viewpoints and consider these alternative perspectives. As you consider the evidence, you should learn to be open to rethinking your stance rather than simply digging in your heels and sticking with your initial position.

Research is a process.
A researcher gathers information, reviews it, and then seeks to fill information gaps. You will use scholarly, peer-reviewed journals and books as resources, taking a variety of sources and analyzing or synthesizing the material into an integrated whole. Sometimes the most helpful part of an article will be the bibliography, so make sure you read the works cited thoroughly and track any useful sources. Not all sources will be available in SMU's libraries, but if you start researching early enough, then you can request them through interlibrary loan. For most of your classes, you will be responsible for planning your research/writing schedule. Remember that research will usually take at least twice as much time as you think it will, so plan accordingly. As you progress through your academic career, you will learn that the most convenient and familiar resources are not necessarily the best choices. The best databases for an introductory course will not be adequate for an upper-level seminar.

    Research is challenging, but also exciting and rewarding.
    Ask a librarian for help. We are here for you.

Rebecca Graff
Research Librarian
SMU Central University Libraries

Computers on Campus

Your instructors will expect you to have access to a computer and a printer. For students who do not own a computer or whose computer malfunctions or crashes, SMU maintains several labs where students may use personal computers or receive assistance in using unfamiliar equipment or software. Among the places you'll find computers: Fondren Library, the Business Library, the Altshuler Learning Enhancement Center, and residence halls. Students may print in these labs from the public computers or from their laptops using their SMU identification card. Check in advance for information on specific locations and hours of availability, as these may change.

Do not expect your instructors to help you with computer-related problems. For help with computer, printer, or Canvas problems, call the Help Desk at 214-768-4357, e-mail them at help@smu.edu, or go in person to the Help Desk in Fondren Library next to Starbucks. For information about hours, check the Help Desk Web site at help.smu.edu. The Help Desk makes every effort to respond to each request the same day it is received.

As a rule, instructors will not excuse late or missing work resulting from computer malfunctions. It is your responsibility to back up all your files in a safe place, not just on the hard drive of your computer.

On Grading

I do not . . . grade on potential, talent, improvement, effort, motivation, intention, behavior, personality, weight, height, sex, race, accent, appearance. I grade on accomplishment. . . . As represent exceptional work, far above average. Bs represent good work, above average. Cs represent average work. Ds below-average work. And Fs exceptional work in the wrong direction.

It is the work I am grading, not the student. It is work that can be shown to the student, to colleagues, to administrators; it is work that relates directly to the quality of the reference that would be given for the student when that student applies to more advanced courses or for a job. It is a grade that represents my evaluation of what the student has accomplished and demonstrated at the end of the course after the student has had the benefit of extensive writing and extensive reaction to that writing.

From A Writer Teaches Writing, *by Donald Murray*

D&D Rubric for Evaluating and Grading

Accomplishment level	Content	Organization	Style	Usage	Sources
	SLO 1: Students will state and defend a thesis with adequate attention to analysis and evidence.	SLO 2: Students will demonstrate an understanding of essay and paragraph development and organization.	SLO 3: Students will craft sentences with attention to audience, purpose, and tone, as well as sentence variety and diction.	SLO 4: Students will demonstrate proper use of grammatically and mechanically correct English.	SLO 5: Students will incorporate and document sources correctly and appropriately.
EXEMPLARY 5 A	Thesis demonstrates significant controlling idea or assertion. Thesis clearly answers assignment's demands. Supporting evidence is concrete, relevant, and accompanied by substantive analysis. Topic sentences provide structure with strong and meaningful assertions.	Organization reveals strong attention to symmetry and emphasis. Paragraphs are focused, coherent, and led by a controlling argument. Logical transitions reinforce the progress of the analysis. Introduction strongly engages initial interest; conclusion closes essay in compelling fashion.	Sentences varied, purposeful, and emphatic; diction fresh, precise, economical, and idiomatic. Tone complements and conveys the authorial persona and suits the audience.	Few, if any, mistakes in grammar, syntax, punctuation, and/or spelling. Close attention to detail and a mastery of mechanics and presentation. Overall adherence to conventions highlights content and credibility.	Quoted material incorporated effectively and correctly. In-text citations and reference list contain few, if any, errors.
ACCOMPLISHED 4 B	A less discerning thesis with a controlling idea or assertion is supported with mostly concrete and relevant evidence. Analysis present but not always thorough. Topic sentences generally provide insight and structure.	Organization reveals attention to symmetry and emphasis. Paragraphs are coherent and do not digress from controlling idea. Logical transitions signal changes in direction. Introduction engages initial interest; conclusion supports without merely repeating.	Sentences generally varied, purposeful, and emphatic; diction appropriate and idiomatic; tone suits the subject, persona, and audience.	Few mistakes in grammar, syntax, punctuation, and/or spelling. Attention to detail and a fair level of mastery of mechanics and presentation. Minimal number of errors provides little distraction from overall content or credibility.	Quoted material incorporated correctly, with minimal errors. In-text citations and reference list generally correct.

DEVELOPING 3 C	Thesis has little ambition or complexity and is too broad to lead a focused essay. Assertion is general, limited, or obvious. Some supporting evidence is repetitious, irrelevant, or jumbled, with little analysis. Topic sentences contain little insight and offer little structure.	Organizational efforts apparent, but not entirely successful, and sense of emphasis may be weak. Paragraphs' focus and coherence breaks down at times. Transitions functional but often obvious or formulaic. Introduction and/or conclusion may be mechanical rather than purposeful or insightful.	Sentences competent but lacking emphasis and variety; diction faulty at times; tone acceptable for the subject.	Several mistakes in grammar, syntax, punctuation, and/or spelling. Little attention to detail and lower level of mastery of mechanics and presentation. Multiple errors distract from content and undercut credibility.	Occasional errors in quoted material. In-text citations and reference list contain several errors.
BEGINNING 2 D	Thesis is superficial or vague. Logical incoherence and faulty claims present in the main idea. Evidence is insufficient, obvious, contradictory, or aimless with no attempt at analysis. Topic sentences contain no insight or structure.	Organization unclear or inappropriate, failing to emphasize central idea. Paragraphs fragmented or underdeveloped. Transitions unclear, inaccurate, or absent. Introduction merely describes what is to follow; conclusion merely repeats what has been said.	Sentences lack necessary emphasis and variety; diction vague and unidiomatic; tone inconsistent with or inappropriate for the subject.	Frequent mistakes in grammar, syntax, punctuation, and/or spelling. Lack of attention to detail; mastery of mechanics and presentation is marginal. Errors obscure content and diminish credibility.	Quoted material incorporated incorrectly. In-text citations and reference list contains multiple errors.
ABSENT 1 F	No discernible idea or assertion controls the random or unexplained details that make up the body of the work.	Organization and emphasis indiscernible. Paragraphs lack controlling idea, transitions, and coherence. Neither the introduction nor the conclusion satisfies any clear rhetorical purpose.	Incoherent, rudimentary, or redundant sentences thwart the meaning of the essay; diction nonstandard or unidiomatic; tone indiscernible or inappropriate for the subject.	Frequent and serious mistakes in grammar, syntax, punctuation, and/or spelling. No attention to detail; no mastery of mechanics or presentation is apparent. Serious errors undermine content and credibility of the work, rendering it meaningless.	Quoted material, if present, incorporated carelessly and aimlessly. In-text citations and reference list either not present or incorrect, causing work's loss of credibility.

Avoiding Bias

In early editions of *The Elements of Style*, their classic guide to effective writing, William Strunk and E. B. White argued for the appropriateness of using "*he* as pronoun for nouns embracing both genders," writing that "*he* has lost all suggestion of maleness in these circumstances" (60).

More recent research by linguists and psychologists, however, suggests that readers do tend to envision male characters when reading *he* or *man,* even if the rest of the passage contains no references to gender, and that these assumptions affect the readers' understanding of and appreciation for what they are reading. Today, then, almost all handbooks and style manuals recommend that writers rely on gender-neutral word choice and on constructions that carry no specific designation of femininity or masculinity when no specific references are intended. These handbooks contain extensive practical and stylistically graceful suggestions for ways to avoid gender-biased language.

Bias-free writing extends beyond gender. As a writer, you want to consider both if and how you should refer to someone's age, ethnicity, appearance, physical abilities, religion, or sexual preference. Include this information if it is relevant to your context and point, and be consistent. For example, if you wouldn't refer to one person as a "heterosexual," why would you describe another as a "lesbian"? If you haven't described one character as "someone's husband," why would you describe another as "someone's wife"? If you haven't mentioned your European-American history professor's ethnicity, why would you mention the ethnicity of your African-American economics professor? When such references are appropriate, be sure that your descriptions are neither stereotypical nor degrading. For example, avoid references to "inscrutable" Asians, and refer to someone as "using" a wheelchair, rather than as "confined" to it.

Some may be concerned that avoiding biased language is merely a form of political correctness, an attempt to change beliefs or limit free exchange of ideas. Others may denigrate the issue by making jokes about "person-hole covers," but, in fact, good writers use bias-free language because it is more concise, more accurate, and more persuasive since it eliminates distracting and irrelevant observations and assumptions. All language is persuasive: Through language, we do not describe the world; we create the human experience of the world—both for ourselves and for our listeners and readers, who are affected in one way or another by our words. As a writer, you want neither to reveal your own unacknowledged or unintended biases nor to trigger unintended biases in your readers.

Works Cited

Strunk, William and E. B. White. *The Elements of Style*, 3rd ed. McMillan, 1979.

On Plagiarism

Plagiarism is literary burglary. At its worst, it involves an outright intent to deceive, to pass off another's work as one's own. More often, it is the result of carelessness or ignorance. But whether intentional or unintentional (the distinction is often hard to draw), plagiarism is always an error, and a serious one (Stone and Bell 214).

Copyright laws exist to protect authors' rights to their own ideas as well as their actual words. In addition, scholarly ethics demand that writers make accessible to their readers the research materials they have used to develop their written argument or presentation. Student writers are expected to observe at all times both the limits of the copyright laws and the ethics of scholarly research. To this end, all written work submitted in any course should be organized according to an original plan. <u>Words taken from anyone else's work—spoken or written, in print or online—must be quoted and cited, and ideas taken from someone else's work, whether paraphrased or summarized, must be cited as well.</u>

While the purpose of any argument should be to express an original idea and point of view, it is often desirable for students to draw information or ideas from responsible sources and to use those ideas to support or enhance their own observations and conclusions. <u>All quotations and borrowed material must be properly credited to their sources.</u>

Copying published material or borrowing the words of another person without acknowledging indebtedness constitutes plagiarism. SMU students who plagiarize may be subject to failure in the course and to any other disciplinary actions the Honor Council may impose.

Works Cited

Stone, Wilfred and J. G. Bell. *Prose Style: A Handbook for Writers.* McGraw-Hill, 1968.

Statement on Academic Honesty

Southern Methodist University has an Honor Code; students are expected to pledge that any work that they turn in is the product of their own minds and efforts. When you sign your name to the Honor Pledge—"On my honor, I have neither given nor received any unauthorized aid on this work"—you offer your own character as evidence that you have abided by SMU's Honor Code.

Each time you submit written work in your DISC class (or in any class), you automatically subscribe to the following:

1. You have not taken any words from any other piece of writing—published, unpublished, or online—without putting quotation marks around such words and indicating their source. This pledge pertains to phrases as well as whole sentences, and even to significant single words, such as those that express opinion or judgment.
2. You have not taken ideas from any source—including an online source—even if you express them in your own words in summary or in paraphrase, without giving credit to that source.
3. You have organized your material according to a plan of your own creation, based upon your own thorough exploration of the assignment.
4. While you may have asked someone for an opinion about your paper, you have received only suggestions. You have neither asked nor allowed someone else to write, revise, edit, proofread, or otherwise modify your work in any way.

SMU students understand that a violation of the Honor Code results in severe penalties. One minimum penalty given by the Honor Council is a notation of "Honor Violation" for the course, which will remain on a student's official transcript for three years after graduation. Other penalties recommended by the Honor Council can include deferred suspension for one calendar year, indefinite suspension, or even expulsion from the University.

The Revising and Editing Process

Rewriting encompasses a wide spectrum of activities, from extensive modifications in content and structure to minor changes in form. As you move from a loosely constructed first draft to the final polished essay, rewriting forces you to backtrack constantly, changing your meaning and refining your intention. **Revising** refers to substantive textual alteration—significant rhetorical changes in content, focus, organization, and meaning. Revising, then, implies that you discover your subject by writing about it. **Editing** refers to refinements in diction and sentence structure that make a text not only more correct but also more readable, more stylistically engaging, and rhetorically appropriate. **Proofreading** refers to manuscript preparation; you eliminate distracting minor errors from the final copy of the text.

In DISC, we want you to revise your drafts substantially; only by examining your writing with a critical and careful eye can you know what further writing you need to do. Although we can't outline a specific procedure that applies to all writers or all projects, the following model does suggest ways in which practiced writers evaluate their prose.

I. **After the first draft:**
   a. ask yourself if you have followed the assignment directions closely;
   b. select a provisional title that will help you identify your subject's limits and develop a point of view towards it;
   c. emphasize cutting; keep writing until you have enough material to cut;
   d. mark your good passages with a check;
   e. figure out your main point; reformulate the thesis statement if necessary;
   f. add pieces that are missing and cut pieces that present unnecessary or unrelated matters;
   g. put the good passages in some kind of order reflecting a provisional pattern of organization: chronological, logical, cause/effect, etc.;
   h. write out the next draft.

II. **During the intermediate drafts:**
   a. continue to clarify through cutting; try reading your draft aloud to experience the writing from a reader's point of view;
   b. ask yourself if you are saying what you mean; do your words mean what you think? If not, keep writing and cutting until you achieve clarity and precision;
   c. consider your paragraphs; do they build confidence in your thesis? Are they fully developed? Have you made transitions between paragraphs?

d. ask yourself if you have used too many words to make a point: circle prepositions and revise sentences that pile on too many prepositional phrases; circle "to be" forms and substitute precise verbs; circle passive constructions and shift to the active voice; circle expletive constructions and revise to emphasize agency and action; combine and subordinate choppy sentences;
e. correct grammar, punctuation, and spelling errors.

Priorities in Evaluating an Essay

Whether you are revising your own draft, discussing a draft with your instructor, or responding to a classmate's draft, the following priorities should help you evaluate work in progress.

- Clear and concrete articulation of a thesis (a central idea, proposition, or assertion)
- Analysis or defense of that thesis in a series of points; careful development of those points into a series of paragraphs (logical and purposeful organization)
- Selection of relevant supporting evidence (concrete details)
- Clear transitions within and between paragraphs
- Style appropriate to the subject, purpose, and audience
- Effective sentences (logical relationships emphasized through combining, subordinating, and condensing)
- Effective diction (precision and purpose; special attention paid to nouns and verbs)
- Mechanical accuracy* (conventional grammar and punctuation; correct spelling, typography, and format)

---

*Mastery of the conventions of the language must be assumed in college work; that is, you must clear the static before a reader can begin to receive your message.

Revision Worksheet

Revision is the process of looking over what you have written and making substantial changes in such areas as organization, development, voice, argument, thesis, or evidence. Revision involves a careful rethinking of purpose and a reconsideration of audience. Think about the following questions as you revise or help another revise.

1. Is the **purpose** of the writing clear in its first paragraph? (If not, why not?)
2. Can you identify the **audience** for whom this is written? (Look for cues in the writing: tone, style, and word-choice.)
3. How is the paper **organized**? (Look for a pattern here: chronological, topical, logical, compare/contrast, cause/effect, general to specific, specific to general, most important/least important or vice versa.)
4. Is each body paragraph focused and unified by a topic sentence that supports the paper's thesis? (If not, why not?)
5. Is **evidence** used to support generalizations? (Look for examples, specific details, and concrete descriptions.)
6. Do the ideas in the paper move smoothly one from another, both within and between paragraphs? (Look for appropriate transitions, for movement out of the familiar into the unfamiliar.)
7. Can you summarize the **main point** of the paper in a sentence or two? (Does the introduction or conclusion do this?)

Editing Worksheet

Editing is the process of fine-tuning your prose. In editing, you turn your attention to sentence-level matters of diction, tone, economy, emphasis, and precision. Think about the following questions as you edit or help another edit.

1. Do you use **active verbs** wherever you can? (Do you "decide" rather than "make a decision"?)
2. Do you have good reasons for using **passive constructions**? If not, make them active. (Not: "The liquid was poured into the test tube by the chemist." Instead: "The chemist poured liquid into the test tube.")
3. Have you cut all the **dead wood** from your sentences? (Not: "It is interesting to note that editing is easy." Instead: "Editing is easy.")
4. Have you avoided wordy, vague "there+be verb" and "it+be verb" constructions? (Not: "There are many interstate highways in need of repair." Instead: "Many interstate highways need repair.")
5. Can you use a **smaller or precise word** where you have used a big one? (Not: "In today's society, the economic situation is often an important factor." Instead: "Today, money often determines a person's social class.")
6. Do you find any **clichés** in your sentences? ("Can you cut through the red tape and get on the ball?" Or, "Do you finish what you start?")
7. Can you **combine** any sentences to avoid repetition? (Not: "The water is brown. It is flowing fast. It is polluted." Instead: "The brown, polluted water rushes by.")
8. Do you express parallel ideas in parallel forms? (Not: "I love walking and to swim and go sailing." Instead: "I love walking, swimming, and sailing." Or: "I love to walk, swim, and sail.")
9. Do you have any one-sentence **paragraphs**? (You shouldn't.)
10. Are your **references, documentation,** and **calculations** complete and precise?
11. Have you proofread the paper to correct **punctuation, spelling,** and **grammar**?

Basics:
Some Conventions of Correct Writing

Because observing the conventions of grammar, syntax, and punctuation helps a writer achieve clarity and precision, every writer needs to learn and follow these conventions.

While the following ten principles, or "Basics," are by no means inclusive, most experienced writers consider them essential to achieving and communicating clear thinking in almost any writing but particularly in professional, business, and academic writing.

1. **Learn to recognize and construct sentences.**

   The simple English sentence contains a subject and a predicate. Compound and complex sentences combine clauses and must contain appropriate conjunctions and punctuation.

   A. **Avoid sentence fragments.**

   Faulty: The woman who works hard and therefore will triumph in the end.

   Correct: The woman works hard and therefore will triumph in the end.
   The woman who works hard will triumph in the end.

   Faulty: When I go to New York, I want to visit the Museum of Natural History. Because I have always been interested in dinosaurs.

   Correct: When I go to New York, I want to visit the Museum of Natural History because I have always been interested in dinosaurs.

   B. **Avoid fused sentences and comma splices.**

   Faulty: The topic is difficult to write on it doesn't interest me.
   The topic is difficult to write on, it doesn't interest me.

   Correct: The topic is difficult to write on, and it doesn't interest me.
   Because the topic doesn't interest me, it is difficult to write on.

2. **Use the correct form of the verb.**

   Many English verbs change form to indicate person, number, tense, voice, and mood.

   A. **Subject and predicate must agree in person and number.**

   Faulty: Neither she nor her partner have left a message.

   Correct: Neither she nor her partner has left a message.

Faulty: The truth about his many accomplishments are going to be revealed at this afternoon's meeting.

Correct: The truth about his many accomplishments is going to be revealed at this afternoon's meeting.

B. Use the tense that best expresses your idea or logically completes a sequence.

Faulty: Last night my roommate and I reviewed our homework, took a practice test, and plan to get plenty of sleep.

Correct: Last night my roommate and I reviewed our homework, took a practice test, and planned to get plenty of sleep.

3. **Avoid misplaced or dangling modifiers.**

Any word, phrase, or clause used as a modifier should be placed so it cannot appear to modify the wrong word or element in the sentence.

Faulty: While still warm, roll the cookies in powdered sugar.

Correct: While the cookies are still warm, roll them in powdered sugar.

Faulty: The girl who looks bored with red hair is my date.

Correct: The redhead who looks bored is my date.

4. **Avoid faulty parallelism.**

Use the same grammatical construction for parts of a sentence that are similar in function.

Faulty: He prides himself on his originality, looking chic, and acting macho.

Correct: He prides himself on being original, looking chic, and acting macho.

He prides himself on his originality, his stylishness, and his machismo.

5. **Avoid vague or faulty pronoun reference.**
   A. A pronoun should agree with its antecedent in person, number, and gender.

   Faulty: Everyone should turn in their essay on Friday.

   Correct: Everyone should turn in his essay on Friday.

   Everyone should turn in her essay on Friday.

   Everyone should turn in his or her essay on Friday.

   Students should turn in their essays on Friday.

B. **The antecedent of a pronoun should be apparent.**

Faulty: If you can't identify phrases and clauses, this will be a handicap to you.

If you can't identify phrases and clauses, it will be a handicap to you.

Correct: The inability to identify phrases and clauses will be a handicap to you.

If you can't identify phrases and clauses, you will be at a disadvantage.

6. **Use commas correctly.**

Commas should be used intentionally, to clarify or to emphasize the meaning of a sentence.

A. **Use a comma before a coordinating conjunction to join independent clauses of a compound sentence.**

Faulty: Right now we consider the situation tragic but in time we'll be able to laugh about it.

Correct: Right now we consider the situation tragic, but in time we'll be able to laugh about it.

B. **Use a comma between all terms in a series.**

Faulty: We had our choice of sandwiches: chicken salad, salami, ham and cheese.

Correct: We had our choice of sandwiches: chicken salad, salami, ham, and cheese.

We had our choice of sandwiches: chicken salad, salami, or ham and cheese.

C. **Use a comma to set off introductory words, phrases, and clauses.**

Faulty: Frightened he dialed the emergency number.

Correct: Frightened, he dialed the emergency number.

Faulty: After a long evening of study in the library my roommate and I went out for a hamburger.

Correct: After a long evening of study in the library, my roommate and I went out for a hamburger.

Faulty: Because I forgot to set my alarm I was late to class.

Correct: Because I forgot to set my alarm, I was late to class.

D. **Use a comma, or a pair of commas, to set off parenthetical expressions and non-restrictive words, phrases, and clauses.**

Faulty: I had taken some aspirin. My headache, however was getting worse.

Correct: I had taken some aspirin. My headache, however, was getting worse.

Faulty: My teacher who was beginning to lose his patience repeated the instructions.

Correct: My teacher, who was beginning to lose his patience, repeated the instructions.

7. **Use the semicolon correctly.**

   A. **The semicolon joins closely related independent clauses.**

   Faulty: Good intentions are not enough, intelligence is also required.

   Correct: Good intentions are not enough; intelligence is also required.

   Faulty: I had taken some aspirin, however, my headache was getting worse.

   Correct: I had taken some aspirin; however, my headache was getting worse.

   B. **A semicolon sometimes replaces a comma when the stronger mark of punctuation is needed for clarity.**

   Example: I looked at my mother hopefully, trying to find some sign of encouragement; but before I could utter a word, Ms. Taylor's secretary appeared from nowhere and asked us to follow him.

   Example: Attending the conference were Ms. Adams, the president; Mr. Byers, the secretary; and Mrs. Whelan, the treasurer.

8. **Learn the correct use and formation of the possessive.**

   The possessive is usually formed by adding an apostrophe plus *s* to the singular form of a noun or by adding an apostrophe only to a plural noun ending in *s*. The possessive form of personal pronouns does not contain an apostrophe.

   Faulty: The childrens uniforms were furnished by the Parents Club.

   Correct: The children's uniforms were furnished by the Parents' Club.

   Faulty: Its time you got the plant it's fertilizer.

   Correct: It's time you got the plant its fertilizer.

APPENDIX 257

9. **Assure that pronouns appear in the correct case.**
   A. **Use the NOMINATIVE CASE for subjects and predicate nominatives.**

   Personal Pronouns:

Person	Singular	Plural
1st	I	we
2nd	you	you
3rd	he, she, it	they

   Faulty: It was me who asked the question.
   Correct: It was I who asked the question.
   Faulty: No one is a more reliable friend than her.
   Correct: No one is a more reliable friend than she.

   B. **Use the OBJECTIVE CASE for objects of prepositions, indirect objects, and direct objects.**

   Personal Pronouns:

Person	Singular	Plural
1st	me	us
2nd	you	you
3rd	him, her, it	them

   Faulty: The duchess invited my friend and I to tea.
   Correct: The duchess invited my friend and me to tea.
   Faulty: Virginia Woolf is a writer who I admire.
   Correct: Virginia Woolf is a writer whom I admire.

10. **Combine words logically.**

    In every clause, the subject and the predicate must combine to make a logical statement.

    A. **Be sure the subject, verb, and direct object make sense together.**

    Faulty: The ball, stolen from an SMU player, allowed an Aggie to score two points.
    Correct: Stealing the ball from an SMU player allowed an Aggie to score two points.

    Having stolen the ball from an SMU player, an Aggie scored two points.

B. **When you use "to be" to assert the identity of two terms, make certain those terms are logically and grammatically equivalent.**

Faulty: Waiting in line is when I get impatient.

Correct: Waiting in line makes me impatient.

When I have to wait in line, I get impatient.

Discernment and Discourse
Department-Wide Grading Scale

A	94 or above
A−	90–93
B+	87–89
B	83–86
B−	80–82
C+	77–79
C	73–76
C−	70–72

Anything below 70 is failure of a DISC course, and the student must retake the class.

Your Name (First Last)   Last Name 1

Your Professor's Name

Course Number

Due Date (D/M/YYYY)

Centered, Original Title with Proper Capitalization

    This page is designed to show you exactly how your essays for DISC courses should be formatted. Use MLA style, as indicated in your course syllabus. The margins are 1" on all four sides, which is probably different than your computer's default. Text is left-aligned, not justified, so the right edge will be uneven. Every line of the document, including your heading and title, should be set to double (2.0) spacing. In order to avoid breaks that are too large between paragraphs or sections, you must check the box that says, "Don't add space between paragraphs of the same style," which is found under "Home/Paragraph" on your Word program. Indent each paragraph by hitting "Tab" one time. Use Times New Roman font (size 12, black) for the entire document. Either one or two spaces between sentences is acceptable in MLA, as long as you are consistent and following your professor's requests. Do not embellish with bold, italicized, or underlined text unless required by MLA norms. If turning in paper copies, always staple your essay before turning in; never ask your professor for a stapler the day your essay is due. Do not use a report cover or other type of binding unless requested.

    Your heading in the upper left corner should look like the one above, with your information substituted in the order indicated in parentheses. Your last name only, followed by *one* space and then the page number, is used in a header, which you can access by double-clicking above the top line of your heading. Use "Insert/Page Number" to have the number automatically inserted, but you will likely still need to adjust the font on your name and the page number—yes, the header needs to match the rest of the document! This header will appear on every page of the document.

 Familiarize yourself with this page, any writing handbooks assigned by your professor, and MLA's online "Style Center," which includes templates and sample papers for your reference. These resources will be crucial to accuracy as you format your essays, create reference lists, and insert in-text citations. Once you have fine-tuned your formatting, save yourself time and energy by creating a template to use for all subsequent DISC essays. Fondren Library also hosts regular workshops on MLA style, as well as other styles you may use in your various courses. The IT Help Desk, found in Fondren Library or at 214-768-HELP, can help you with any computer, printer, or Canvas questions as you write, print, and upload your essays.

Southern Methodist University (SMU) will not discriminate in any employment practice, education program, education activity, or admissions on the basis of race, color, religion, national origin, sex, age, disability, genetic information, or veteran status. SMU's commitment to equal opportunity includes nondiscrimination on the basis of sexual orientation and gender identity and expression. The Executive Director for Access and Equity/Title IX Coordinator is designated to handle inquiries regarding the nondiscrimination policies, including the prohibition of sex discrimination under Title IX. The Executive Director/Title IX Coordinator may be reached at the Perkins Administration Building, Room 204, 6425 Boaz Lane, Dallas, TX 75205, 214-768-3601, accessequity@smu.edu. Inquiries regarding the application of Title IX may also be directed to the Assistant Secretary for Civil Rights of the U.S. Department of Education.

[1] Title IX of the Education Amendments of 1972, 20 U.S.C. §§ 1681–1688.

CPSIA information can be obtained
at www.ICGtesting.com
Printed in the USA
LVHW041336180219
607881LV00001B/1/P